French Music
in the Fifteenth
and Sixteenth Centuries

AV-IOVR-D'HVY il y ha peu d'hommes qui ſa-
chent bien ſonner de la trompe, et parler aux
Chiens en cris et langages plaiſans, comme faiſoyent
les anciens : car a preſent ie veoy que les Piqueurs
ne prenent pas grand plaiſir a veoir courir, ne faire
chaſſer et requeſter les Chiens : mais ſeulement leur
ſufiſt de veoir prendre et mourir vn Cerf, pour auoir
la bonne grace de leur maiſtre, et faire leur
profit : et deſlors qu'il eſt lance, n'en deſirent que la

French Music
in the Fifteenth
and Sixteenth Centuries

Isabelle Cazeaux

PRAEGER PUBLISHERS · NEW YORK

Published in the United States of America in 1975
by Praeger Publishers, Inc.
111 Fourth Avenue, New York, N.Y. 10003

Library of Congress Cataloging in Publication Data
Cazeaux, Isabelle.
    French music in the fifteenth and sixteenth centuries.

    Bibliography: p.
    Includes index.
        1. Music—France—History and criticism.   2. Music—
History and criticism—Medieval, 400–1500.   3. Music—
History and criticism—16th century.   I.   Title.
ML270.2.C36   781.7'44   73-15168
ISBN 0-275-53710-2

PRINTED IN GREAT BRITAIN

TO MY MOTHER
for her seventy-fifth birthday

Contents

Acknowledgments

A grant from the Martha Baird Rockefeller Fund for Music has enabled me to prepare this book. For this help I am most grateful.

Frontispiece taken from Du Fouilloux's *La Venerie* (Poitiers, 1566), courtesy of the Spencer Collection, The New York Public Library (Astor, Lenox and Tilden Foundations).

Foreword

As recently as 1930, Maurice Cauchie told us that 'up to now, French musicians of the sixteenth century have been studied very little. Their lives in particular, except for those of two or three among them, have not given rise to any serious research, whereas those of most of the German and Italian musicians of the same period are known in great detail. As for the works, only those of the end of the century have been the subject of important publications.'[1] What he said then might also have applied to a certain extent to French music of the fifteenth century. This may be somewhat of an exaggeration, in view of the studies which had already appeared by 1930: those of Michel Brenet, and some by Charles van den Borren and by André Pirro (though he was to do his most important work on the Renaissance later). Even much younger persons, such as Geneviève Thibault, had begun to have works printed by then. Certainly none of these studies could be considered anything but serious research, and their quality cannot be questioned. There is more than a kernel of truth in Cauchie's statement, however, because the quantity of pertinent publications at the time was still relatively small.

We are happy to report that times have changed somewhat—one might even say radically—and although there are still more than a few gaps in our knowledge of French musicians of the fifteenth and sixteenth centuries and their music, we are not quite so ignorant as we used to be, thanks largely to the efforts of scholarly private presses, such as the American Institute of Musicology, one of whose continuing series, *Corpus Mensurabilis Musicae*, includes *Opera omnia* of French composers, the Editions de l'Oiseau-Lyre, the Société de Musique d'Autrefois, and several university presses. Within the last twenty-five years or so, a significant number of doctoral dissertations and other monographs or essays have been devoted to specific elements of French music of the

[1] Cauchie, *Guilliaud*, p. 6.

Renaissance—composers, musical genres, publishers and their work, collective manuscripts or prints, musical centers, etc. Substantial articles about French composers are becoming the rule rather than the exception, not only in France but in other countries too, in such reference works as *Die Musik in Geschichte und Gegenwart* and the forthcoming sixth edition of Groves's *Dictionary of Music and Musicians*. Important sections of more general histories treat French music of the fifteenth and sixteenth centuries, and in this category, though it would not be possible to list all of them, we cannot fail to mention Pirro's *Histoire de la musique de la fin du XIVe siècle à la fin du XVIe*, Paul Henry Lang's *Music in Western Civilization*, Gustave Reese's *Music in the Renaissance*, Roland-Manuel's edition, *Histoire de la musique*, in the *Encyclopédie de la Pléiade*, the *New Oxford History of Music*, and F. W. Sternfeld's edition, *Music from the Middle Ages to the Renaissance*.

We realize, thanks to Brenet and Pirro, those pioneers of French Renaissance music research, that it was not in the third quarter of the twentieth century that some of the more conservative members of society first became concerned about men's hair styles. In 1514, at the Sainte-Chapelle in Paris, for example, a barber was paid to trim the choirboys' hair every week.[2] In the fifteenth century, at the Cambrai cathedral, members of the singing personnel were sometimes reproved for wearing their hair too long; the proper length was considered to be no lower than the level of the middle of the ear.[3] And François Lesure, bless him, even regales us, in a slice of a 'dictionary of musicians who are not in any dictionary'[4] and in numerous other sources, with succulent morsels of information on some of the lesser known French musicians, such as the Huguenot Richard Crassot, who left Troyes in 1560, 'without even paying his respects to the master at whose house he had lived, and left behind some debts' besides; and Jean Bastard, who was 'bastard by name but legitimate son of the Almighty Father,' according to the reassuring words of a contemporary poet. To be sure, Lesure and other musicologists with a flair for archival studies and paleography give us other details that are more important than these for the

[2] Brenet, *Sainte-Chapelle*, p. 67.
[3] Pirro, *Cornuel*, p. 197.
[4] Lesure, *Minor*, pp. 538–544.

history of music, but such seemingly trifling data also help us to place these composers within their historical and social context and bring back to life for us the times in which they made music. It takes more than concentration on a limited number of significant compositions by so-called great masters to achieve a meaningful understanding of a musical era.

We now have a reasonable amount of information available, scattered though it may be, and if I may venture to make a prediction, I am convinced that Lesure—and Helen Hewitt, Daniel Heartz, Howard Brown, and many others—will continue to provide us with valuable new material on French Renaissance music as long as they live. That should take care of us for the next fifty years at least. What more can we ask for?

From time to time, someone points out that in spite of serious studies devoted to a given subject, its definitive history remains to be written. I shall not add a similar complaint about French music in the fifteenth and sixteenth centuries, nor shall I propose to write its definitive history. In fact I think that history is rarely, if ever, definitive. The discovery of new facts may cause us to change our perspective of what happened in the past and the reasons for these happenings.[5] I well realize

[5] That we have problems in treating such a vast subject is all too evident. For one thing, not everyone agrees as to what one should call some of the musicians of the fifteenth and sixteenth centuries who have contributed to the musical life of the region that corresponds roughly to present-day France. They themselves do not seem to have been unduly concerned about their haphazard designations by contemporaries in such terms as *Galli* or *Belgae* (*see* H. Expert, in Bibliothèque nationale, *Musique*, p. 35). Musicologists have spoken of Netherlanders to include composers from the northern provinces which eventually reverted to France, as well as from Belgium and Holland. Other broad designations have included 'Burgundian' and 'Franco-Flemish', based on either the place of birth of a given musician or his language. For stylistic considerations, Guillaume de Van has even suggested that the expression 'Franco-Italian style' be substituted for 'Franco-Flemish' (Van, *Pédagogie*, p. 80). Then one also hears of narrower subdivisions, such as the Parisian chanson, which centers around the productive years of a small number of printers from the French capital and has little to do with the regional origins of its composers. Perhaps we can also refer to a school of Lyon, or even of Toulouse. Concerning the vexed problem of proper designation, Herbert Kellman (his *Links, Abstracts*, p. 23) has lucidly explained that 'though France and the Empire were politically hostile for the better part of the period 1500–1530, their sovereigns' courts admired many of the same composers and favored music of one general style. The term "Franco-Flemish" quite aptly

that we do not yet know all that was going on, musically, in every corner of France during two of its most colorful centuries.[6] My aim has not been to write a straightforward, more or less chronological history of French Renaissance music in English. This has, after all, been remarkably well done by some of the authors mentioned earlier—Lang, Reese, and the contributors to the *New Oxford History of Music*, among others. These books are far from obsolete and must be consulted by anyone interested in the subject. It did not seem worthwhile to follow the same basic pattern, adding, along the way, a new fact or two which may have come to light since the publication of these works. Rather, it has been my aim to provide a companion

expresses both our inability to make significant distinctions between music north and south of Hainaut, and our view of a kind of common market in musicians and music in the region consisting of northern France and the Low Countries.'

[6] Paule Chaillon (*Louis XII*, p. 66) rightly points out some of the things we do not know about music in aristocratic circles when she writes, in relation to the court of Louis XII: 'In order to have an exact idea of the state of this music, it would be necessary to know the tastes of the important personages who surround the king. Unfortunately, no study has been devoted to this subject, and the accounts of the various houses have not always been preserved for us.' And this could well apply to other courts and less exalted milieus. H. M. Brown states that 'a history of musical life in Paris remains to be written' (Haar, *Chanson*, p. 2) and that 'a definitive history of sixteenth-century instrumental music has not yet been written' (Brown, *Instrumental*, p. 1). Lesure would like to see more studies devoted to the history of French *maîtrises* (Lesure, *Sociologie*, p. 338, written before the appearance of Becker's dissertation on the subject) and finds, in relation to French religious music, that 'there are still too few texts available, too many essential problems still unexamined (such as the study of liturgical usages and of the provincial choir-schools, and the clearing-up of the uncertain boundaries between Catholic and Protestant music) for us to be able to pick out the most significant personalities and works of the last two thirds of the [sixteenth] century, or to describe with any precision the evolution of the religious style in France' (*Oxford*, IV, p. 253). Mr. Kellman's remarkable archival findings about the circumstances of Josquin's death and his probable place of birth (*Josquin in Condé: discoveries and revisions*; paper read at the thirty-ninth annual meeting of the American Musicological Society, 9 November 1973) as well as Craig Wright's similar documents about Dufay (papers read at the fortieth annual meeting of the society, November 1974 and at the Dufay quincentenary conference, 7 December 1974) show how much we still need to know, even about major historical figures—not to speak of so-called minor masters.

volume which deals with French matters in a manner analogous
to that employed by such scholars as Nanie Bridgman in *La vie
musicale au quattrocento,* where she shows the place of music in
Italian history and social life of the times. Similarly, I shall try to
show some ways in which music permeated the life of the French
in the fifteenth and sixteenth centuries. One cannot pretend, of
course, to deal with all aspects of so fascinating a subject in the
present volume. It is my hope, however, that it may give rise to
similar investigations.

FOOTNOTES

In order to save space in the footnote references, bibliographical
citations are kept to a minimum. They include the author's surname
followed by a catchword or abbreviated title (since words are usually
more intelligible than sigla). Lesure, *Minor,* for example, stands for
François Lesure, 'Some Minor French Composers of the 16th
Century,' in *Aspects of Medieval and Renaissance Music: a Birthday Offering
to Gustave Reese,* ed. by Jan La Rue, New York: Norton, 1966.
Complete author and title listings are given in the bibliographical
section at the end of the volume, together with corresponding short
titles (pp. 261–291).

The catchword title is qualified by the addition of the designation
'edition' or 'article' when an author has served as editor of a
manuscript or of a composer's works and has in addition written an
article about the subject in another publication. Examples include
Lowinsky, *Medici* (edition) for Edward E. Lowinsky, ed., *The Medici
Codex of 1518* . . . Chicago, London: University of Chicago Press,
1968, 3 vols. *Monuments of Renaissance Music,* 3–5), and Lowinsky,
Medici (article) for his 'The Medici Codex . . .' in *Annales
Musicologiques* V (1957), pp. 61–178.

PART ONE

Music and French Society
in the
Fifteenth and Sixteenth Centuries

Introductory note

The heart was a favorite symbol among French poets and musicians of the Renaissance, despite Stravinsky's assertion that 'the heart in music is an invention of the eighteenth century.'[1] From Dufay's *Mon cueur me fait tout dispenser* to Thessier's *Mon cœur, ma chère vie* (on a poem by Ronsard), one finds few courtly texts which do not mention it, however briefly.[2] Scribes sometimes made a drawing of a heart instead of writing the word for it. An example of this can be seen in *MS. 564 (olim 1047)* of the Bibliothèque du Musé Condé, Chantilly, in the course of the *rondeau Belle, bonne, sage, plaisant et gente*, by Baude Cordier, whose name, incidentally, contains the word *cor*, an old form of *cœur*. This often-represented piece seems to imply a double interest in the subject on the part of its copyist, because it not only contains a picture of a heart within the literary text, but it also has its music laid out so that the whole composition looks like a heart.[3] The

[1] Roth, *Business*, p. 199. It may be somewhat unfair to quote out of context this pronouncement, which was made to an audience of young composers in Russia. Stravinsky was probably not concerned with visual and poetic aspects of the heart in music, but with its popular use as a virtual synonym for 'emotion,' or even 'sentimentality,' as opposed to an intellectual approach. The statement undoubtedly reflects his often expressed conviction that music is not meant to portray one's personal feelings; it runs counter to certain views expressed in the Renaissance, by Glarean, for example, who appreciates Josquin partly on the basis of his ability to express the emotions in music (see his *Dodecachordon*, 1965, p. 17), and occasionally even in the Middle Ages, as in Machaut's letter to Péronne d'Armentières, in which he assures her that 'Qui de sentiment ne fait, Son dit et son chant contrefait.'

[2] The heart is often present even in poems not specifically related to courtly love, such as the meditative *rondeaux* of Charles d'Orléans. One of them, *Dedens mon livre de pensée,/ J'ay trouvé escripvant mon cueur . . .* mentions the word twice.

[3] Various hypotheses have been advanced as to the provenance and date of the Chantilly Manuscript. Most scholars believe that it was copied in Italy, though Apel questions this, and suggests that it was made in France in the late fourteenth century (Apel, *Fourteenth*, p. 7). Reaney, on the other

chansonnier cordiforme (Paris: Bibliothèque nationale, *MS. Rothschild 2973*) on the other hand, has normally-notated music, which lies in straight instead of curved lines, but then the entire manuscript is cut and bound in the shape of a double heart. It also contains the diagram of the heart within the text, as a

hand, proposes a Florentine origin, and doubts that it was copied earlier than 1400 (Reaney, *Chantilly*, p. 85). In any case, the heart-shaped piece that interests us is in a French fifteenth-century hand, and was possibly copied out, by Cordier himself (Apel, *op. cit.*, p. 23). Cordier, whose name could be translated as 'string man', may have been the harpist Baude Fresnel (Wright, *Tapissier*, p. 186). This work and the composer's canon in the shape of a circle, for which Meylan (*Réparation*, pp. 68–71) proposes a new solution, have generally been considered later additions and not part of the original manuscript, although Wright (*op. cit.*, p. 187, note 139) disagrees. He believes that the manuscript was compiled before 1397–98. Besseler dated *Belle, bonne* about 1420, because of its notation in *tempus perfectum diminutum* (Blume, *Musik*, v. 2, col. 1666), and Reaney finds that an even later date would not be unreasonable (Reaney, *Fifteenth*, p. ii). Thus it seems that this manneristic approach to the depiction of the heart in music is very much a fifteenth-century phenomenon. Preoccupation with the heart is probably not limited to France. Scribes sometimes drew capital letters to look like one. The initial B of Busnois's *Bel accueil*, the opening piece of the beautiful Mellon chansonnier (New Haven, Yale University), which Leeman Perkins believes to be of Italian origin (in his paper read at the Toronto meeting of the American Musicological Society, 7 November 1970) reminds us of a heart, albeit slightly distorted. And it is used for a French piece.

The heart was not the only symbol represented visually and musically in the Chantilly manuscript. There is also the well-known circle canon, Cordier's *Tout par compas suy composés*—which remind one slightly of coil poems, such as will be found later in the anthology *Witt's Recreations* (1640; *see* Church, *Pattern*, pp. 132, 136). Another piece from Chantilly 564 (olim 1047), *La harpe de mélodie*, by Senleches, appeared in another source, a lost manuscript from Vienna, notated in harp shape (Reaney, *Chantilly*, p. 82).

Diamonds, then as now, were occasionally cut in the shape of a heart. Anne of Brittany bought 'deux cueurs de dyamans assiz sur ung souvenez-vous de moy' (Leroux de Lincy, *Anne*, p. 108). Stylized hearts sometimes appeared as watermarks on French paper (*see* Bibliothèque nationale, *Livre*, p. 29), and apparently also as bread. An exhibit outside a bakery shop in Paris (14 rue de la Michodière) showed bread of various forms from different periods of history. Among the oddities was bread in the shape of a heart, which according to the undocumented caption, had been made for Ronsard following the publication of his *Amours*. Since there was a musical supplement to the original edition of these poems in 1552, we can once more connect the heart with Renaissance music, but this time in a gastronomical context.

substitute for the word *cueur*. Another heart-shaped manuscript
—but not a musical one—is a fifteenth-century book of Hours
for the use of Amiens (Paris: Bibl. nat., *MS. lat. 10536*).

These beautiful manifestations remind one of other
ideograms, but in which music does not take part—pattern
poems such as the heart shaped *Charitie*, by the seventeenth-
century poet Nathanael Richards.[4] In France, the outstanding
example that comes to mind is of course Apollinaire's
Calligrammes, which he originally called figurative verse, or
ideogrammatic poems, or lyrical ideograms.[5] In Apollinaire's
case, my earlier statement regarding the absence of music may
not apply strictly, because every one of his poems has an
undeniable musicality;[6] but this quality is perceived not in the
appearance of a given poem but in its sound, when it is read.
In other words, unlike the fifteenth-century musical hearts,
shaped poetry does not normally include visual aspects of
music—i.e., musical notation—and cannot properly be called
musical composition.[7] It has been said that Apollinaire
replaced 'some of the sound qualities of a sign by its visual
qualities, thus adding a sort of . . . iconopoeic palette-knife to
the orthodox onomatopoeic plectrum.'[8] Pattern poems, we
are told, stem from a penchant for the ornate, which
Quintilian defines as

something which goes beyond what is merely lucid and
acceptable. It consists in forming a clear conception of what

[4] Church, *Pattern*, p. 317.
[5] Themerson, *Ideograms*, pp. 17–18.
[6] As Themerson aptly expresses it, 'Apollinaire was a singing poet. And
he didn't cease to be a singing poet when, later, he tried to use the visual,
spatial quality of signs to express the same, his own thoughts and
sentiments, to create the same, his lyricism' (*ibid.*, p. 17).
[7] Technopaegnia, the method of writing pattern verse which by the
varying length of its lines forms a picture or design, has been used to
portray musical instruments, such as pipes, or drums, from time to time, in
Greece, in the Orient, and then in Europe (*see* Church, *Pattern*), but here
again the musical element is not present to the same degree as in the
fifteenth-century heart pieces, because nothing indicated that the poems
were to be sung. Even if it was the poets' intention to have them performed
musically—which is not improbable—the music is still not shown
graphically, and therefore is not part of the ideogram.
[8] Themerson, *Ideograms*, p. 16.

we wish to say, secondly in giving this adequate expression, and thirdly in lending additional brilliance, a process which may be correctly termed embellishment.[9]

In relation to a later era, the pattern poem is described as 'a baroque toy where form in itself becomes an art apart from meaning [and it serves] both to unite and to separate content and form.'[10] All these statements can apply to the fifteenth-century heart pieces and help explain their *raison d'être*.

There have been several figurative pieces in French literature between the Chantilly manuscript and Apollinaire's *Calligrammes*—Panurge's bottle-shaped prayer to the divine bottle, in Rabelais's *Pantagruel*, for example, which occurs for the first time in the 1565 edition of Book V, of doubtful attribution.[11] The minor French poet Etienne Tabourot implies, in *Les Bigarrures et touches du Seigneur des accords* (Paris, 1608) that when he was a student in Paris in 1564, he wrote a poem in the shape of a kettle.[12] And in 1763, Charles François Pannard wrote the drinking pieces *Le Verre* and *La Bouteille* in the shape of a glass and a bottle, respectively.[13] A poem entitled *La Tour de 300 mètres construite en 300 vers*, by Armand Bourgade (1889) is appropriately enough shaped like the Eiffel Tower.[14]

It would be a gross exaggeration to claim that the source of inspiration for all these fanciful ideograms was the Chantilly manuscript, because quite probably none of their authors had

[9] Church, *Pattern*, p. x.

[10] *Ibid.*, p. 215. The best-known examples of shaped poetry are George Herbert's *The Altar* and *Easter Wings*. In her excellent study, Miss Church traces the genre back to its probable Alexandrian origins, *ca.* 300 B.C. and gives examples from subsequent Greek, Oriental, and Latin authors (Fortunatus, Alcuin, and Abbon of Fleury, among those who lived in Gaul or France). She then concentrates on English pattern poetry after it was introduced into England in 1573, under some influence from Italy and France. Richard Willis, for example, wrote his poem in the shape of pan-pipes (*Pastoriciam fistulam*) in Paris, though he published it in England in 1573 (Church, *Pattern*, p. 53).

[11] *See* Bibliothèque nationale, *Livre*, p. 69.

[12] Church, *Pattern*, p. 103.

[13] *Ibid.*, pp. 214, 413.

[14] André Billy, in his preface to Apollinaire, *Œuvres*, p. xli. Other examples of ideograms appear in Bibliothèque nationale, *Livre*, pp. 66–71.

ever seen it. Still I believe that it belongs in the history of the genre in France and in the French language. The heart music—and the circle canon—are more than pattern poems because they combine not only language and pictures, but also music, thus amalgamating three elements instead of two. (Music is hardly the same as a language, regardless of how often it is called a universal one.) Themerson tells us that

> language is one species of the genus 'sign' and pictorial representations are another species of the same genus. These two species can be wedded to each other. They can be wedded either politely and conformably (as when an illustration is married to a text, or a caption to a drawing) or they can start an illicit liaison so intimately integrated that one doesn't know any more who is the bride and who is the bridegroom.[15]

In the fifteenth-century heart pieces, there is nothing illicit in the relationship of the three closely integrated elements; but the marriage must of necessity be a polygamous one.

We have often been informed that sixteenth-century chanson texts are more earthy than those of the preceding century. While this may be true on the whole, there are texts written before 1500 that might cause a fireman to blush, and conversely, there are many pieces written after that date and much later which are perfectly respectable, even by Victorian standards. The lyrical repertoire seems to be at least as important as the other (although I have not made a count of all extant chansons in order to find the ratio of Rabelaisian songs to more tender ones) and shows a renewal of interest in courtly poetry during the high Renaissance. With the advent of the sixteenth century, much of the preciosity that one associates with fifteenth-century hearts disappears, certainly; but the heart is still fashionable as a subject for writers and musicians, although they do not emphasize its decorative aspects as much as before.

Mid sixteenth-century authors of serious Calvinist texts, to be sung to pre-existent secular tunes, were not overly concerned with hearts or similar emblems suggestive of

---

[15] Themerson, *Ideograms*, pp. 11–12.

human love. Yet one of the best-known of these writers of contrafacta, the poet-musician Eustorg de Beaulieu, seems reluctant, in his collection *Chrestienne resjouyssance* (1546) to reject *le cœur* when he alters some of Clément Marot's amorous poetry to suit his purpose. And so he transforms *J'ayme le cueur de m'amye* into *J'ayme le cœur de Marie*, and *Le cueur de vous ma présence désire* into *Le Sainct Esprit mon paouvre cœur désire*.

Calvin himself has something to say about the heart in relation to religious music. He asserts, in his *Institution de la religion chrétienne,* that speaking and singing for the purpose of prayer are not appreciated by God and are of no value unless they proceed from affection and from the bottom of the heart, and that the use of the tongue without the heart should be highly displeasing to Him.[16] In the preface of the psalter of 1543, he recommends the singing of the psalms, for by the addition of music, the words 'pierce the heart' much more strongly and enter it 'in a like manner as through a funnel, the wine is poured into the vessel; so also the venom and the corruption are distilled to the depths of the heart by the melody.'[17]

At some point in the century, the heart ceases to dominate the chanson poetry, although it does not entirely renounce its rights. Other parts of the body will become rivals for its position. The *blasons anatomiques*, such as Clément Marot's *Blason du beau et du laid tetin*, are extreme cases of explicit description. In more discreet chansons, however, we find more and more allusions to the eye—almost as much as to the heart in earlier times. An anonymous poem, *Est-ce au moyen*, with music by Claudin de Sermisy, tells us why, and shows us the relationship between the two: 'Parce que l'œil est du cueur la fenestre,/ Et le profond du cueur il fait congnoistre' (Because the eye is the window of the heart,/ And makes known the abyss of the heart). Until the end of the century, the heart apparently lost little of its appeal in France.

[16] Pidoux, *Psautier*, I, p. xiii.
[17] Hamersma, *Pseaumes*, p. 4.

I

Royal courts and music

Music has always been closely associated with the French royal circle—kings, queens, princes, and royal mistresses. Though some of the kings are known to have had more genuine interest in the art than others—some of them even sang with their choristers, or actively promoted the dissemination of new music—all of them were exposed to music, either by their educators, in their childhood, or by practical musicians in the service of their family. They heard High Mass frequently—almost every day, in fact—sung by the personnel of whatever church they were attending, or by the members of their own chapel, which was ambulatory and followed the kings wherever they went—Paris, the provinces, or abroad, in time of war or on the occasion of important political meetings. Whenever they made a solemn entry into one of the cities of their realm, the kings were offered some sort of musical tribute.

Charles V is best known to musicologists because he was a patron of Guillaume de Machault, who, according to unsubstantiated legend, wrote his *Messe de Nostre Dame* for the King's coronation. Charles had a musical chapel and liked to hear the music of soft instruments after meals.[1] He seems to have manifested interest in theoretical aspects of music too, since he had a French translation made for him of Aristotle, which included passages on music.[2]

His love for music was transmitted to his mentally ill son, Charles VI, who reigned from 1380 to 1422. In 1383, the duke

---

[1] Pirro, *Charles VI*, p. 1.

[2] Pirro, *L'Enseignement*, p. 30. It was by Nicole Oresmes, bishop of Lisieux and director of the Collège de Navarre, a well-known translator in his time. Becker, *Maîtrise*, p. 56, notes that 'his remarks and allusions to the practice of the time rendered the text fully intelligible to the people of his world. For example, they should appear to be "accessible-to music"; to refuse to do so was an "insensible vice." The work was widely circulated and stimulated in the nobility the desire to surround themselves with music in courts and chapels.'

of Burgundy sent the young king a brass flageolet, probably because he was aware of his interest in things musical. On the occasion of a visit from Gaston Phébus, count of Foix, in Toulouse, 1389, the king listened to instrumental music with his guest for two hours. He maintained a musical chapel which, in 1399, consisted of eleven singers, headed by Jehan du Moulin (d. 1421), a canon of Notre-Dame de Paris, and in 1422, of fifteen chaplains under the direction of Adam Maigret. His instrumental musicians included a harpist, Pierre Julian. It was perhaps for him that he paid one hundred *livres tournois*, in 1413, for a well-made harp with his device.[3]

In 1401, Charles VI created a court of love, a confraternity in which poets and musicians participated. The 'prince of love,' arbiter of taste in that court, had recourse to musicians who, according to Guillebert de Mets, knew how to compose and sing 'all types of chansons, *ballades, rondeaux, virelais*, and other love poems, and how to play instruments melodiously.' Their main festivals were held on Saint Valentine's day, and were marked by the celebration of a Mass 'with music, to the sound of the organ, chant and discant, and with the best singers that could be had.'[4] Whether or not the unfortunate king was fit to appreciate music as much as would have been desirable, he certainly was surrounded by things musical, and the 'Hôtel de Saint-Pol in Paris, where the royal family and some of the princes of the blood resided, must have been a favorite haven for singers and other musicians.'[5] Charles VI sponsored regulations for various musical groups. In 1401, he issued a charter of reformation for the Sainte-Chapelle du Palais, in Paris, in an attempt to correct some of the usual abuses of the choristers—e.g., absenteeism at the celebration of the Office Hours—and in 1405, he made the dignity of *chantre*, or chief singer, an elective one, with the provision that the incumbent should be musically and otherwise qualified. The *chantre* became the musical director of the Sainte-Chapelle and was responsible for the proper performance by the chaplains and clerics of the readings, plainchant and polyphony.[6]

[3] Pirro, *Charles VI*, pp. 5, 13, 20, 27, 34, and Marix, *Histoire*, pp. 148–149.
[4] Pirro, *Charles VI*, p. 24, and Marix, *Histoire*, pp. 98–99.
[5] Apel, *Fourteenth*, p. 16.
[6] Brenet, *Sainte-Chapelle*, pp. 25–26.

The king gave royal letters patent, in 1401, to the Confraternity of Saint-Julien-des-Menestriers, the Parisian association of instrumental musicians.[7] His interest in religious instrumental music was manifested on 26 June 1394, when he gave two hundred francs to the chapter of Notre-Dame de Paris to pay for the reparation of the organ.[8]

His queen, Isabeau of Bavaria, who is best remembered today for her part in handing over France to England by the Treaty of Troyes in 1420, was fond of music. She played the harp[9] and in 1416 ordered strings for it as well as for her *echiquier*. Whenever she travelled from residence to residence, the organ of her chapel was taken along with her.[10] Among the musicians of her household, in 1410, was a lady *menestrelle*, Gracieuse Alegre, from Spain.[11]

The dauphin Louis, duke of Guyenne, who died young in 1415, after a life spent in 'shameful idleness and frivolous pleasures, such as the sound of the organ and the noise of drums,'[12] had a fine chapel, and spent his nights playing the organ in a special room which he had constructed at the Louvre. His excesses, musical and other, provoked riots among the people of Paris, as well the censure of his uncles, who complained that he refused to replace his sick father at council meetings.[13] His sister, Catherine of France, who married Henry V of England in 1420, had also learned to play the harp.[14]

When one considers that Charles VII was born into such a musical family, it should come as no surprise to learn that he was exposed to music at a very tender age. Indeed, his mother Isabeau had instrumentalists play before the future king's

[7] Bowles, *Processions*, p. 156. It had been 'organized in Paris in 1321, when 37 jongleurs established duties and privileges and petitioned the provost to sanction their charter.'

[8] Rokseth (*Orgue*, p. 23) suggests that the purpose may not have been solely musical and that Charles was, perhaps, trying to placate God for his sins.

[9] *Loc. cit.*

[10] Pirro, *Charles VI*, p. 27.

[11] Pirro, *Histoire*, p. 25.

[12] Sauval, *Antiquités de Paris*, quoted in Rokseth, *Orgue*, p. 24.

[13] Rokseth, *Orgue*, p. 24.

[14] Pirro, *Charles VI*, p. 31.

cradle when he was only one year old.[15] His activities as king of France, 1422–1461, which included among other feats the retaking of France (except for Calais) from the English, with help from Joan of Arc, the repression of the Praguerie, a revolt of the nobles in which his own son the Dauphin (later Louis XI) took part, and the establishment of stable institutions for the government, probably left him little time for music-making. Still it was under his patronage that Ockeghem began his tenure as leader of the royal chapel, a position which he was to keep under the reign of three successive kings, and became treasurer of Saint-Martin de Tours, which was a most enviable and lucrative honor.[16] Whether Charles VII met Ockeghem's great predecessor Dufay or not is uncertain, but it does not seem impossible, because according to a letter dated 22 February 1456, Dufay had shortly before followed the Duke of Savoy to France, where the latter had had a meeting with the king.[17] The monarch, towards the end of his life, had fourteen chaplains, including one organist, who performed Mass for him every day.[18]

[15] Rokseth, *Orgue*, p. 24.

[16] This distinction made him curator of the collection of relics and treasures, as *maître de chapelle* of the king. Ockeghem was probably the most admired musician in France before Josquin Desprez, judging from the poetic and musical tributes paid to him after his death, such as the *Deploration* by Guillaume Cretin. The most famous of these laments, at least among musicians, is Josquin's *Deploration*, on a text by Molinet, which in one version describes Ockeghem as 'learned, of handsome appearance, and not stout' (Lowinsky, *Medici* article, pp. 79–80). He must indeed have been elegant in his fur-trimmed robes—though he sometimes wore a plain black robe and hood (Brenet, *France*, pp. 32, 36). Perhaps more than for his compositions he was highly regarded at the time on account of his voice, which Erasmus describes as 'golden'. Tinctoris more specifically places him 'intre bassos contratenoristas' and considers him the finest bass singer he has ever heard (Pirro, *Histoire*, p. 102, and Reese, *Fourscore*, p. 35). It has been noted that Renaissance musicians were generally paid not so much according to their talents as composers, but according to the beauty or rarity of their voices, or so it seems. The reasons for the salary scale of chapel musicians sometimes elude us. Galeazzo Maria Sforza, for example, gave Josquin only five ducats a month during his stay at his court in 1474–76, whereas he paid L'Abbate, who is to us a more obscure musician, fourteen ducats. Perhaps the duke of Milan liked L'Abbate's voice more than Josquin's (Bridgman, *Mécénat*, p. 20).

[17] Borren, *Etudes*, p. 43.   [18] Rokseth, *Orgue*, p. 42.

Louis XI (reigned 1461–1483) undoubtedly heard some good music at his father's court, but he was not there too often, because the relationship between father and son was not a most harmonious one. Louis's initial unsuccessful revolt when he was sixteen years of age and participated in the Praguerie was followed by a brief reconciliation with his father, during which he was made governor of Dauphiné. But mutual distrust soon caused Louis to seek refuge at the court of Philip the Good, where he stayed for almost five years. There he could not have avoided hearing some of the most beautiful music available in Europe, since the duke of Burgundy, according to all contemporary reports, had perhaps the most sumptuous court in all of Christendom, and not the least of his expenses was allotted for his music. Louis was not by far so artistically inclined as his cousin Philip, nor so extravagant (except in matters of bribery, when it was politically expedient for him to resort to the practice), but after he became king, he did maintain a fine chapel, which Ockeghem continued to direct. His second wife, Charlotte of Savoy, had her own chapel, with six singers.[19]

A music book written for Louis XI but now lost contained works by Ockeghem and Busnois among others.[20] On a somewhat lower level, among the king's accounts of 20 February 1470 is a listing for thirteen *sols*, nine *deniers tournois* to be given to 'a drummer to provide for dancing around the bonfire on the eve of the feast of Saint John.'[21] King Louis was extremely devout, and occasionally heard as many as five Masses a day. His own chapel performed at daily Mass and Vespers.[22] In 1474, he made a provision for six choirboys at the Church of the Holy Innocents in Paris, and gave a fine organ to Notre-Dame d'Embrun in honor of the Virgin Mary, to whom he had always been particularly devoted. On 6 July 1482 he founded at the same cathedral a daily and perpetual Mass requiring one hundred participants, including instrumentalists.[23]

[19] *Ibid.*, p. 44.   [20] Brooks, *Busnois*, p. 2.
[21] Cimber, *Archives*, 1ere sér., t. 1, p. 94.   [22] Rokseth, *Orgue*, pp. 42–43.
[23] *Ibid.*, p. 43. His selection of the church of the Holy Innocents as the recipient of his gift may have stemmed from a particular devotion which he had for the Holy Innocents. He followed a custom rather prevalent in his

After Louis's death, we enter into an altogether new era. Though it was not without numerous links with the past, life at the French court seems to have become less austere. As H. M. Brown convincingly sums it up:

> Beginning with the reigns of Charles VIII and Louis XII, but especially under Francis I, the importance of the court in the intellectual and artistic life of the country increased enormously. At the court the advance guard of the nation assembled; the newest philosophy, art, music, and literature were fostered and flourished in the king's household.[24]

It is true that by then, although the spirit of its musical chapel was still present in the establishments of the Habsburg dynasty, the Burgundian court had ceased to exist and was replaced by the royal court as a French cultural center.

Charles VIII (reigned 1483–1498) almost married two very musical ladies, Mary of Burgundy, and later her daughter, Margaret of Austria,[25] and finally wedded another duchess

---

time, according to Calmette (notes to Commynes, *Mémoires*, II, pp. 57–58), which consisted in abstaining from all business transactions on the day of the week corresponding to the Feast of the Holy Innocents celebrated the preceding year. In 1475, every Wednesday was considered the 'Innocents' day' by Louis XI, because 28 December 1474 had fallen on a Wednesday. On that day, Commynes tells us, the king 'did not discuss any of his state affairs, nor did he want to; he considered it very bad luck if anyone spoke to him about business and he became very angry with those who were his familiars and who knew about his custom.'

Even on his deathbed he did not lose faith in the Blessed Virgin Mary. As Commynes (II, p. 325) reports: 'He said that he hoped not to die before Saturday and that Our Lady would grant him this grace, since he had always placed his trust in her, was very devoted to her, and had prayed to her. . . . And so it happened as he had wished it, for he died on Saturday, the last day in August, 1483, at eight o'clock in the evening, at Plessis, where he had taken ill the previous Monday.'

[24] Brown, in Haar, *Chanson*, p. 2.

[25] The marriage project between Charles and Mary, who was more than twenty years his senior, was not considered seriously for long, though Mary was eager to become a member of the ruling house of France. Her first lady-in-waiting, Jeanne de Hallwin, however, maintained that the duchess's subjects needed a man and not a child (Commynes, *Mémoires*, II, pp. 251–252). As for Margaret, daughter of Mary of Burgundy and

with musical interests, Anne of Brittany. During his Italian campaign in 1495, Charles heard High Mass at the church of Saint John, in Naples; it is true that it was celebrated not by a Neapolitan, but by 'Master Robinet, canon of Rouen.'[26] The same year at Poggibonsi, on Corpus Christi day, the singers of his chapel joined the local clergy in celebrating the occasion; they were followed by players of high instruments.[27] His court chapel, with Ockeghem at its head, included such outstanding musicians as Loyset Compère, who was *chantre ordinaire* in 1486, and Alexander Agricola. That the king cared for the music which these people provided is shown by an anxious letter from Charles to Piero de' Medici, in Florence, entreating him to send back to him Agricola, his singer, who had left the royal chapel for Florence, along with a good lutenist, in the days of Piero's father Lorenzo. The king wants Agricola and the nameless lutenist to return and promises to treat them well.[28]

Louis XII (reigned 1498–1515), formerly duke of Orléans, came to the throne from a collateral line, since Charles VIII lost his small son the dauphin, who might otherwise have succeeded him. Louis's father was Charles d'Orléans, many of whose poems were set to music by fifteenth-century musicians. By the standards of Francis I and in retrospect, Louis XII's court may have appeared a trifle sober; yet it led the way to what was to become the golden age of the French musical Renaissance. In 1496, Louis had a collection of chansons made for him (Paris, Bibl. nat., *MS. fr. 2245*) which included works by Ockeghem, Josquin, and Prioris.[29] The latter was to become the head of his royal chapel in 1507. Among the musicians who served in that institution were Antoine de Longueval, who became its *maître de chapelle* under Francis I, and is perhaps best known today for his probable authorship

Maximilian I of Austria, she was taken to France at the age of three, where she remained for several years as the Dauphin's fiancée, until her engagement was broken. During her French sojourn, she was given the title of Queen of France.

[26] Cimber, *Archives*, 1ère sér., t. 1, p. 351.

[27] Thoinan, *Origines*, p. 75.

[28] Picker, *Agricola*, p. 668. The letter is at the Morgan Library, New York, and is undated. Picker believes it may have been written *ca.* 1492.

[29] Lowinsky, *Medici* (edition), v. 3, p. 47.

of the early motet-passion formerly attributed to Obrecht,[30]
Jean Braconnier, called Lourdault, Antoine de Févin,
characterized by Glarean as Josquin's emulator, and by Jean
Mouton, his colleague at the royal chapel, as 'gentil.' The king
appreciated Févin's music so much that in 1507 he sent a letter
from Italy to request one of his chansons, so that he might
show it to the ladies.[31] According to Zarlino, Mouton was the
teacher of Adrian Willaert, whose compositions led the way in
Venetian polychoral writing, though he can no longer be
considered the originator of that practice.

Louis XII, and Francis I after him, were the first to name as
canons at Saint-Quentin members of the Royal Chapel who
were eligible for retirement and deserving of some reward for
past services.[32] Mouton was so honored. He died at Saint-
Quentin and was buried there in 1522, near Compère.[33] It has
been noted that whereas there were many Italian dancers,
instrumentalists, and organ builders in France, the court
singer-composers under Louis XII were not Italian, but hailed
from the northern provinces.[34] The king took a personal
interest in the dissensions between the Sainte-Chapelle and his
own chapel, as to which official, the king's *maître de chapelle*, or
the treasurer of the Sainte-Chapelle, should supervise the
personnel of the Saint-Chapelle. Since the two institutions had
become more distinct than in the past—in fact they were by
then completely separate, although some of the members of
the Sainte-Chapelle might also have had duties in the royal
chapel, as Claudin de Sermisy was to have from 1532 on—and
considering that the king's chapel had become ambulatory,
Louis XII decided, by letters of 1511, that the treasurer of the
Sainte-Chapelle was to have supreme authority there.[35]

Glarean's anecdote about Louis XII's lack of musicality and

---

[30] Reese (*Renaissance*, pp. 273–274) sums up the arguments for
Longueval's authorship. The late Lucien van Hoorn, in his book on
Obrecht, was still convinced that Obrecht was the author, owing, perhaps,
to his great enthusiasm for that composer, on whom he had spent so many
years.
[31] Chaillon, *Louis XII*, p. 66.
[32] Raugel, *Saint-Quentin*, p. 54.
[33] Finscher, *Compère*, p. 19.   [34] Chaillon, *Louis XII*, p. 66.
[35] Brenet, *Sainte-Chapelle*, pp. 20, 54–56. This ruling apparently did not
prevent an inspection and visitation of the Sainte-Chapelle's house for the

thin voice is probably apocryphal. According to the *Dodecachordon* (1547), Josquin wrote the unpretentious *Lutuichi regis Franciae jocosa cantio* (with a two-part canon in the upper voices, a long held note in the next lower voice [labelled *regis vox*] and an ostinato bass on two notes a fifth apart—the second of which is at the octave of the *vox regis*), at the king's request, so that he could somehow perform in a polyphonic group without losing his place or his pitch. The piece, which Glarean gives without words, appears in an earlier source, the *Liederbuch* of Johannes Heer (St. Gall: Stiftsbibliothek, *MS. 462*) under the title *Carmen gallicum Ludovici XI regis Francorum*, with the date 1510, and the text 'Guillaume s'en va chauffer . . .' There is no designation of *regis vox* in the third voice. Unless an absent-minded scribe erroneously wrote *XI* instead of *XII*, the king in question was Louis XI. Clinksdale points out that Heer, who lived in Paris in 1510, under the reign of Louis XII, was not likely to have mistaken him for a king dead twenty-nine years. Since the manuscript gives no indication that the third voice was sung by the king—it is called simply contratenor—it does not show any conclusive proof to bear out Glarean's story concerning its composition.[36]

Anne of Brittany was twice a queen of France. The first time it was as the wife of Charles VIII, after an earlier marriage by proxy to Maximilian of Austria had been broken. Thus the duchy of Brittany, Anne's dowry, was united to the French crown, although it was not formally annexed until 1532. The widowed queen's second valid marriage was to Charles's successor, Louis XII, after the latter had his first marriage to Louis XI's daughter, Jeanne of France, dissolved.[37] Anne descended from a music-loving family on both sides; her father was Francis II, last duke of Brittany, and her mother Marguerite of Foix. As a young girl she learned Greek and Latin as well as music. We know that she sang and accompanied herself on the mandora. When she came to the

children from being made in 1517, under Louis XII's successor, not by the treasurer of the Sainte-Chapelle, but by Antoine de Longueval, in his capacity as Master and first chaplain of the king's chapel (*ibid.*, p. 65).

[36] *See* Glarean, *Dodecachordon*, 1965 ed., I: p. 3, II: p. 284, Clinksdale, *Josquin*, pp. 67–69, and Brown, in Haar, *Chanson*, p. 12.

[37] She was canonized by the Roman Catholic church in 1950.

French court, she surrounded herself with poets, painters, and musicians, whom she protected. Among the better known of the poets were Jean Meschinot, Jean Marot, and Jean Lemaire de Belges. Her secretary, André de Lavigne, wrote a history of Charles VIII. Her musicians included the singer Prégent Jagu, who became honorary *valet de chambre* to the king in 1501, a cornettist, trumpeters, a drummer, a rebec player, a clavichordist, a lutenist from Como, and other instrumentalists, some of whom came from Brittany. She liked beautiful manuscripts and spectacles. The theatrical troupe *Galans sans soucy* occasionally performed for her, as did a Florentine woman dancer. She had an organ imported from Naples to Amboise. In 1511, she provided for the reconstruction of the organ of the cathedral of Saint Maurice in Angers, which had been destroyed by lightning in 1451. On the new organ-case was the portrait of the benefactress, wearing an ermine-trimmed dress;[38] this undoubtedly called to mind the ermine of the coat-of-arms of Brittany. After Anne's death at the age of thirty-seven, Louis XII married King Henry VIII's sister Mary Tudor, in the hope of obtaining a son who could succeed him to the throne. Daughters he had, but in France women could not inherit the crown.[39] Louis's wish was not granted, and his marriage was short-lived, for he died in 1515, not more than a year after Anne, but not before being treated to a musical offering by his young queen, who used to sing and play the lute at the foot of his bed.[40] And so with the accession of Francis I (reigned 1515–1547) to the crown, a collateral line was once more called into play, and 'the salamander of the Valois-Angoulême replaced the porcupine of the Valois-Orléans.'[41] The many contributions of

[38] *See* La Laurencie, *Bretagne*, pp. 6–13, and Chaillon, *Louis XII*, pp. 63–64.

[39] Commynes (*Mémoires*, II, p. 257) approves of the custom as far as great powers are concerned, because a ruling queen might select a foreign lord as her consort (or he would be selected for her), who would then be the *de facto* ruler of her land; and this, in the memorialist's opinion, might be most inconvenient for the kingdom.

[40] Lowinsky, *Medici* (edition), v. 3, p. 44.

[41] Barbier, *Histoire*, I: p. 48. The founder of the house of Angoulême, Jean d'Orléans (1455–1482), had several singers in his private chapel (Thoinan, *Origines*, p. 67).

Francis I to learning are well enough known not to require much elaboration here; suffice it to mention his foundation of the Collège de France, his creation of royal professorships in various disciplines, and his establishment of special categories of royal printers for particular subjects, which included music. He attracted to his brilliant court some of the most distinguished artists and men of letters from France and abroad, such as Clouet, Clément Marot, and Albert de Rippe (from Mantua). It was for these things that he most wished to be remembered, apparently, for at his funeral on 22 May 1547, on his last journey through the streets of Paris, the twenty-four town criers stopped periodically to say: 'Pray to God for the soul of the most high, most powerful and most magnanimous Francis, first of his name, by the grace of God most Christian king of France: clement prince, father of arts and sciences.'[42] In a double homage to beauty, the king is supposed to have said: 'A court without ladies is a springtime without roses,' and 'I can make a nobleman; God alone can make a great artist.'[43] He was a poet and his works were set to music by contemporary composers; not all the poems ascribed to him in one source or another are necessarily his, however. It has been suggested, on the basis of an attribution of a chanson from one of Attaingnant's prints to 'Françoys', that the king may have been its composer.[44] It is not impossible that this was so, given the king's great interest in music, but François was by no means an unusual name at the time and could also have referred to any number of people of lesser renown. Some of the literary manuscripts containing his poems ascribe them more clearly to 'le roy.' Whether or not he composed, he has been depicted as playing a pedal organ.[45]

He was so eager to have a good chapel that he sometimes closed his eyes to exactly how singers were recruited for him. In 1517, for example, two boys were kidnapped from the *maîtrise* at Rouen for the king. This custom was not uncommon

---

[42] Heartz, *Attaingnant*, p. 139. This was probably Francis's idea as much as that of his mourners, for kings, before they die, often make provision for the ceremonial pertaining to their funeral. We know, for example, that Louis XI did so in great detail (Commynes, *Mémoires*, II, pp. 324–325).

[43] Erlanger, *Diane*, p. 32.

[44] Heartz, *Attaingnant*, p. 103.   [45] Rokseth, *Orgue*, p. xi.

in the Renaissance—Lassus was one of its victims—but not everyone practiced it. Jean Conseil, who was leaving Cambrai for Rome, did not dare take with him a young singer whom his colleagues would not let him have.[46] Anne of Brittany, who wanted one of the little singers from Chartres, Le Fève, used gentle and ladylike means to obtain the boy whose voice had pleased her; she gave the cathedral a big bell in return. It was in 1510. When the canons granted her wish, she is supposed to have told them: 'You have given me a little voice, but I want to give you a big one.'[47]

Francis I gave a charter of reformation to the Sainte-Chapelle in 1521 and provided for two scholarships to be used by its choirboys at the Collège de Navarre. These grants were in effect many years after his death, for on 22 December 1570, the music master of the Sainte-Chapelle was delegated to confer with the king's confessor about their assignment, in accordance with 'the charity of King Francis.'[48]

It was under his reign that his household musicians, apart from the chapel, were classed as members of *musique de la chambre* and *musique de l'écurie*. The chamber musicians from 1516 to 1538 included soloists such as the lutenists François de Bugats, Jehan Paulle, Hubert d'Espalt, and Albert de Rippe, who were in the category of honorary domestics, as well as cornettists, fifers and drummers. The *écurie* (literally, stable) comprised violins, oboes, and sackbuts. At some time between 1530 and 1540, the singer Anthoine Le Riche (possibly the same person as the composer Divitis, who was in the royal chapel in 1515) appears among the members of the *musique de la chambre*, although royal singers were normally associated only with the chapel. It has been assumed that he was a solo singer. In 1535 or thereabouts, Francis created a small vocal group to sing chansons, to which he added some instruments, such as flutes and oboes, and organs. And so a new

[46] Pirro, *Histoire*, p. 306.

[47] It was one of the four large bells of Notre-Dame de Chartres and was named Anne in honor of the queen. Through her protection Le Fève eventually became a canon at Chartres. He gave 3,000 *livres* to the chapter so that the queen's bell might be rung from the Sunday after Easter until Trinity Sunday, for one hour each day (La Laurencie, *Bretagne*, p. 13).

[48] Brenet, *Sainte-Chapelle*, pp. 71, 118.

organization for the *musique de chambre* included the domestic officers, singers, instrumentalists, cornettists, and fifers and drummers. The last category (fifes and drums) occasionally included harps and rebecs. We can thereby see that the classification was indeed a loose one and that divisional names were not meant to be taken seriously. This set-up was kept by Henry II and his successors, with minor changes, such as acceptance of violins in the chamber group, probably under Charles IX. By 1609, the violins were twenty-two in number. The musicians of Francis I's *écurie*, on the other hand, were not soloists; they were more comparable to members of a small band. The wind players were on the whole foreigners, and the violinists French.[49] These hardy men who made music for balls, parades, and other such festivities seemed to have had a lower social position than their more pampered confrères from the king's chamber. When they accompanied the sovereign on some of his trips, they were not provided with first-class accommodations or the most comfortable means of travel. In fact, they probably followed the royal retinue on foot, although the king occasionally gave them a special allotment so that they might 'have a horse.'[50] Guillaume Telin, in *La Louenge de musique*, 1533, excuses this apparent lack of consideration for musicians with diplomacy, on the grounds that horses and music are not good enough to carry these worthy men, who will eventually be borne on clouds and consort with the angels.[51] Until that time comes, however, musicians must walk.

Queen Claude lived in a musical atmosphere all her life, at the court of her parents, Louis XII and Anne of Brittany, and of her husband Francis I; she could hardly have failed to have had some musical training. Her governess had been Jeanne de Polignac, mother of the music-loving Cardinal de Tournon. At the time of the birth of Claude's daughter Louise,

[49] After Francis's death, Henry II brought in more Italian violinists (Boyden, *Violin*, p. 21).

[50] Prunières, *Chambre*, pp. 219–247.

[51] 'One hardly sees musicians ride horses or mules nowadays. And that is because such a mount is not worthy of supporting them; but if some of them now travel on foot, a time will come when they shall be raised on clouds and placed with the consort of angels, in whose glory they participate' (Telin, *Louenge*, fol. 77no).

the poet Jean Marot composed a laudatory epistle for the queen, in which he depicts musicians giving praise to the celestial court for the event by playing on various high instruments.[52] The king's second wife, Eleanor of Austria, sister of Emperor Charles V and widow of Manuel I of Portugal, was an accomplished musician. She had been a keyboard student of the famous organist Herry Bredemers, and had received a 'clavicenon' in 1512. She also played the lute and sang so well in ensembles that 'it was a pleasure to see and hear her.'[53] Although she could hardly have been called the most elegant woman of her time, she so charmed Francis, when she danced a 'moorish sarabande' for him in 1525, while he was her brother's prisoner in Madrid, that for this and for other reasons, more political in nature, he asked for her hand in marriage.[54] And so he obtained his liberty, although it was hardly unconditional, and he had to send his two sons as hostages in his place. By 1530, four years after the treaty of Madrid, Francis I carried out his promise to marry Eleanor, when she came to France, accompanied by his recently released sons.[55]

The king's sister, Marguerite of Navarre, was as interested as her brother in arts and letters. She gathered around her some of the most original thinkers of her time, including the poet Clément Marot, in an atmosphere permeated with the ideas of religious reformers and humanists. They were influenced by the writings of Marsilio Ficino, which some scholars consider to be at the root of the French academies, beginning with Baïf's *Académie de poésie et de musique*.[56] A poetess of no mean value, Marguerite had many of her works set to music. Some of her little plays refer to fashionable tunes of the day, and some of the tales of her *Heptameron* also refer to music. Her first husband, the duke of Alençon, used to have a fine chapel.[57] As

---

[52] François, *Tournon*, p. 28, and J. Marot, *Œuvres*, p. 160. Bernstein (*Couronne*, pp. 48–50) has suggested that Queen Claude's sister Renée, duchess of Ferrara, and her three children were associated with the Venetian collection *La Couronne et fleur des chansons a troys* (1536[1]) and its principal composer, Willaert.

[53] Picker, *Marguerite*, p. 28.

[54] Erlanger, *Diane*, pp. 79, 91.

[55] François, *Tournon*, pp. 86–87.

[56] Yates, *Academies*, p. 49.   [57] Rokseth, *Orgue*, pp. 105–106.

for the two favorites among Francis's favorite ladies, Françoise of Foix, countess of Châteaubriand, the king's official mistress since 1515, who was probably murdered by her husband after the king gave her up and sent her back to him, and Anne de Pisseleu, duchess of Etampes, who supplanted her in 1526 and kept her authority over the king until his death, both were given musical tributes. The first was the recipient of a beautiful chanson manuscript (London, Brit. Mus., *MS. Harley 5242*) and may also have been the subject of two dance tunes; the second probably had a *basse-danse* named after her.[58]

Henry II (reigned 1547–1559), though less artistically gifted than his father, nevertheless may have written a poem which was set to music by Sandrin, as well as music for Marot's translation of Psalm 128.[59] He liked to sing, and perhaps occasionally to read theoretical treatises on music. (He had a copy of Glarean's *Dodecachordon* in his library.)[60] Seated at the side of his Egeria, Diane de Poitiers, he played tunes for her on the guitar.[61] Like his father, he helped music printers in their work by granting them privileges, and by creating new royal printers for music, Le Roy et Ballard, after Attaingnant's death; and for this printers and musicians were grateful. Thus Albert de Rippe's first book of lute tablature, published posthumously at the press of Fezandat in 1552 by Guillaume Morlaye, contained a dedicatory epistle to the king by the latter musician.

Frenchmen have often and a bit indiscriminately attributed the faults of his queen, Catherine de' Medici, to her Italian blood, though a few have on occasion praised her for it. But she was only partly Italian, since her mother was Madeleine de

[58] *See* Chaillon, *Françoise*, and François, *Tournon*, p. 178 on Mme de Châteaubriand. Daniel Heartz (*Preludes*, p. lxxv) suggests that the *basses-danses Chasteau brient* and *Foués* (corresponding to the sixteenth-century pronunciation of Foix) might have to do with Françoise, and that the basse-danse *La Brosse* refers to the second lady. Her husband was Jean de la Brosse, count of Penthièvre, whom she married in 1534. In order that she might become a duchess, he was named duke of Etampes (Erlanger, *Diane*, p. 104).

[59] Heartz, *Attaingnant*, pp. 102, 141.

[60] Bibliothèque, Nationale, *Musique*, p. 38. It does not mean, of course, that he necessarily read it.

[61] Erlanger, *Diane*, p. 221.

la Tour d'Auvergne, a princess from the house of Bourbon.[62]
What authority Catherine lacked during her husband's reign,
she more than compensated for when her three sons came to
the throne successively. Her love for music and the dance was
proverbial, as was her part in the establishment of the French
ballet de cour; and she knew how to mingle music and politics
effectively. The *Ballet des provinces françaises*, her musical
spectacle in honor of the Polish ambassadors, for example,
was presented on the occasion of the election of her son Henry
to the throne of Poland, before it became necessary, through
his brother Charles's death, for him to become king of France.
The seventeenth-century historian Mezeray tells us somewhat
disapprovingly that when the queen mother accompanied her
son Charles IX to the siege of Saint-Jean d'Angely in 1569,

> she always took along with her all the apparatus for the
> most voluptuous entertainment, and particularly one
> hundred or so among the most beautiful women from the
> court, who led with a leash twice as many courtiers. It was
> essential, as Montluc [marshal of France and persecutor of
> Calvinists] used to say, that in the greatest troubles of the
> war and [state] affairs, the ball should go on. The sound of
> the violins was not stifled by the sound of the trumpets: the
> same band dragged ballet machines and war machines; and
> within the same field could be seen the combats in which the
> French cut each other's throats and the carrousels in which
> the ladies took their pleasure.[63]

Catherine's famous *escadron volant*, whose name may derive
from a triangular dance formation, reminiscent of a squadron
of flying cranes, in which Hélène de Surgères and other court

---

[62] It was for Madeleine's marriage to Lorenzo de' Medici, in May 1518,
at Amboise, that the beautiful *Codex Medici*, containing motets associated
with the French court repertoire, was undoubtedly commissioned. By
whom is not easy to determine. Lowinsky, in his magistral study and
edition of that manuscript, believes Francis I to have been the donor,
whereas Leeman Perkins, in his review of Lowinsky's edition (pp. 262–265),
hypothesizes that it was not the French king, who was already doing the
groom a favor by letting him have a wealthy bride far above him in social
standing, but Pope Leo X.

[63] Quoted in Kastner, *Militaire*, p. 100.

ladies participated, and which was described by Ronsard, was probably less scandalous than loose tongues would have it, as Frances Yates points out. These ladies took part in court spectacles which the queen mother encouraged, but it was in order to promote the cause of peace. And at least once, Catherine encouraged propriety in musical spectacle, when she suggested to Baïf that he avoid lasciviousness in plays that his academy was planning to present. These works were to be composed of *vers* and *musique mesurés*, with corresponding dance steps which would reflect the long and short syllables of the text and attempt to recapture the spirit of Greek drama.[64]

The queen mother had her own chapel, and one of her singers, Michel Fabry, from Provence, won a prize at the music contest in Evreux in 1577.[65] She received the dedication of Janequin's *Octante deux pseaumes de David* (1559), translated into French, with an epistle in verse by the composer, and the second book of Jean Maillard's motets (1565), with a poem by the royal publishers, Le Roy and Ballard.

It is true that her chief rival during her husband's lifetime, Diane de Poitiers, also had psalms by Certon dedicated to her (Le Roy et Ballard, 1555), as well as other musical collections, such as the *Chansons nouvelles* by the precocious poet-composer from Marseille, Barthélemy Beaulaigue, who wrote words and music to these chansons at the age of fifteen or so. This was published by Robert Granjon at Lyon in 1559, and represented the printer's first venture into *musique en civilité* (rounded notes). It has been suggested that *MS. Q 19* of the Civico Museo Bibliografico Musicale in Bologna was made for Diane.[66]

She had been a lady-in-waiting to Queen Claude and then married to Louis de Brézé, grand seneschal of Normandy and grandson of Charles VII and Agnès Sorel, a man forty years her senior. Henry II was twenty years her junior. At the beginning of his reign, Diane, who had dressed in black since her

[64] Yates, *Academies*, pp. 251, 60–61. Baïf mentions this in verses which he had addressed to Charles IX during an absence of the king. Whether these plays were ever written, we do not know.

[65] Bonnin, *Puy*, p. 54.

[66] Lowinsky, *Medici* (edition). Perkins, in his review, pp. 266–267, is not convinced that this was so.

widowhood in 1531, and would do so to the end of her days, assumed publicly an air of austerity which she tried to impose on the court. The feasting, dancing, and music-making which had been characteristic of Francis I's era were curtailed somewhat, and his son's court was supposed collectively to engage in good and virtuous thoughts.[67] These fine intentions, however, were only skin-deep. Diane was very fond of music. She played the lute and sang. And she never travelled without her spinet, which was taken care of by a special servant. She sang psalms in French, as did everyone else at court. Her favorite piece was Marot's *De profundis (Du fond de ma pensée)* which she sang to the cheerful tune of *La volte*.[68] Also in the manner of a *volte*, that is, in rapid ternary meter, she sang the psalm of Théodore de Bèze, *Ainsi qu' on ouït le cerf bruire*.[69]

Francis II (reigned 1559–1560), the French husband of Mary Stuart, queen of Scotland, died at the age of sixteen; and so it is difficult to determine whether he would have continued in the tradition of his father and grandfather as a protector of the arts. But Ronsard, in his dedication to the young king of his *Livre des mélanges*, published in 1560 by Le Roy et Ballard, expresses the hope that God will

> increase more and more the virtues of Your Majesty and . . . continue you in the kindly affection which you are pleased to have for music and for all who study to make flourish again under your sway the sciences and arts which flourished under the empire of Caesar Augustus.

He believes that Francis II takes after his father Henry, who

> so honored, loved, and esteemed music that all in France who today remain well-disposed toward this art, have not, all combined, so much affection for it as he had alone. You also, Sire, as the inheritor both of his realm and his virtues, show that you are his son, favored by Heaven, in so perfectly loving this science and its accords, without which nothing of this world could remain whole.[70]

[67] Erlanger, *Diane*, p. 210.
[68] Lowinsky, *Medici* (article), p. 102.
[69] Lesure, *Eléments*, p. 172.
[70] Strunk, *Readings*, pp. 96–99.

After the premature death of Francis II, his brother Charles IX was called upon to reign, from 1560 to 1574, with his mother as regent until 1563. At Mass, according to Brantôme,

> he got up very often and, imitating the late King Henry his father, who used to do the same, he went to the lectern with his singers; and he stood among them and sang his *taille* [tenor] part and the *dessus* [top part] quite well; and he was fond of his singers, and particularly Etienne Le Roy ... who had a very beautiful voice.[71]

A *haute-contre* of the king's chapel was the composer Eustache du Caurroy, who also served under Charles's two successors, Henry III and Henry IV. In 1578, Du Caurroy's title was 'sous-maître,' but until the seventeenth century, the musical director was called *sous-maître*, or *premier sous-maître* when two persons of that rank existed. The title of *Maître* was honorary and was usually held by an outsider whom the king wished to favor.[72] Du Caurroy became royal chamber composer in 1595. He is best known for his motets and instrumental fantasias. Charles's lutenist and *valet de chambre*, Vaumesnil, was celebrated by many poets; his *Fantaisie* was printed in Besard's *Thesaurus Harmonicus* (1609).[73]

The king was fond of Ronsard's poetry.

> He often passed a great part of the night in reading his verses or having them recited, for which he would employ Amadis Jamyn, Estienne Le Roy, Abbé de Saint Laurent, the master of the music of his chamber, and other of his domestic servitors.[74]

[71] Quoted in Verchaly, *Desportes*, p. 276. This singer had belonged to the Sainte-Chapelle and left it in 1570 to become Abbé of Saint-Laurent. He is mentioned in *La Galliade* of Guy Le Fevre de la Boderie (1578): 'Et soit de Saint Laurent la haute et douce voix/ A jamais agréable aux oreilles des rois' (quoted in Brenet, *Sainte-Chapelle*, p. 115).

[72] Pierre, *Chapelle*, p. 14.

[73] Bibliothèque Nationale, *Musique*, p. 76.

[74] Quoted from Arnauld Sorbin, *Vie de Charles IX*, in Yates, *Academies*, p. 49. Miss Yates adds: 'This sounds like a performance in which Le Roy, the famous castrato singer, collaborated with Jamin in a musical presentation of Ronsard's verses.' This indeed corresponds to Ronsard's and the Pleiade's ideas of how verses should be presented with music.

Charles liked the music of Lassus, whom he tried to lure to his court as his chamber composer. The lutenist-publisher Adrian Le Roy tells Lassus, in a letter dated 14 January 1574, that the king found Orlando's chanson *Ung jeune moine* most agreeable to hear. Apparently Charles also had more sophisticated tastes in music, for Le Roy relates further that he had enjoyed a chromatic piece by Vicentino, and had exclaimed that surely 'Orlando could not compose such chromatic music.' The publisher replied that indeed he had written some, and had the king listen to an example, after which he was 'so entranced that I cannot describe it.'[75]

Le Roy et Ballard wrote a Latin dedication to the king in Maillard's *Modulorum* (1565) and addressed a dedicatory ode to him in their publication of Lassus's *Novem quiritationes divi Job* (1565, and re-edition 1572), in which they spare no praise of the Flemish composer, whose music, it seems, could singlehandedly put France back on its feet. The compliment to Lassus appears to be temporarily at the expense of 'vulgar' French music, whatever that means:

> . . . Votre France n'a pas affaire
> De notre musique vulgaire;
> Affin de la remettre sus
> Il faut, pour amollir l'audace
> De ce facheux temps, que la grace
> Et l'accord, vienne de Lassus.[76]

The publishers surely did not mean to be unpatriotic. They were perhaps only trying to cater to the king's taste. Or possibly they had a bit of trouble finding a word that would rhyme with 'affaire;' and so they used 'vulgaire' without thinking too much about the matter. *Vulgaire* does not necessarily mean 'vulgar,' of course; it can mean 'vernacular.' I believe that the first meaning applies, however, and that the publishers were not suggesting total abandonment of music with French words.

Charles IX cooperated with Baïf in the foundation of his *Académie de poésie et de musique*, and made laws for it by letters

[75] Lesure, *Le Roy*, p. 37.
[76] *Ibid.*, p. 32.

patent. The Parlement made difficulties about ratifying them, but the letters were eventually accepted, largely through the king's insistence. Since the *Académie* developed *vers mesurés* and *musique mesurée*, an essentially French humanistic manifestation, the king can be considered in some ways responsible for the launching of a French national musical style, though it was through patronage rather than creation—as Isabella d'Este had done many years before, in Mantua, when she promoted the frottola, which became an important Italian national genre. The aims of Baïf's *Académie* were considered a governmental matter, for its by-laws state that the music of a country mirrors the social state of the nation.[77]

After Charles's death, the institution which he had helped to found gave way to the *Académie du Palais* (so named because its seat was in the Louvre instead of in Baïf's house) under Henry III (reigned 1574–1589). Its members included the poet from the South, Guy du Faur de Pibrac, Ronsard, Tyard, Baïf, Agrippa d'Aubigné, grandfather of Mme de Maintenon, and some women, such as the duchess of Retz and Marguerite de Valois, first wife of Henry of Navarre, the future Henry IV of France.[78] Henry III maintained a good chapel; its four adult *dessus*, six pages, seven *hautes-contre*, seven *tailles*, and eleven *basses-contre* with two flutes and cornets in 1578 compare favorably with one *dessus*, eight *hautes-contre*, four *tailles*, and five *basses-contre* which had comprised the personnel in 1532. In 1578 Henry gave them a list of duties to perform: all the singers and canons are bound to sing at a High Mass every day, on the hour selected by the king, unless they are excused by their director. They are to participate in all the canonical hours at stated times during the year, such as for Christmas, Easter, feasts of the Blessed Virgin Mary, and during Lent. Vespers and Compline they must celebrate every Saturday and Sunday, and on the eve and on the feasts of the Apostles, as well as at other specified times. For the services, the performers were to present themselves in long robes, surplices, almuces, and round bonnets 'in the manner of churchmen, and as properly as possible.' Among the many responsibilities of the *sous-maître* were the supervision of the food for the little pages,

[77] Lesure, *Musicians,* pp. 93–94.
[78] Yates, *Academies,* pp. 32–33.

and the upkeep of the chapel's pack animal 'which served ordinarily to follow the king, carrying trunks which contain clothes, blackboards for writing, books to study, and other personal belongings and necessities of the said pages.'[79]

The king's organist was Nicolas de la Grotte, one of Ronsard's musicians, who was important in the history of the *air de cour* and the *chanson mesurée*. The text *Despité/J'ay quitté* . . ., which first appeared in Chardavoine's chanson collection (1588 edition), has been called in another collection, *La fleur de toutes les plus belles chansons*, 1614: *Chanson du Roy Henry 3*.[80] Whether the king had anything to do with its authorship is not known.

France had been plagued for many years with religious conflicts between Catholics and Protestants, and the royal family often found itself divided over where its sympathies lay. At any rate, under the influence of the Catholic Counter-Reformation, Henry III considered that his kingdom was ready for some austerity, and in order to set the proper tone for this new way of life, he cut down on court entertainments, created congregations of penitents, and organized nocturnal processions in which he and his nobles took part, unattended, and dressed in sackcloth. Musicians followed, in the same apparel, chanting 'the litany in fauxbourdon.' The penitents proceeded from church to church until they reached Notre-Dame, where the chapel sang the *Salve Regina*.[81] Some of Henry III's religious confraternities included the *Confrérie d'Hieronymites*, whose members had cells in the Bois de Vincennes, and the *Congrégation de l'Oratoire de Notre Dame de Vie Saine* (a pun on *Vincennes*). Two of the members had to be musicians, in order to help with the cult. Meanwhile, in these difficult times, the *Académie du Palais* at the Louvre may have exhausted itself and continued in a more sacred context, which led to the devout humanistic movement of the seventeenth century.[82]

[79] Pierre, *Chapelle*, pp. 4–5.

[80] Verchaly, *Chardavoine*, p. 211.

[81] Brenet, *Processions*, p. 9.

[82] Yates, *Academies*, pp. 159–161, 176. Miss Yates maintains (pp. 34–35) that 'there is very good reason to think that the "congrégation" which [Henry III] established at Vincennes about 1584 . . . was a kind of

Henry's queen, Louise de Lorraine, participated in the religious movement by having her own processions. We realize, however, that splendor was not entirely absent from the court, when we recall the *magnificences* which were organized for the marriage of the duke of Joyeuse to Mademoiselle de Vaudémont, sister of Queen Louise, and the *Balet comique de la royne*, which was perhaps the high point of the festivities. Salmon, one of the musicians who collaborated in this spectacle, may have belonged to one of the king's religious confraternities.[83]

François duke of Anjou (1554–1584), fifth son of Henry II and younger brother of the last three kings mentioned, was not always sure where he stood in matters of religion, and his allegiance vacillated between Catholics and Huguenots. In matters musical, however, he knew what he wanted, and attracted to his residence some of the most talented musicians in France, such as Claude le Jeune, who began his career in 1582 as master of the children at François's household.[84] In 1575 the duke took into service his brother Charles's lutenist Vaumesnil.

Henry IV (reigned 1589–1610), the first of the Bourbon kings, was the grandson of Marguerite of Navarre. His father, Antoine de Bourbon, husband of Marguerite's daughter Jeanne III d'Albret, queen of Navarre, had in his service Nicolas de la Grotte. During Henry IV's reign, music and ballet became once again a very important part of court life. This was especially true after 1598, when the peace of Vervins had been established, as well as the Edict of Nantes, which granted religious freedom to Protestants. (The king himself had once been a Huguenot.) The twenty-two violins which were part of his chamber ensemble in 1609 were the precursors of the famous Twenty-four Violins of the king (Louis XIII),[85] which group has been considered to be the first genuine permanent orchestra in France. It has been noted that

continuation of the Palace Academy in a religious form. It was Henri III's religious foundations, such as the order of the Holy Spirit and the *Congrégation de Notre Dame de Vincennes* which probably did most to preserve the academic spirit during this period of utter confusion.'

[83] Yates, *Academies*, p. 161.   [84] Levy, *Le Jeune*, pp. 22–23.
[85] Boyden, *Violin*, p. 57.

Henry IV's influence was not felt to any great extent in the music of his own chapel, although he intervened in a dispute between his singers and those of Notre-Dame de Paris, on one occasion when he was at the cathedral.[86] Since the royal chapel accompanied the king practically everywhere, and that included Notre-Dame, the singers considered that they were entitled to celebrate Mass in his presence regardless of where they happened to be. The singers of Notre-Dame, on the other hand, did not see why they could not sing Mass in their own church. The king settled the singers' argument by asking each group to sing a different section of the Mass.

His first queen, whom he repudiated in 1599, was Marguerite de Valois (often called *la Reine Margot*), daughter of Henry II and Catherine de' Medici. Brantôme depicts her as a writer of very fine poetry

> which she has some of her little child singers perform (or even sings herself, for she has a beautiful and pleasant voice, mingling it with the lute, which she plays rather nicely). And thus her unfortunate days are spent, without doing anyone harm, living the quiet life which she has chosen for the best.[87]

We recall that she had participated in sessions of the *Académie du Palais* in 1576. It was on the occasion of Henry of Navarre's marriage to Marguerite, 20 August 1572, that the spectacle *Paradis d'Amour* was presented. It was a joint effort by some of the most famous poets and musicians of the time, such as Baïf, Ronsard, Courville, and Claude le Jeune, and was an important precursor of the *ballet de cour*. The music, unfortunately, has not survived.

Henry IV's marriage to Marie de' Medici, in 1600, at the Palazzo Pitti in Florence, prompted the presentation of Peri's and Caccini's *Euridice*, considered by most historians to be one of the first real operas ever written. But it would be beyond the scope of this study to dwell upon that memorable occasion, which is well-known to all lovers of opera, for it marks the beginning of another era, and it belongs to Italian history.

[86] M. Garros, in Roland-Manuel, *Histoire*, I: p. 1592.
[87] Quoted in Verchaly, *Desportes*, p. 276.

2

Music in non-royal circles: ducal, aristocratic, ecclesiastical

Aristocratic circles other than the royal court also gave impetus to musical manifestations. Many of the persons from these milieus were in some way related to the kings of France, but they did not necessarily work in harmony with them at all times, musically or politically. Late mediaeval dukes of Burgundy, for example, though they had a common ancestor with the kings in the person of John the Good, king of France from 1350 to 1364, ocassionally forgot that by feudal law, they held the duchy as a fief from the crown of France, which could (and did) repossess it upon the death of the last male heir, and therefore owed allegiance to the king as ultimate suzerain; and so they openly made alliances with enemies of France, and made war against its ruler. The last Burgundian duke, Charles the Bold, even held the French king, Louis XI, a virtual prisoner at Péronne in 1468. But by that time, feudalism was beginning to lose some of its original force. The subjects of France and of Burgundy were hardly inspired by nationalistic feelings on one side or the other. Those who fought the wars were often mercenaries from foreign countries—Switzerland, for example, in the case of France. High-ranking nobles, including Louis XI's brother, Charles, duke of Berry, and his sister Yolande, duchess of Savoy, wavered in their allegiance between France and Burgundy, and took the side of whoever appeared to be the stronger at a given time.

The duchy of Burgundy, which became the leading musical center of Europe during the fifteenth century, was transmitted to Philip the Bold as his *appanage* in 1363 by his father John the Good. In the following generations, John the Fearless, who was duke from 1404 to 1419, had his cousin Louis of Orléans, brother of Charles VI, murdered, and then tried to make peace with the Dauphin, the future Charles VII; he was in turn killed by the Dauphin's advisers. John's only son, Philip the Good, because of his alliance with England, allowed the

English king to succeed Charles VI, in place of the French Dauphin. The regent of France, the duke of Bedford, brother of Henry V of England, became Philip's brother-in-law by marriage to his sister Anne of Burgundy. Philip did not trust the English entirely, however, for in 1427, at Lille, he tried to show that they had plotted to kill him, although his suspicions were probably unfounded.[1] He was eventually reconciled with Charles VII and even befriended Louis XI, at least outwardly, but his heart did not seem to be in it.

The history of the county of Burgundy (Franche-Comté) is intertwined with that of the duchy, because it was part of the possessions acquired through marriage and inheritance by the dukes of Burgundy. After Duke Charles's death, most of the county passed into the hands of the French, for a time, owing mostly to the skillful negotiations of Louis XI. The county, however, unlike the duchy, did not stem from the French crown, but had the Holy Roman Emperor as its ultimate suzerain. With Margaret of Austria, daughter of Mary of Burgundy and Emperor Maximilian, it reverted to the house of Austria, and was not finally reunited to the French crown before the reign of Louis XIV. The duchy, on the other hand, remained under French rule since 1477, although the kings did not always find it easy to keep. Emperor Charles V, for example, wanted it very much, and almost got it back from Francis I, but it was saved for France at the Treaty of Cambrai in 1529 (the Ladies' Peace, arranged by Francis's mother, Louise of Savoy, and by her sister-in-law, Margaret of Austria, who was Charles V's aunt; the ladies had been childhood

---

[1] Parris, *Binchois*, pp. 11–12. About 1429, during the English occupation of France, the duke of Bedford, who, it is believed, once had Dunstable in his service, made a tangible contribution to French music, or at least to one French musician, by offering two *écus* of gold at the chapter Mass in Rouen, on a day when the receipts from the collection were traditionally allotted to the music master of the cathedral. How firmly this custom was established we do not know, and apparently neither did the music master, for it is reported that he immediately bought wheat with the regent's money, before the chapter changed its mind as to the two *écus*' final destination. And he probably acted wisely, because shortly afterwards, the canons, contrary to tradition, stipulated that henceforth offerings of gold would go directly to them instead of to the music master (Becker, *Maîtrise*, pp. 188–189).

friends at the French court) and once again at the Treaty of Crépy, in 1544, when Charles renounced his claims to the duchy.

The region of France now called Burgundy, with Dijon as its capital, which is famous among other reasons for its fine wines and large edible snails, is only a pale reflection of the possessions that were once in the hands of the dukes of Burgundy. Charles the Bold was master not only of Burgundy proper, but of parts of Lorraine, Luxembourg, Picardy, Artois, Flanders, Hainaut, Brabant, and Gelderland. In other words, his territories included parts of present-day Belgium and Holland. And so Flemish was spoken in part of the realm. The language of the court, however, was French, and the poetess Christine de Pisan reminds us that the French tongue is 'la plus commune par l'universel monde.'[2] Most of the court musicians, too, had French-sounding names—Pierre Fontaine, for example, who served under three Burgundian dukes. In fact, by 1419, a good many of the singers had been trained at Notre-Dame and at the Sainte-Chapelle in Paris, and so the musicians of the Burgundian court performed in the Parisian fashion.[3]

Philip the Bold's chapel in 1389 consisted of eleven singers and six clerics directed by Jehan de Chartres. By 1404, the year of the duke's death, his chapel had as many as twenty-one chaplains, three clerics, and four *sommeliers*, and was reputed to be superior in number and in quality to that of the king of France and of the popes at Avignon.[4] The divine service was celebrated day and night 'in the royal manner.'[5] John the Fearless is reported to have taken on four boy singers who had formerly belonged to the duke of Berry; their leader was the Paris-trained Nicole Grenon. Unlike some private ambulatory chapels, the duke's chapel did not always follow him in his travels.[6] Duke John once had a Christmas celebration pre-

[2] Bethel, *Burgundian*, pp. 20–21.   [3] Marix, *Musiciens*, p. xii.

[4] The duke also employed seven *menestrels* (mostly shawm players), a trumpeter, a harper, and an organist (Wright, *Tapissier*, p. 178).

[5] Marix, *Musiciens*, p. xi.

[6] Wright (*op. cit.*, p. 181) reports that when John the Fearless was in Ghent during Easter week in 1407, he called upon four choirboys from the church of Saint Pierre in Lille, instead of his own singers, to perform the divine service at court.

sented before King Charles VI, with all sorts of instruments, including flutes, harps, *vielles*, drums, and trumpets. After dinner, a performance was given by the singers of the royal chapel and the players of high instruments.[7]

The social situation of the ducal musicians was much the same as that of the royal musicians. The singers of the chapel and the instrumentalists formed very distinct and unequal groups. The trumpeters and other *menestrels* were members of the duke's household on the same footing as heralds or cup-bearers, and they sometimes also served as heralds, waiters, messengers, etc. The chaplains, on the other hand, were well-to-do churchmen, provided with substantial prebends, and belonged to the duke's intimate circle. In addition to their positions as singers, they doubled as secretary, almoner, or ordinary *valet de chambre* to the duke.[8] Singers and instrumentalists had little to say to each other, and they were sometimes pointedly segregated, as at the famous musical Banquet of the Oath of the Pheasant, given on 17 February 1454 at Lille, when the chaplains were put in an improvised construction that represented a church, while the *menestrels* were gathered in a huge *paté*.[9]

When Philip the Good became duke of Burgundy, after the assassination of John the Fearless at Montereau-Faut-Yonne in 1419, he took over his father's chapel, which consisted of fifteen chaplains, three children, and other personnel. Philip had learned to play the harp. He took a personal interest in the music at his court and did not trust others to choose his musicians for him. Others might recruit them in various provinces, but the duke heard them sing before engaging them. He sent back many and kept few. Robinet de la Magdalaine he heard during all of Easter Week before hiring

[7] Pirro, *Charles VI*, pp. 20, 28–29. At the time, instruments were categorized as high or low, according to their loudness or softness of sound, rather than according to their range.

[8] The composer Jean Tapissier, for example, honorary *valet de chambre* to Philip the Bold, had his own personal valet and two horses. On 24 October 1396, he was given 'one hundred *écus* to help defray the expenses he had recently incurred in marrying off a sister,' and in December 1399 he received 'a cloak of mink fur valued at 39 francs, 5 *sous* to cover his livery during the winter season 1399–1400' (Wright, *op. cit.*, pp. 179–180).

[9] Marix, *Musiciens*, p. xiii.

him. His instrumentalists included Jehan Facien, 'king of the *menestrels* of France,' since the death of Charles VI, and Antoine le Blanc, formerly a royal trumpeter, as well as German musicians. His wife Isabella of Portugal brought with her a lutenist and a *vielle* player, both of whom were blind.[10] The duke, who had an exceptionally fine library, included music manuscripts among his holdings. In 1468 he paid twenty-four *solz* for 'three new Masses with music.' Philip has been compared to Pope Eugene IV as a patron of music; he founded *maîtrises* with a master and four choirboys at the Sainte-Chapelle in Dijon, on Christmas Day 1424, and at Saint-Pierre de Lille in December 1425. The children were to be 'innocent and of good morals.' The master was expected to be honest, and was to teach them good doctrine as well as music: plainchant, discant, and counterpoint. The boys were also to learn grammar and to have a reading and speaking knowledge of Latin.[11] In 1424, the duke provided for the celebration of a Mass in honor of the Virgin Mary every Saturday, to be sung with discant and organ. In 1431, he founded another High Mass at the Sainte-Chapelle of Dijon, to be sung with discant, except when it was a Requiem. In each of his castles was an organ.[12]

The most outstanding among the fifteenth-century composers were associated with Duke Philip's court. Dufay, though we do not know precisely whether he was there, and if so when, or what his duties were, was listed as singer to the duke of Burgundy. The title may have been purely honorary but it implies some relationship with the court.[13] Binchois was there for many years. He was considered to be the equal of Dufay and Dunstable, and Tinctoris sees in these three men the leaders of the musical art of their time. In addition to musical services, Binchois occasionally helped in matters of a more occult nature; in 1437 he supplied the duchess of Burgundy

[10] *Loc. cit.* Isabella must have been familiar with English music when she came to Burgundy, for Sarum use had been introduced to Portugal through the marriage of her parents, Philippa of Lancaster and John I of Portugal. On the continent there were several English chapels which used the Salisbury rite (Parris, *Binchois*, pp. 58–59).

[11] Marix, *Histoire*, pp. 19, 22, and Becker, *Maîtrises*, pp. 43–51.

[12] Rokseth, *Orgue,* pp. 33–34.   [13] Borren, *Etudes,* p. 40.

with a ring that allegedly cured toothaches. Eloy d'Amerval mentions him in his *Livre de la Deablerie*.[14]

Charles the Bold, like his father Philip, learned music at an early age, and he played the harp when he was only seven years old. He was also taught singing and the rules of composition, and occasionally practiced both. It has been suggested that Dufay could have been one of his teachers. At any rate, the two men were certainly acquainted, because an inventory of Dufay's possessions after his death lists 'six books of various pieces to be sung,' which the composer had promised the young man, but the use of which he had retained until his death.[15] Robert Morton taught Charles music, as did Antoine Busnois.[16] Morton, an Englishman, is one of the possible originators of the tune *L'Homme armé*, which became extremely popular in France (and later elsewhere) as a basis for other compositions. If the tune is not his, he is at least the author of one of its earliest settings.

Charles was closely related to the English and spoke their language fluently. He had kinship with the Lancastrian line, through his mother's side, and at the time of the War of the Roses had always secretly favored the house of Lancaster over the house of York. That did not prevent him from helping King Edward IV, however, when it seemed politically expedient to do so; and he married the king's sister, Margaret of York. It is not surprising, therefore, that English musicians were welcome at the Burgundian court.

To return to Charles's musical talents, much has been made of his poor voice, which was publicized by Olivier de la Marche. The chronicler is quick to add, however, that in spite of this handicap, Charles liked music and was gifted in it, and that he composed several good chansons.[17] He is also supposed to have written a motet that was sung at the cathedral of Cambrai, after a Mass which he attended on 23 October 1460, when he was still count of Charolais.[18]

[14] Marix, *Musiciens*, p. xvi.   [15] Borren, *Etudes*, p. 42.
[16] Brooks, *Busnois*, pp. 3–4.
[17] Marix, *Histoire*, p. 19. In 1502, the anonymous author of *L'Art, science et pratique de plaine musique* was still mentioning that Charles of Burgundy loved music and had written several chansons. No mention is made of his singing voice.   [18] Snow, *Mass*, p. 313.

Whatever the quality of his voice, he was evidently not shy about letting it be heard, for he used to sing, along with the members of his chapel, once in a while. He treasured his chapel, which sang Mass and the Hours for him every day, and accompanied him on his trips. His musician Busnois, therefore, was present at the siege of Neuss in 1474.[19] Another famous composer who had been in the duke's service was Hayne de Ghizeghem. Though he was not a formal member of Charles's chapel, he was court singer and honorary valet de chambre. In 1472, he accompanied the duke to the siege of Beauvais. His chanson *De tous biens playne* was one of the best-loved pieces of the Burgundian school, and parts of it were often borrowed by other composers. He and Morton were mentioned in a *rondeau* from Dijon, Bibl. publique, *MS. 517, La plus grant chiere de jamais,* as having been warmly received in Cambrai.[20] The duke's musicians had at one time included twenty-four adult singers, children, an organist, a lutenist, an oboist, and string players.[21] In 1477, at his death, the chapel numbered forty persons 'including a bishop confessor, three other priests, many chaplains, singers, various clerical officers and servants, and an organist.' The organization of the Burgundian chapel was maintained by the Habsburg rulers.[22]

Jean Molinet gives Charles credit for having gathered around him the most famous singers in the world, and for maintaining a chapel of such 'harmonious and delectable voices that, after celestial glory, there was no other pleasure.'[23] Inventories of his library show that he possessed 'Ung livre de chançons notées,' and 'Ung livre de chançons et choses faictes'[24] (*res facta,* or written out counterpoint).

In spite of his undeniable interest in music, Charles the Bold, who did justice to his appellation, did not show that music tempers the passions, for by all reports, he was not a mild man. His daughter Mary was extremely gifted musically, but did not have a chance to develop her talent to any great

---

[19] Brooks, *Busnois,* p. 6.
[20] Droz, *Poètes,* p. 9.
[21] Rokseth, *Orgue,* p. 47.
[22] Picker, *Marguerite,* p. 22.
[23] Molinet, *Chroniques,* quoted in Linden, *Molinet,* p. 167.
[24] Barrois, *Bibliothèque,* p. 119.

extent, owing to the difficult time she had, when she became
Duchess of Burgundy after her father's death, in trying to
control her territories. She had to contend not only with Louis
XI, but with hostile local governments, and her husband
Maximilian apparently was too inexperienced to help in the
political situation. She had studied the clavichord, and her
music teacher had been Busnois.[25] Her daughter, Margaret of
Austria, inherited her mother's and her grandfather's love for
music. It was not under their influence that she enfolded her
musical taste, however. Charles the Bold died before her
mother's marriage, and Mary herself died at twenty-five, as a
result of a fall from a horse, when the little girl was only two
years old. The following year, Margaret was taken to the court
of France as the Dauphin's fiancée, and her education,
supervised by his sister, Anne de Beaujeu, was entirely French.
But she did not stay in France, for her marriage plans were
altered; and after becoming twice a widow (first of the Infante
Juan of Castille, son of Ferdinand and Isabella, and later of
Philibert II of Savoy), she served as a governess of the Low
Countries for her nephew, Emperor Charles V. But her
language was French, and she never learned Flemish very well.
She was an important patroness of music and had several
music manuscripts made for her. Pierre de la Rue was
probably her favorite musician.[26]

John, duke of Berry (1340–1416), third son of John the
Good and brother of King Charles V and of Philip the Bold of
Burgundy, is probably best known today for the *Très riches
heures du duc de Berry*, the beautiful book of Hours that was
made for him and is now located in the Bibliothèque du
Musée Condé, at Chantilly. His love for the arts extended to
music—particularly that for the organ.[27] He had several
menestriers in his household, and included them among his
valets de chambre.[28] The musician Solage had been at his court,
and wrote the ballade *S'aincy estoit* in the duke's honor.[29]

'Good' King René of Sicily and Aragon, duke of Anjou, Bar,

[25] Brooks, *Busnois*, p. 4, and Rokseth, *Orgue*, p. 127.
[26] *See* Picker, *Marguerite*.
[27] Pirro, *Charles VI*, p. 21.
[28] Rokseth, *Orgue*, p. 17.
[29] Apel, *Fourteenth*, pp. 2, 16.

and Lorraine, and count of Provence (1409–1480), had never managed to conquer his kingdoms, but he consoled himself by patronizing the arts. He was a brother-in-law of Charles VII. His mother, Yolanda of Aragon, had already manifested an interest in music by donating a small organ for the cathedral of Angers to the musician Cesaris, in 1417.[30] René, after his unsuccessful Italian expeditions, remained in Anjou and in Provence, where he was well liked because of his artistic tastes. He founded his chapel in 1449, and had singers recruited in Picardy and in Italy. Charles d'Orléans sent him a singer in 1452. The organist and singers wore the ducal livery: red robes lined with grey fur. In his castle of Angers was a clavichord.[31] By the time of his death, he had in his residence in Provence seventeen instrumental musicians, including an organist, five trumpeters, and five 'haulx menestriers'. The latter group played the sackbut, *douçaine, chalumeau, musette*, or bombard. In addition, René had four drummers, lutenists, and other instrumentalists.[32]

René's singers were highly regarded at the time. Octovien de Saint-Gelays, uncle (or probably father) of Mellin de Saint-Gelays, wrote about them in *Le Séjour d'honneur:* 'Chantres avoit, doulx et organisans,/ Tous approuvez en nouvelle musique.' After René's death, his nephew Louis XI sent for his singers and took them into his service. Eight singers from Provence, who had formerly been in René's chapel, performed at a Mass which Louis had founded at the Sainte-Chapelle in 1481. That institution's ecclesiastics differed from other music lovers in their appreciation of the Southerners; they did not like them, because they considered them intruders.[33]

Brown suggests that a morality play with music, *Le Messatgier, Argent, Bon Advis*, which seems to have been in the repertoire of a troupe of actors in Avignon active about 1470, may have been performed before King René.[34]

The good king indirectly and posthumously helped the cause of modern musicology. It was largely by means of a

[30] Reaney, *Fifteenth*, v. 1, p. i.
[31] Rokseth, *Orgue*, pp. 39–40.
[32] Rokseth, *Instruments*, pp. 207–208.
[33] Brenet, *Sainte-Chapelle*, p. 37.
[34] Brown, *Theater*, p. 19.

piece that alludes to the death of René that it became possible to date the monophonic Bayeux manuscript (Paris: Bibl. nat., *MS. fr. 9346*) as not earlier than 1480.[35]

Charles d'Orléans (1391–1465), son of King Charles VI's brother Louis, and father of King Louis XII of France, was a gifted poet, whose works were often set to music in his time, and occasionally later (such as Debussy's *Trois chansons de Charles d'Orléans*). He played the organ and the harp, as had his mother, Valentine Visconti. He seems to have been particularly fond of the latter instrument, because he had a harper, Jehan Petitgay, in his service in 1413. Many years later, in 1457, his secretary, Vilot, undoubtedly realizing that the duke's interest in the harp had not diminished, offered him one. From England Charles once brought back 'four folios with several notated chansons.'[36] In 1414, he ordered a robe to be made for him, with sleeves on which the one hundred and forty-two notes of the chanson *Madame je suis plus joyeux* were embroidered with five hundred and sixty-eight pearls.[37] The members of his musical chapel at Blois wore robes of grey cloth.[38] On the first of the year, the town musicians of Blois used to come to his court and serenade his wife and small son.[39]

Anne of Brittany's ancestors from Foix and Brittany had been music lovers. Gaston Phébus, count of Foix, in the fourteenth century, had encouraged musicians, and several pieces of the Chantilly *manuscript 564* were written in his honor. Reaney believes that the collection of which *MS. 564* is probably a Florentine copy, came from the territories of Foix and Aragon.[40] All the fifteenth-century dukes of Brittany had a musical court, beginning with John V, who increased the number of his *ménétriers* from four to seven, between 1404 and 1426. He also had singers, four of whom he brought with him to Rouen, on the occasion of a meeting with King Henry V of

[35] *See* Gérold, *Bayeux*, pp. xi, 104. The chanson contains the lines: Celuy qui nacquit sainctement/ . . . / Veuille mener a saulveté/ L'ame du bon feu roy René.

[36] Marix, *Histoire*, p. 31, and Droz, *Poètes*, p. 8.

[37] Pirro, *Histoire*, p. 26.

[38] Rokseth, *Orgue*, p. 39.

[39] Chaillon, *Louis XII*, p. 65.   [40] Reaney, *Chantilly*, pp. 82–85.

England in 1419. John's court fool, Coquinet, numbered singing among his accomplishments, and performed for his master's friends in 1424. John's son and successor, Francis I of Brittany, was 'one of the most handsome men in the duchy. . . . He honored and loved the ladies more than anything else, as well as dances, jousts, and listening to singing.' Along more serious lines, he left in his will, on 22 January 1449, an endowment for the foundation of a Mass with music at a church in Saint-Nicolas-de-Redon. Peter II made a solemn entry to music into Nantes, 8 October 1450. He had received a fool named Denis as a gift from the queen of France, and Denis had been provided with a 'garderesse,' a sort of governess named Elizonne, who watched his language and his gestures. Peter II numbered among his instrumentalists clarions, war trumpets, and one dulcimer player. His wife, Françoise d'Amboise, was an accomplished musician and played the lute to perfection, but this did not prevent her husband from subjecting her to brutal treatment—another proof that music does not always soothe the savage breast.

The next duke, Arthur III, was old and sick when he came to power. He maintained nine clerics and nine trumpeters in his establishment. Jean Meschinot used to write *ballades* for him. Francis II, last duke of Brittany (ruled 1458–1488), husband of Marguerite of Foix, father of Queen Anne, and lover of a former mistress of Charles VII, had eight trumpeters in his household, all of whom played at the *béguin*, or mourning, for his death. For his burial in Notre-Dame des Carmes, at Nantes, each was given three ells of cloth worth one hundred *solz* per ell.[41]

The court of Savoy had been a brilliant one, particularly in the 15th century, under Duke Amadeus VIII (1383–1451) and his son Louis. Amadeus, an ardent bibliophile, had been elected antipope in 1439 by the Council of Basle, and had abdicated his dukedom in favor of his son. Dufay had belonged to the Savoyard chapel and occasionally also rendered non-musical services to the rulers. Louis's wife, Anne of Cyprus, of the Lusignan dynasty, thanked Dufay, in 1451, for having sent her some fine cloth.[42] The duchess had been

[41] La Laurencie, *Bretagne*, pp. 2–6.   [42] Borren, *Etudes*, pp. 36–39.

raised in an atmosphere of French music in Cyprus; it has been suggested that she brought an important corpus of this music (*MS. J. II. 9* from the Biblioteca nazionale in Turin) with her to Savoy in 1434, at the time of her marriage to Amadeus's son.[43]

Many members of the house of Lorraine were closely associated with the royal court, its politics, and its music—Queen Louise, wife of Henry III of France, for example, and her sister, whose marriage to the Duke of Joyeuse was the occasion for the *Balet comique de la royne*. Cardinal Jean de Lorraine, a generous patron of the arts, had in his household some Italian violinists, who were presented with a gift by Francis I, in 1543.[44] Cardinal Charles de Lorraine had as head of his chapel Arcadelt, who had also been a royal musician.[45] In their own court in Lorraine, the dukes maintained a respectable chapel and promoted music in various ways. *MS. fr. 1597* of the Bibl. nat., Paris, has the arms of René II de Vaudémont, duke of Lorraine (ruled 1475–1508) and his son Antoine (ruled 1508–1544). René II, turned out of his territories by Charles the Bold, returned to Lorraine and defeated the duke of Burgundy at Nancy in 1477, where Charles was killed in battle. René wanted Provence, which he thought should have been his inheritance from his maternal grandfather, Good King René, but the French court maneuvered so that he never obtained it.

The ducal chapel of Lorraine consisted of adults and choirboys under the direction of Pierrequin de Thérache from 1499 to 1527. The chapel musicians took an active part in the production of mystery plays and liturgical drama. In 1478 they performed a Saint Nicholas play by Jacquemin Berthemin, notary of Nancy, in the duke's chapel. The actors known as *Galans sans souci* also performed for him mystery plays, mostly by the famous Pierre Gringore, who had worked for both René and Antoine. Instrumental music was provided at court

[43] Hoppin, *Cypriot* (edition), p. ii.

[44] Heartz, *Attaingnant*, p. 83.

[45] It was not unusual for high-ranking churchmen to have their own chapel. Georges II d'Amboise, archbishop of Rouen in 1510 and cardinal in 1545, had his private *maîtrise*, and took interest in the music at the cathedral as well (Rokseth, *Orgue*, p. 79).

by Swiss, Spanish, German, and French players. The preludes to the mystery plays were performed by lutes and small drums. René had a particular predilection for the drum, and requested a drummer to accompany chansons. Other instruments at court included rebecs, *vielles*, violins, harps, organs, flutes, psalteries, trumpets, and fifes. A violin master, Jehan Darmurot, was employed there.

René had the first large pneumatic organ built in Nancy, in 1487, for the Collégiale Saint-Georges. It was transferred to the Cathedral of Saint Pierre in 1744.

Antoine added singers to his chapel and provided sixty francs a year for each child's education and general care. After Pierrequin's death, his *maître de chapelle* was Mathieu Lasson. His organists included Jehan de Sermaize and Mathieu de Milleville.[46]

Music was not only made but also discussed in the salons of many French aristocrats with humanistic interests. They attracted some of the leading philosophers, poets, and musicians of their time, and frequently provided meeting-places for these men, which resulted in collaboration among them. Catherine de Clermont, duchess of Retz, received the writers Pontus de Tyard, Desportes, Jamyn, and Jodelle, as well as the musicians Costeley and Adrian Le Roy. The latter dedicated to her a book of *airs de cour* by Nicolas de la Grotte. Tyard and the musician Cléreau met at the house of the marquis of Elbeuf, and Anthoine de Bertrand had discussions with the poet Robert Garnier in the circles of the *jeux floraux* at Toulouse. The Maecenas Jean de Brinon may have been responsible for bringing together Ronsard and Goudimel.[47]

Perhaps as important as the various secular courts and other aristocratic circles as centers of music-making were the French ecclesiastical establishments; and their music was available to anyone who came to the services. There were often musical interrelationships between church and court in the sense that court musicians had sometimes been trained in a church. Some musicians worked concurrently for a religious institution and for a king or nobleman. Then, too, the king often had his word to say in the assignment of ecclesiastical

---

[46] Shipp, *Lorraine*, pp. 20–23.
[47] Lesure and Thibault in Roland-Manuel, *Histoire*, I: pp. 1060, 1316.

benefits to musicians. It was the visit of the Queen of France to the cathedral of Rouen in 1444 that prompted the personnel to perform a motet and thus break the tradition of pure plainchant there.

During the performances of the choir, canons generally sat on the top stalls, with the lesser clergy—such as vicars—on lower stalls or on floor level. The choirboys sat on benches or stools on the floor before the lectern. At Bayeux and Chartres, the boys were provided with low chairs placed around the altar. The choirboys' titles varied from church to church. Though the generic term for them was *enfants de chœur* almost everywhere, they were also called *pueri clericuli, choriaux, heuriers, clergeons, enfants d'aube, chantonnots, feriales,* and *nourissons de l'église.*[48]

In the early fifteenth century, Paris seems to have been the chief training place for good church musicians. It was to a Parisian priest that the duke of Burgundy entrusted his five choirboys in 1409.[49] Notre-Dame had been an important musical center for many centuries, as is well known, since it gave its name to a whole period of composition—that of Léonin and Pérotin. Though it was not to keep its universal fame—the circle of the Avignon popes attracted some talented musicians too—it nevertheless was in favor among singers and composers for many years. Roger de Breauté, a member of the Burgundian chapel, moved to Notre-Dame de Paris in 1418.[50] Ockeghem was admitted there as a canon in 1463, but owing to his work for the king, the musician was not often seen at Notre-Dame and eventually gave up his prebend there.[51] Notre-Dame had a *maîtrise*, or choir school, long before the fifteenth century, but it was not before 1455 that the choirboys had a house they could call their own. Previously, they lived at the houses of various canons. In 1402, one of them, Nicolas de Bol, offered to lodge, feed, and dress the eight boys for twenty francs each. Organ was taught at the cathedral, and occasionally students were sent there from Chartres.[52] It was at

[48] Becker, *Maîtrise*, pp. 87–88, 132–134.
[49] Pirro, *Charles VI*, p. 28.
[50] *Ibid.*, p. 32.
[51] Lesure, *Ockeghem*, pp. 147–149.
[52] Becker, *Maîtrise*, pp. 53–54, 104.

Notre-Dame that important religious ceremonies connected with the royal family took place.

The Sainte-Chapelle du Palais, in Paris, dedicated in 1248, was founded by Saint Louis in order to house the Holy Relics brought back from the Crusades, which included the Holy Crown of Thorns—and according to an inventory made in 1534, in the presence of Claudin de Sermisy, canon of the Sainte-Chapelle and director of the royal chapel, also wood from the Holy Cross, blood of Our Savior, and milk of the Blessed Virgin Mary.[53] The leader of the personnel was a master chaplain, who was later given the title of treasurer, and he was assisted by an ever increasing number of principal chaplains, or canons, and other clerics and choirboys. The boys went to sing before the king on special feast days or at other times, at his pleasure, even if it required travelling. Otherwise, the children were not to sing except in the Sainte-Chapelle. It was forbidden to sing in the street. The Sainte-Chapelle had its problems, financial and musical. On 28 September 1566, it was decided that the organist's verbal request for bread, the *pain de chapitre*, to which the choristers were entitled, could not be granted, for lack of means. Many of the singers found it necessary to work in the fields, in addition to performing their duties at the Sainte-Chapelle. As long as it did not happen too often or without permission, they were granted paid leave for that purpose. The composer Pierre Certon and a colleague, who had gone to the fields the preceding week, were granted their full week's salary on 22 March 1570. The same ruling was made on 13 October 1599 in favor of the previously censured music master Renvoyré, who had been absent for a week to gather his grapes, because 'it was not his custom to miss the divine service.' But on 20 April 1569 the chapter took a dim view of Adrian Le Keu's frequent unexcused absences for the purpose of going to the fields, and of his appearance wearing a cloak. It was explained to him that it was neither decent nor proper garb for a churchman, and that henceforth he should dress according to his estate.[54]

In matters musical, it was sometimes difficult to maintain the excellent standards of the choir, owing to absenteeism on

[53] Félibien, *Histoire*, III, pp. 150–151.
[54] Brenet, *Sainte-Chapelle*, pp. 11–19, 110, 113, 116, 149.

the part of those members who also belonged to the king's chapel. Internal conflicts occasionally occurred between the music master and the canons who wished to have their music performed. On 24 May 1600, Le Roy complained that the music master refused to have a Mass of his sung. The chapter decided that any time that Le Roy or another canon might wish to have music performed, they could do so 'without the said music master being able to stop them.'[55]

The Cambrai cathedral was to become one of the most important musical centers of Europe in the fifteenth century. It belonged to the old county of Hainaut. Its members were recruited by the canons, following the advice of the music master, mostly from the surrounding regions, and many, though not all, of its best singers and composers came from northwestern France.[56] Nicole Grenon, Richard de Locque-ville, Dufay, and Obrecht were among those who held positions there at one time. Composers from Cambrai frequently were recruited for the pontifical chapel or other Italian courts, and achieved an international reputation.

Mediaeval choirboys, according to an edict of Pope Clement IV, were to have the Office of the Martyrs performed at their funeral, rather than the Requiem, 'propter durissimos labores.'[57] This surely must not have applied to Cambrai, where life at the cathedral seems to have been far from monotonous for the young ecclesiastical singers, or the young at heart. They had much music to perform, it is true, but certain mischievous clerics managed to avoid some of the tediousness of repeating the same plainchant formulae day after day by adapting original and most unliturgical words to them. In 1476, some chaplains were reprimanded for having composed, to the tone of the Preface, a song in which they mocked several servants of the church, whom they mentioned by name. On 31 December 1492, at a lesson for Matins, another chaplain substituted his own unofficial trope: 'Fabri, you are a very bad boy,' which he intoned with a Northern accent. In order not to be lonely in church, one day in 1497, a cleric brought along his dog to the service, and protested

[55] *Ibid.*, pp. 145, 149.
[56] Borren, *Musicologie*, pp. 20–22.
[57] Pirro, *Pour l'histoire*, p. 51.

because a canon pushed the animal with his foot, five times. The ecclesiastics were apparently well-fed, because on 9 September 1493, they had pieces of meat and bones left over from dinner, which they threw at each other during the Office. The 'little vicar' and composer Jean Cornuel was once brought before the chapter because he owed the wine merchant twenty-seven and one half *patards*. It was decided to withhold half of his salary until the creditor had been paid. Instead of singing at Vespers, one clergyman went bowling. Another practiced archery. A vicar was accused of having abducted a married woman; another admitted that he visited *loca inhonesta*. In 1492, an ecclesiastic grew so bold as to appear for dinner in the company of a lady named Symonetta.[58]

These non-musical activities, which are by no means atypical of conduct at other ecclesiastical establishments, were probably practiced by a minority of the personnel, at Cambrai as elsewhere. These incidents were recorded because they were not condoned. They obviously did not prevent the choir members from learning and performing some of the most beautiful music of their age, and Cambrai of rivaling and possibly supplanting Paris as a center of polyphony for a time. A particularly impressive occasion must have been the last solemn consecration of the cathedral to the Blessed Virgin, with Pierre de Ranchicourt, bishop of Arras, officiating. He was probably a friend of Dufay, at whose house he lodged. It has been suggested that the Mass performed on that day was the composer's *Ave Regina*.[59]

The dukes of Burgundy took an interest in the cathedral of Cambrai, but it was only one of many places where they heard music. They were otherwise at Dijon, Lille, and other towns, where their chapel often followed them.

The cathedral of Chartres followed the Parisian custom in matters of music, and had a good working relationship with Notre-Dame de Paris.[60] A category of singers older than the choirboys was called *heuriers-matiniers* and sang the Offices. The youngest were eighteen years of age. Some of them also served as canons, or as masters of music or grammar. Before

[58] Pirro, *Cornuel*, pp. 191–197.
[59] Planchart, *Dufay*, p. 21.
[60] Pirro, *Charles VI*, p. 21.

their investiture, they swore by the head of Saint Anne that they were born of legitimate marriage, and that they would perform at all times the daily and nocturnal Offices from beginning to end, under penalty of having their emoluments withheld. During the fifteenth century they were theoretically twenty-four in number, but in practice, they were between ten and twenty. One of the best-known of them was Antoine Brumel, who was *heurier-matinier* from 1483 to 1486. Until 1504, these singers participated in the Feast of Fools on the first of January, during which they parodied the religious services and made fun of higher churchmen. This feast was not peculiar to Chartres, of course. From the Middle Ages, it was celebrated everywhere in France—as was the Feast of the Innocents, during which the younger choirboys elected a bishop for the day and held a mock service. In Chartres, this custom was continued until the eighteenth century.

An occasion for merriment which was special to the *heuriers-matiniers* of Chartres and the choirboys was their traditional donkey ride to a leprosarium, the priory of Grand-Beaulieu, where they sang the *Regina coeli, De profundis,* and other prayers for the memorial service in honor of the deceased lepers. All sorts of excesses took place during the trip, and occasionally on the premises, where the prior was expected to provide food and drink for the singers, their valets, and of course, the donkeys.

The cathedral of Chartres celebrated five daily Masses, of which three were High Masses, sung at the high altar, with deacon, sub-deacon, and *chanoines semainiers* (two canons selected each week to read the Gospel, and two to read the Epistle). On certain occasions, such as the eve of particular saint's days, the *heuriers-matiniers* took part in processions within the cathedral, after Vespers. The Magnificat was sung with its antiphon. At the end of the procession, the participants were dedicated to the Blessed Virgin.[61]

Another important center was Saint-Quentin, at which many well-known composers received their musical training and sang, or became canons—among them Josquin Desprez, Loyset Compère, Jean Mouton, and Simon Alard. Some of the canons evidently maintained good relations with their Parisian

[61] Goldine, *Chartres,* pp. 161–172.

confrères, for in 1559, when Saint-Quentin was besieged by the Spanish forces, they fled to Paris, where the canons of Notre-Dame de Paris allowed them to hold meetings in their chapter. They also assembled several times at the house of Claudin de Sermisy, canon of the Sainte-Chapelle and head of the king's chapel. It was there that they decided to return to Saint-Quentin as soon as possible, after the Treaty of Cateau-Cambrésis, which returned Le Catelet, Ham, and Saint-Quentin to the king of France.

Owing to a series of wars in which Saint-Quentin had become involved, the *Eglise collégiale* was so poor, in 1509, that it could no longer afford a good polyphonic choir. It was therefore decided by the king that one prebend should be cancelled in favor of a music master and eight choirboys. Whereupon an altruistic and music-loving canon, Blavet (who really deserves to have his name mentioned) 'freely and voluntarily' gave up his prebend into the hands of the king. About 1550, another canon provided for the performance of Josquin's *Stabat mater* at the end of the Good Friday Office each year. On Christmas day 1597, a future pope (Leo XI), who was then Cardinal Alessandro de' Medici, archbishop of Florence and legate in France, and who was trying to bring about peace between the kings of France and Spain, sang the High Mass at Saint-Quentin, which he celebrated with the same ceremonial as the pope; and 'it was a great honor for this church.'[62]

Some of the composers who were at one time choirmasters at major cathedrals include Jean Mouton at Amiens, Nicolle des Celliers d'Hesdin at Beauvais, Pierre Cléreau at Toul, Guillaume Le Heurteur and the Huguenot Richard Crassot at Tours, Jean Bastard at Bourges, Raimond de la Cassaigne at Toulouse, and Claude Petit Jehan at Metz. The latter, who should not be confused with Petit Jehan de Lattre, was also choir director at Verdun, and was called upon to participate in the funeral of the duchess of Lorraine in 1575 at Nancy, along with the singers from Toul and Verdun.[63]

Music of a simpler sort and performed without the help of a professional choir could be heard in the French church of

---

[62] Raugel, *Saint-Quentin*, pp. 53–55.   [63] Lesure, *Petit*, p. 156.

Strasbourg, where Calvin established himself in 1538. Gérard
Roussel, former almoner to Marguerite of Navarre, one of the
first French preachers to be won over to the ideas of the
Reformation, had followed Lefèvre d'Etaples to Strasbourg in
1525, and reported that, at the time, psalms were sung in the
vernacular by men and women together. This was presumably
not polyphony, but one-line singing at the octave. Calvin
wrote to Guillaume Farel on 19 December 1538 that he would
soon publish some of these psalms in French (the collection
Aulcuns pseaulmes et cantiques mys en chant [1539?], which
antedates the Geneva psalter by several years), but with pre-
existent German psalm tunes, because they were pleasing to
the faithful of Strasbourg. He did not always use the corresponding German melody for a given French psalm—*Psalm 46*
has the tune of German *Psalm 25*, for example—nor did he
always adapt the tunes well to the French language, but he
was not burdened by aesthetic considerations, and he used
music in order to attract people to the word of God in a
medium which they could understand and in which they
could participate.[64]

A Walloon student described psalm singing in the 'little
French church' in 1545: 'When I heard the singing, I could
not help weeping with joy. You would not hear a single voice
projecting over another. Everyone has a music book in hand,
whether man or woman. Everyone praises God.' By 1553, the
church numbered five or six hundred parishioners.[65]

[64] Rokseth, *Chants*, pp. 10–18.
[65] *Ibid.*, pp. 19–20.

3

Occasional music: personal and political

Since religious and secular aristocracy did so much to help musicians, it was fitting that musicians in turn should compose music to honor these people or to commemorate special personal or political events in their lives—births, baptisms, marriages, deaths, coronations, or peace treaties. In the case of high-ranking persons of the ruling class, it is hardly possible to separate personal and political occasions. Persons honored by specific pieces include non-noble political figures, poets, and other musicians, but in these instances, the tributes generally though not invariably came after their death. Closely related to music about special persons or personal events in their lives, was music for various occasions in which important figures took part—political interviews, receptions and ceremonies. Finally there is a category of political music directed against certain individuals or groups.

Several pieces were composed (or altered) to render homage to a given important person without necessarily including clues about what occasion, if any, prompted their writing. Most of the time the person's name appears in the text or in the title. Other times, it can be deduced by implication. The Chantilly manuscript contains several pieces in honor of French noblemen. Two pieces by Trébor and one by Cunelier are addressed to Gaston Phébus. A *ballade* by Solage was written in praise of 'bon Jhean, duc gentilz de Berry,' his valor, and his noble heart, which make him 'la flour du monde.' Reaney suggests that Gilet Velut's allegorical ballade, *Un petit oyselet*, which mentions a 'fauconnier de grant eage,' might refer to the aging king of France, Charles VI.[1] Motets in honor of Joan of Arc by Eloy d'Amerval, master of the choirboys at the church of Saint-Aignan, were sung at Orléans on 8 May of each year during the procession commemorating the deliverance of the city. The music has not been preserved.[2] Several *rondeaux* and one *bergerette* by Busnois were composed in honour of Jacqueline d'Hacqueville, wife of

[1] Reaney, *Fifteenth*, v. 2, p. vi.   [2] Brenet, *Processions*, p. 8.

a counselor at the Parlement of Paris and sister of its president. Her name or surname appear as acrostics or puns.[3]

Some basses-danses were probably named in honor of duchesses of Burgundy—*La Portingaloise* for Isabella of Portugal, third wife of Philip the Good, and *La Margarite* for Margaret of York, third wife of Charles the Bold.[4] Three *rondeaux* were composed on Anne of Brittany's device, *Non mudera*. The poet François Robertet was the author of two, which appear with anonymous music in the *chansonnier* of Françoise de Foix, and possibly also of the third.[5] Françoise was Anne's cousin and it was the queen who had married her to Jean de Laval-Montmorency, lord of Châteaubriand in 1509; it is therefore not surprising to find veiled homages to Anne in the manuscript. A further allusion to the queen is the reference to grey and black, which became her colors after the death of Charles VIII, in the chanson *Si j'ay perdu par mesdisans*, from the same source. In order to convert the piece into a tribute to the widowed queen, a line of poetry from an earlier and better rhymed version, which mentions yellow, green, and blue, was altered to allude to the more somber royal tints. Three chansons from the same collection, which may have been offered to Mme de Chateaubriand by Charles de Bourbon, before she became the official royal mistress, refer to 'Françoise' instead of 'ma belle amye', which appears in other sources.[6]

The anonymous *France par consolation*, from Attaingnant's *Vingt et huit chansons* (RISM 1531[1]), mentions the 'très noble roy François' and ends with the greeting: 'Vive le roy des fleurs de lys.' Gascongne's motet *Non nobis, Domine* (Attaingnant, 1535[3]) has as the text of its second part: 'Conserva regem Franciscum.' Two chansons by Costeley, *Ma douce fleur, ma Marguerite,* and *Muses, chantez le loz de la princesse,* are presumed

[3] G. Thibault, in Roland-Manuel, *Histoire*, p. 912. The pieces, with commentary, are in Droz, *Chansonniers*.

[4] Borren, *Closson*, p. 15.

[5] Droz, *Poètes*, p. 11. One of the pieces, *Non mudera ma constance et firmesse*, was sung to her when she visited Lyon in 1500 (La Laurencie, *Bretagne*, p. 11).

[6] Chaillon, *Françoise*, pp. 3–5, 64.

to have been written for Marguerite de Valois and her mother Catherine de' Medici respectively, possibly for their anniversary.[7]

Among the motets or other pieces composed for births or baptisms of high-ranking babies, one should mention *Nove cantum melodie* of Binchois, in which he lists several contemporary composers by name. The motet was for the birth of Antoine (1430–1432), son of Isabella of Portugal and Philip the Good.[8] Binchois also wrote a motet for the birth of Mary of Burgundy in 1457.[9] Mouton's *Non nobis, Domine* was written in 1509, in honor of the birth of Renée, second daughter of Louis XII and Anne of Brittany.[10] The young lady was to become duchess of Ferrara and a protector of Huguenots. On 19 April 1518 it was reported from Amboise to the duke of Ferrara that 'Johannes Mouton went to Paris these days to compose music to celebrate the birth of the Dauphin.'[11] The prince in question was François (1518–1536), son of Francis I and Queen Claude. It has been conjectured that he was the same Dauphin who was honored somewhat less formally in a quodlibet by Gaspar van Weerbecke (no. 49 in *MS. Basevi 2442* of the Biblioteca del Conservatorio, Florence), which contains the verse: 'Sonnez la bienvenue de Monsigneur le Dauffin.'[12]

As for the christening of Antoine, son of René II of Lorraine and Philippa of Gelderland, we do not know precisely what pieces were composed—this is a common gap in our understanding of what happened at Renaissance ceremonies—but we do know that they were performed

[7] Godt, *Costeley*, I, p. 70.

[8] Marix, *Histoire*, p. 28, and *Musiciens*, pp. 212 ff.

[9] Marix, *Musiciens*, p. xvii. The motet is not known, but it is recorded that Binchois was paid for it.

[10] Chaillon, *Louis XII*, p. 64, and Thoinan, *Origines*, p. 85. Renée's first-born daughter, Anna d'Este, was also to be honored in music, on the occasion of her marriage to Louis de Bourbon in 1548. Cypriano de Rore's *En voz adieu*, though it does not mention her by name, is supposed to have been written for Anna's wedding (Bernstein, *Couronne*, p. 50, after B. Meier, 'Staatskompositionen . . .' in *Tijdschrift van de Vereniging voor nederlandse Muziekgeschiedenis*, XXI (1968–70), pp. 88ff.).

[11] Lowinsky, *Medici* (edition), v. 3, p. 38.

[12] Brown, *Chansons*, p. 65, and Hewitt, *Chanson*, p. 384.

during dinner, on drums, fifes, trumpets, and 'all sorts of instruments.'[13]

Royal and princely weddings were no small affairs. The marriage of Catherine of France, daughter of Charles VI, to Henry V of England had been the subject of a clause in the treaty of Troyes, 9 April 1420; and on 2 June in the same year, it was celebrated in great pomp at Troyes. Musicians preceded the chariot carrying Catherine and her mother, and played trumpets, clarions, and 'many other instruments, in the hundreds and thousands.' Philip the Good of Burgundy attended this wedding and gave money to the musicians of Henry V and of the English lords.[14] For the wedding of the Dauphin Louis (the future Louis XI) and Margaret of Scotland, his first wife, at Tours in 1436, the organ of Saint-Martin accompanied the choirboys in a motet of welcome in honor of the lady.[15] For the same occasion, but at a different time, a moresca was performed before the Dauphin and the Dauphine by three dancers with multicolored bedsheets.[16]

Anne of Brittany married Charles VII at Langeais, in Touraine, on 6 December 1491. On 13 December, the town of Rennes gave festivities in honor of the couple. Morescas were danced, and music was performed with four trumpets, two small drums, a rebec, and other instruments. Anne's marriage to Louis XII was celebrated in Nantes, 8 January 1499, at the castle's chapel. The musicians of the royal chapel sang together with the bride's musicians. The king had brought Josquin Desprez for the occasion. After the ceremony, a delegation of young ladies from the locality sang *Madame la mariée* for the queen.[17]

When Renée de Bourbon arrived in Nancy in 1516, shortly before her marriage to Antoine duke of Lorraine, a song, *Vive le duc et la duchesse, Dame Renée de Bourbon*, was composed to welcome her. It was performed by singers dressed in blue and green.[18]

---

[13] Shipp, *Lorraine*, p. 22.
[14] Marix, *Histoire*, pp. 23–24, and Bowles, *Processions*, p. 151.
[15] Rokseth, *Orgue*, pp. 37–38.
[16] Pirro, *Histoire*, p. 131.
[17] La Laurencie, *Bretagne*, pp. 6–11.
[18] Shipp, *Lorraine*, pp. 25–26.

Francis I met Pope Clement VII in Marseille, in 1533, to celebrate the marriage of the pontiff's niece, Catherine de' Medici, and the king's son, the duke of Orléans. There was 'much melody of singing and instruments.'[19] It may have been for this wedding that Gascongne composed the motet *Cantemus et laetemur*.[20] Albert Seay has suggested that two anonymous pieces from Attaingnant's *Trente et cinq chansons* (*ca.* 1528[7]), *Las, il fauldra que ung estranger la maine* and *Tous nobles cueurs, venez veoir Magdelene*, were probably written for performance during the festivities connected with the wedding of Catherine's mother, Madeleine de la Tour d'Auvergne, and Lorenzo de' Medici, nephew of Pope Leo X, in 1518.[21]

The marriage of the future Francis II and Mary Stuart took place in Paris in April 1558, to the accompaniment of trumpets, oboes, viols, violins, citterns, guitars, and other instruments, played by musicians dressed in red and yellow. The festivities included a royal ball, masques, and other spectacles, such as a procession by twelve young noblemen mounted on artificial horses adorned with gold and silver cloth, which seemed so natural that 'one would have thought that they were alive.' The people sang 'hymns and canticles in praise of the bridal couple and of marriage.'[22] A poem inspired by the occasion, *Dois-tu pas être aise/ O peuple écossais/ D'être en l'obédience/ Du p'tit roy françoys?* was sung to the tune of *Les bouffons*, but not necessarily in the presence of the royal family.[23]

The most famous wedding spectacles of the French Renaissance were the previously mentioned *Paradis d'Amour*, in honor of Henry of Navarre and Marguerite de Valois, and the *magnificences*, which lasted for about two weeks, in honor of the Joyeuse–Vaudémont marriage. It was during these festivities that Claude Le Jeune presented music in the Phrygian mode, which caused one gentleman to become violent and take up arms, and then a piece in the hypo-Phrygian mode, which

[19] Pirro, *Histoire*, p. 280.

[20] Dunning, *Staatsmotette*, p. 324.

[21] Seay, *Chansons*, pp. 326–328.

[22] Cimber, *Archives*, 1ère sér., t. 3, pp. 252–257.

[23] Barbier, *Histoire*, I: pp. 78–80. The tune appears in Arbeau's *Orchésographie*.

immediately calmed the man. In the *Balet comique*, one of the most important precursors of French opera, the castrato Etienne Le Roy sang the part of a satyr.[24]

The death of royalty and other aristocracy was the occasion for much music-making. English singers performed at the funeral of Anne of Burgundy, duchess of Bedford, in Paris, in 1432, 'very sadly, in the manner of their country.'[25] Molinet, in his poem (without music) *Le Trosne d'honneur*, a deploration on the death of Philip the Good in 1467, calls upon the birds of the fields to sing chant and discant, various instruments to play, and notational symbols (proportions, prolations, and perfections of longs and breves) to arrange their sounds in grave dissonances.[26] It was reported that more than three thousand Masses were celebrated for the repose of the soul of Duke Philip of Savoy within ten days of his death in 1497.[27]

Anne of Brittany's funeral was first observed at Blois, where she died on 9 January 1514, by means of four High Requiem Masses, celebrated by her almoner, monks, and singers of her chapel. Her herald, Pierre Choque, called Bretagne, was put in charge of the ceremonies by order of Louis XII, and wrote about them. After a solemn service at Notre-Dame de Paris, with the participation of the royal chapel singers, the burial took place at Saint-Denis. During the procession, the twenty-four ringers of Paris, dressed in black, sounded their bells constantly, so that all would pray for her. She had wanted her heart to be sent to Brittany. There it was transferred from the church of the Carthusians in Nantes to the church of the Carmelites, in the same city, while a town-crier, wearing a black velvet robe ornamented with four escutcheons bearing the queen's arms, rang two bells at every intersection and proclaimed loudly and mournfully that one and all should say Paternosters for the queen's soul.[28]

---

[24] Yates, *Magnificences*, pp. 241–243, and *Processions*, p. 252, and Walker, *Humanism*, pp. 113–114.

[25] Pirro, *Charles VI*, p. 36.   [26] Brenet, *Molinet*, p. 24.

[27] Fox, *Requiem*, p. 7.

[28] La Laurencie, *Bretagne*, p. 12, and Fouché, *Grandioses*, pp. 250–263. Bretagne's account can be read in Paris: Bibl. nat., *MS. fr. 5094* and other manuscripts.

Several motets were written for her death. Moulu's *Fiere Attropos, mauldicte et inhumaine*, for five low voices, appears anonymously in the *Codex Medici*, and with the author's name in Bologna, *Civico Museo Bibliografico Musicale, MS. R 142*, under the title: *Lamento della regina di Francia*. Both Festa and Mouton wrote motets on the queen's death with the text *Quis dabit occulis nostris*,[29] and the latter also composed *Eu nobis, Domine, defecit Anna* for the same occasion.[30] Josquin's *De profundis clamavi*, for five voices, was the official motet for the funeral of Louis XII, and Costanzo Festa's *Super flumina Babilonis* may also have been written to commemorate the king's death.[31]

It has been suggested that Layolle's *Missa Adieu mes amours* may have been composed for performance after the death of Louise of Savoy, 22 September 1531.[32] An anonymous popular chanson mourns the death of Francis I: *France, aussi la Picardie/ Tu dois bien pleurer et gemir/ D'avoir perdu un si grand prince/ Le noble roy des fleurs de lys*.[33] Two others of the same type, *Plorons, chrétiens, plorons la mort extrême/ Plorons la mort du roy Charles Neuviesme*, and *Pleurez, pleurez, fidelles royalistes*, were composed for Charles IX and Henry III respectively.[34] Eustache du Caurroy's *Missa pro defunctis* was not written for a king's death, but was performed several years following its composition, at the funeral of Henry IV and remained for a long time the official Requiem Mass for the kings of France.[35]

Well-known composers have also written memorial music for non-political figures, such as poets and other musicians. Ockeghem's motet-chanson *Mort tu as*navré de ton dard*, which includes the words 'Pie Jesu Domine, dona eis requiem' in one of the lower voices, is a deploration on the death of Binchois, who is called 'le père de joyeuseté.'[36] Dufay provided in advance for his own funeral music—one of three versions of

---

[29] Lowinsky, *Medici* (edition), no. 43, and III: p. 48, and *Medici* (article), pp. 83–84.

[30] In Paris: Bibl. nat., *MS. nouv. acq. fr. 1817*, and in Municipal Library of Cortona. *See* Bibliothèque nationale, *Musique*, p. 53.

[31] Lowinsky, *Medici* (edition), III: p. 48.

[32] Crawford, *Masses*, p. 87.   [33] Barbier, *Histoire*, I: pp. 76–77.

[34] *Ibid.*, pp. 103, 115–116.

[35] M. Garros, in Roland-Manuel, *Histoire*, I: p. 1592.

[36] Marix, *Musiciens*, pp. 83–85, and Pope, *Montecassino*, pp. 26–27.

Ave Regina Celorum, which he requested in his will to have sung during his dying moments; though it was not sung at the appointed time, being performed after the blessing of his body. It is presumed that the version was the one for four voices, in which he refers to himself as a dying man. The will also mentions Dufay's *Requiem*, now lost, which the composer wished to have sung the day after his funeral.[37]

Ockeghem was honored by what has come to be the most famous deploration in the history of music—Josquin's *Nymphes des bois,* to a text by Molinet, and also by Lupi's *Ergo ne contuicit*, to a text by Erasmus.[38] Antoine de Févin was mourned in Mouton's *Qui ne regretterait le gentil Fevin.* Susato's *Septiesme livre* (1545[15]) contains 'trois epitaphes dudict Josquin,' two on the text *Musae Jovis*, by Benedictus (Appenzeller) and Gombert, and *O mors inevitabilis* by Hieronymus Vinders. A deploration on the death of Claudin de Sermisy, by Pierre Certon, *Musiciens, chantres melodieux,* appears in the latter's *Melanges* (Paris: Du Chemin, 1570). The anonymous poet of the mediocre text calls Claudin 'grand maistre, expert et magnifique compositeur,' and 'le thresor de musique.'

Jean Servin included in his first book of chansons (Lyon: Pesnot, 1578) a six-voice *Epitaphe de Goudimel,* for his fellow Huguenot, who had been killed in the massacre of Saint Bartholomew's day. He refers to him as the 'mielleux Goudimel.' To conclude this account of selected pieces for the deceased, we should mention Jacques Mauduit's *Requiem*, originally composed for the funeral service celebrated in the chapel of the Collège de Boncourt on 24 February 1586, on the occasion of the death of his friend Ronsard (27 December 1585). According to Mersenne, who printed the *Requiem* in his *Harmonie universelle*, it was performed only two other times—for the funeral of Henry IV and for that of Mauduit himself.[39]

Among the political events which called for music were coronations. When Charles VI was crowned in Reims, November 1380, Froissart tells us, there were 'more than thirty

[37] Reese, *Renaissance*, pp. 51, 76, 82.

[38] *Ibid.*, p. 118, and Borren, *Tombeaux*, p. 60.

[39] Bibliothèque nationale, *Musique*, p. 43, and Yates, *Académies*, pp. 76, 177.

trumpets, which sounded so clearly that it was marvellous.'[40]
Busnois's motet *In hydraulis*, written for presentation to
Ockeghem, may have been intended for the probable meeting
of the French and Burgundian singers in 1461, when Philip the
Good and his son Charles attended the coronation of Louis
XI.[41]

When Louis XI left Reims for Paris, on 31 August 1461, he
was accompanied by fifty-four trumpeters. Along the way, the
royal procession was honored by pageants and tableaux with
music. The most memorable one, reported by Jean de Roye in
his *Chronique scandaleuse*, showed a fountain, in which 'three
beautiful girls, representing naked sirens . . . performed little
motets and bergerettes, and near them several low instruments
played most melodiously.' The king, on his arrival at Notre-
Dame de Paris, was welcomed with a *Te Deum* and organ music
at the cathedral, the peals of all the bells of Paris, and the cries
of 'Noël' from the people.[42] The motet-chanson *Resiois-toy terre
de France/ Rex pacificus magnificatus est,* from the Montecassino
manuscript (*871 N*), with concordance in Paris: Bibl. nat, *MS.
fr. 15123 (Pixéré court chansonnier)* may have associations with
Louis XI's accession to the throne.[43]

Charles VIII's coronation at the cathedral of Reims on 30
May 1484 was accompanied by organ and plainchant. By 25
January 1515, when the same ceremony was performed for
Francis I, trumpets had been added.[44] It has been suggested
that Josquin's fanfare *Vive le roy*, with a tenor on a *soggetto
cavato* drawn from the title, was composed for Louis XII's
coronation. The three remaining voices of the piece, which
form an independent canon, derive their thematic material
from an older anonymous three-part composition entitled
Vive le roy et sa puissance in the *Seville chansonnier*.[45] Which king
the earlier piece was intended to honor, we do not know.

Gascongne's motet *Christus vincit* (Vatican: *MS. Pal. lat.*

[40] Pirro, *Charles VI*, p. 4.

[41] Brooks, *Busnois*, pp. 1–2, and Pirro, *Histoire*, p. 114.

[42] Bowles, *Processions*, p. 154. Victor Hugo mentions the three sirens in
Notre-Dame de Paris, but places them in the context of a different and non-
royal *entrée*, which was his prerogative as a novelist.

[43] Pope, *Montecassino*, pp. 24–25.   [44] Rokseth, *Orgue*, pp. 78–79.

[45] Plamenac, *Colombina*, pp. 524–525, 538.

1976–79) may have been composed for Francis I's coronation,[46] as was Mouton's *Domine salvum fac regem*.[47] The coronation of queens took place at the royal abbey of Saint-Denis. It
was there that Queen Claude was crowned on 10 May 1517,
during a Mass performed by the singers of the royal chapel 'to
the sound of many instruments.'[48] Moulu's motet *Mater floreat
modulata musicorum melodia* (no. 17 in *Codex Medici*) names
twenty-four composers, living and deceased, who give praise to
the king and queen with strings and organ; Lowinsky believes
that it was probably intended for Claude's investiture.[49]

At Henry IV's coronation at Chartres in 1594, after the
Office, when the canons of the cathedral had sung Psalm XX
'melodiously in fauxbourdon' and the singers of the church
and of the king's chapel had performed antiphonally,
everyone cried: 'Vive le roy.' And this petition was
accompanied by the sound of musical instruments, 'for
everyone realized that the happiness of each individual
depended upon public and universal felicity.'[50]

Music was often associated with state events having to do
with peace treaties and other political alliances. On the
occasion of the peace conference of Amiens (January 1408),
after the assassination of Louis of Orléans, John the Fearless
met with the representatives of France, John, duke of Berry,
and Louis II, duke of Anjou, in order to reconcile
Burgundians with Armagnacs and avert civil strife. It was
perhaps to help achieve these ends that the Burgundian duke
called his musician Tapissier and four choirboys.[51]

Compère's motet *Quis numerare queat*, with its *cantus firmus
Da pacem Domine*, refers to a recently concluded peace, and
Finscher believes it could be either the peace of Vercelli,
between Charles VIII and Lodovico il Moro (1495) or to the
French occupation of Milan, April 1500. Another motet of
Compère's, *Sola caret monstris* probably has to do with the war
between Pope Julius II and Louis XII (1510–12) and takes the

[46] Kellman, *Links* (lecture) suggests this.
[47] Lowinsky, *Medici* (edition), III: p. 73.
[48] Rokseth, *Orgue*, p. 93.   [49] Lowinsky, *Medici* (article), pp. 87–88.
[50] *Cérémonies observées au sacre et couronnement . . . de Henry IIII* (1594),
quoted in Brenet, *Instruments*, p. 283.
[51] Wright, *Tapissier*, p. 181.

part of the king.[52] Louis XII took his singers with him in his
Italian expeditions in 1507 and 1509. During an interview
which he had with Ferdinand of Aragon at Savona in 1507,
a High Mass was celebrated by the papal legate and sung
by the musicians of both royal chapels.[53] Antoine de Févin's
Gaude Francorum regia corona was probably composed for this
meeting.[54]

Two famous interviews were made with music by the singers
of Francis I and those of his fellow rulers. The first was his
meeting at Bologna with Pope Leo X, on 11–15 December
1515, to establish the bases of the concordat which would be
signed the following year. There the royal and papal singers
performed at Mass, which was celebrated by the pontiff.
Dunning associates Mouton's *Exultet coniubilando Deo* and
Bruhier's *Vivite felices* with the Bolognese events. A similar
manifestation took place at the Field of the Cloth of Gold, at
Guisnes, in June 1520, when Francis I and Henry VIII met.
The French and English singers each sang a different section of
the Mass. They had agreed to sing whenever their organist
began to play. And so Pierre Mouton played the *Kyrie* with the
French chapel, and the English organist the *Gloria* with the
English singers, and they continued in alternation until the
end. It was the Frenchmen's turn to sing the *Agnus Dei*, and
when it was over, they also performed several motets.[55] During
lighter moments of the meeting, the English and the French
exchanged visits, in masks. Henry VIII's Italian pipers played
the *Pavana Ferrarese*, and Francis I danced with an English lady
a dance said to be in the Ferrarese fashion.[56] On 4 May 1527, a
musical entertainment with dances and masked men was
offered to the French ambassador, the marquis of Turenne, at
the English court, at the signing of an alliance between Francis
I and Henry VIII.[57]

Francis I's captivity in Spain was commemorated in a short
motet by Gascongne, *Bone Jesu dulcissime*, in which divine

[52] Compère, *Opera omnia*, v. 3, p. ii.
[53] Thoinan, *Origines*, pp. 87–88.
[54] Dunning, *Staatsmotette*, p. 331.
[55] Brenet, *Instruments*, p. 282. Motets had also been performed at the
beginning of the ceremony (Kast, *Camp*, p. 136).
[56] Gombosi, *Masque*, pp. 5, 17.   [57] *Ibid.*, p. 6.

protection is asked for the kingdom.[58] The best-known piece that celebrated the return to France of Francis I's sons, who had been held as hostages by Charles V when their father was released, was Janequin's *Chantons, sonnons trompettes*. This event also prompted the writing of another piece—an anonymous work from Moderne's *Motetti del fiore* (1532): the secular motet *Letare et exultare*.[59] The news of the deliverance of the children, upon payment of a large ransom, was cause for rejoicing in all of Paris, on 4 July 1530. Notre-Dame offered a *Te Deum* with organ, followed by a Mass in honor of the Blessed Virgin, and the Sainte-Chapelle and other churches held similar services. A feast was held at the Hôtel de Ville, with the usual high instruments. Bonfires were lit everywhere.[60]

The Ladies' Peace and signing of the Treaty of Cambrai in 1529, which made the return of the princes possible, was also marked by musical manifestations. Margaret of Austria had brought her musicians from Malines, which included an organist, Jacques Bucquet, who supervised the transportation of the organs, and additional forces from the imperial court. Louise of Savoy brought instrumentalists from her son's household, including nine Italian oboists.[61] On 14 July 1538, during the interview of Francis I and Charles V at Aigues-Mortes, the king came to fetch the emperor in his room, and both descended to a large room on the ground floor of the house where the emperor was lodging, and there they both heard Mass with 'great music.'[62] For the peace conference between the same two monarchs in Nice, which was arranged by Pope Paul III in 1538, the Spaniard Morales composed a motet for six voices, *Jubilate Deo*.[63]

A ceremony was held at Notre-Dame de Paris in honor of the peace of Vervins in 1598, in the presence of King Henry IV and the papal legate. Two 'honorably upholstered' scaffolds were placed on each side of the altar. The royal chamber

---

[58] Lesure, *Religieuse*, p. 66. [59] Pogue, *Moderne*, p. 125.
[60] Heartz, *Attaingnant*, p. 64.
[61] Picker, *Marguerite*, p. 30. It is believed that the difficult days before the Ladies' Peace were invoked in Sermisy's *Quousque non reverteris, pax orba Gallis* (Dunning, *Staatsmotette*, p. 323).
[62] Cimber, *Archives*, 1ère sér., t. 3, pp. 32–33.
[63] Pogue, *Moderne*, p. 177.

singers, with soft voices, were on the right side, along with the low instruments, lutes, viols, etc., so that the king, who had his pew on that side, could hear their soft sound better. The singers of his chapel, blending their stronger and fuller voices with the brass instruments, were on the left side—the legate's corner—and the two choirs sang alternate couplets. On 20 October 1602, again at Notre-Dame, for the solemnization of the alliance between the king and the Swiss, 'there was very good and excellent music with voices, organ, lute and viols.'[64]

An important part has been given to music in other ceremonies, receptions, and interviews connected with political figures. The duke of Bedford was given a rousing welcome when he entered Paris in October 1424 with his four trumpeters and was received 'as if he were God.' The canons of Notre-Dame sang hymns and praises, and instrumentalists played the organ and trumpets. And all the bells rang out.[65]

Philip the Good created the Order of the Golden Fleece on the day of his marriage to Isabella of Portugal, and called together the Knights of the Golden Fleece on 17 February 1454 at Lille, for the Banquet of the Oath of the Pheasant. It was there that they swore to recover Constantinople, which had fallen to the Turks in 1453—although they never were able to carry out their promise. Much musical spectacle was provided for the occasion: a miniature church in which religious music was sung and the organ was played, and a huge pâté, which housed twenty-eight instrumentalists, who performed secular music in small groups or individually, and accompanied singers in the chanson *Sauvegarde de ma vie* as well as other pieces. A young boy clothed in crimson velvet mounted on an artificial white stag with golden antlers entered the banquet hall and sang the upper part of *Je ne vis onques la pareille* (possibly by Dufay or Binchois), while the stag sang the tenor. A woman wearing a white satin dress with a black mantle of mourning represented Mother Church. She was brought in by an elephant led by a giant, and sang a lament on the fall of Constantinople, which may have been Dufay's *Lamentatio Sanctae matris Ecclesiae constantinopolitanae (Tres piteulx de tout espoir fontaine/ Omnes amici eius)* or one of three other

---

[64] Brenet, *Instruments*, pp. 283–284.   [65] Bowles, *Processions*, pp. 152.

lamentations he claimed to have written. Appropriately enough for the Knights of the Golden Fleece, scenes from the story of Jason were included.[66]

Masses were written for the ceremonies of the Golden Fleece by the chaplain Sancy, who was paid for the purpose. The Masses have not survived.

A feast of the peacock, which may have rivaled Philip's banquet of the pheasant in magnificence, was given at the Abbey of Saint-Julien de Tours on 22 December 1475 by Gaston IV, count of Foix and prince of Viane, in honor of the Hungarian ambassadors who had come to ask King Charles VII for the hand of his daughter, Madeleine, for their king, Ladislas V. During the festivities much vocal and instrumental music was performed. After the third course, several musical *entremets* were presented, such as a simulated castle with boy singers inside (probably choirboys from Saint-Martin de Tours), a tiger fighting a serpent, a stag mounted by a twelve-year old boy, a mountain with young savages dancing a moresca, etc. The banquet ended with the oath of the peacock, after the seventh course. The royal marriage did not take place, because several days later, the news arrived that Ladislas had died of the plague—though in reality he had been poisoned. Four years later, Madeleine of France married the son of Gaston IV who had organized the banquet; and though she did not become queen of Hungary, her granddaughter, Anne of Foix, did, as the wife of Vladislas II.[67]

The organ was played at Notre-Dame de Paris, and the large bells 'Marie' and 'Jacqueline' were sounded for the visit of Radegonde of Piémont, sister of Louis XI, in October 1463. Other visits similarly honored were those of the duke of Savoy, 7 November 1463, and the duke of Berry, 6 March 1464.[68]

Charles VIII, after the death of his infant son, the Dauphin Charles-Orland, at Amboise on 6 December 1495, tried to cheer his wife Anne by means of music and dancing. Several young lords, including the duke of Orléans, the future Louis XII, came to dance before her. The spectacle did not have the

---

[66] Reese, *Renaissance*, pp. 57–59, Pirro, *Histoire*, pp. 84–85, Marix, *Histoire*, pp. 32–33, and Brenet, *Instruments*, p. 280.

[67] Haraszti, *Paon*, pp. 135–143.

[68] Lesure, *Ockeghem*, p. 148.

effect which had been intended. The queen was sadder than ever and it seemed to her (and rightly so) that the duke of Orléans was happy about the child's death because it made him next in line for the succession to the throne. She did not speak to him for a long time afterwards for this reason.[69]

After she had evidently forgiven him (and married him), Anne of Brittany organized a musical banquet to discuss a possible future marriage between their daughter Claude and the son of the Archduke of Austria. The spectacle was in honor of Maxmilian's ambassadors, and included dancing in the manner of France, Germany, Spain, Lombardy, and Poitou, by lords and ladies of the court wearing the national costumes of the regions represented.[70]

When Philip the Fair visited the court at Blois in 1501, on his way to Spain for the first time, the singers of his chapel and those of Louis XII sang Mass in alternation, from two different platforms, and after Mass, they joined in the *Te Deum*.[71] He returned in 1503. It was at these meetings that Philip met Josquin, whose music was included in a choirbook made for his chapel after these events. Musicians who were members of Louis's chapel at the time included Verjust, Verbonnet, and Antoine de Févin.[72] As for Josquin, it is not certain in exactly what capacity he served the French court, although we know that he was associated with it in some way.

During a visit which Francis I made to La Rochelle in 1542, he was first greeted with chansons sung from the tower of the church of Saint-Barthélemy. After supper, musicians sang for him, and when the chansons were over, high instruments were played, 'making so much noise that we could not hear each other speak.' Then the king began to dance.[73]

Brantôme reports that a masque with a rudimentary plot based on the parable of the wise and foolish virgins was presented to the French delegation that escorted the widowed queen, Mary Stuart, to Scotland in October 1561, and that the hosts danced with the French guests.[74] Catherine de' Medici's

[69] Commynes, *Mémoires*, III: p. 257.
[70] Chaillon, *Louis XII*, p. 64.   [71] Picker, *Marguerite*, p. 24.
[72] Kellman, *Links* (abstracts), p. 23, and Gottwald, *Ghiselin*, pp. 109–110.
[73] Cimber, *Archives*, 1ère sér., t. 3, pp. 61–63.
[74] Gombosi, *Masque*, p. 6.

ballet in honor of the Polish ambassadors (1573), which was
mentioned earlier, featured sixteen nymphs who represented
the French provinces. Brantôme considered it the most
beautiful ballet in the world. Some of its music was by Lassus,
and its choreography by Beaujoyeulx (Baldassare da
Belgioioso), who later organized the *Balet comique de la royne*.[75]
Her son Henry returned to France from Poland in 1574, by
way of Venice, and there he witnessed the performance of a
Tragedia with music by Claudio Merulo.[76]

Animals, mostly simulated, often took part in musical
celebrations of the Renaissance. During the wedding banquet
for Charles the Bold and Margaret of York in 1468, a whale
contained two sirens who sang a strange chanson. The 'fair
shepherdess' was greeted by a lion singing tenor and *dessus*.
The beast's musical prowess was surpassed by that of four
donkeys who performed a quartet and three she-goats who
played a motet on shawms, while a he-goat played the
sackbut—not to speak of four wolves who played a chanson on
four flutes.[77] This is most instructive as to the performance
practice of the time. The wolves' feat anticipates Attaingnant's
Vingt et sept chansons musicales a quatre (1533[10]), playable on
flutes, by more than half a century, and shows that although
scribes did not specifically say so, fifteenth-century motets and
chansons were already 'convenables tant a la voix comme aux
instruments.' Live birds often provided 'music' for special
occasions. Isabeau of Bavaria ordered several dozens of
'oisellés chantans'[78] and Anne of Brittany owned a singing
linnet. At Nantes, during feasts, singing birds were placed in
cages on trestles.[79]

All sorts of marine animals—sea horses, tritons, whales,
dolphins—had been constructed to participate in a 'water-
music' episode which never took place. During the *magnificences*
attendant to the wedding of the duke of Joyeuse in 1581,
Cardinal de Bourbon had organized a feast in the course of

[75] Dent-Sternfeld, in *New Oxford*, IV: p. 805. A sonnet by Pierre de
Larivey entitled *La Pologne* (1573), in praise of Henry III appears in a work
by François d'Amboise (Jeffery, *Comedy*, p. 29).

[76] Reese, *Renaissance*, p. 569.

[77] Pirro, *Histoire*, pp. 116, 142, and Marix, *Histoire*, p. 106.

[78] Rokseth, *Orgue*, p. 23.   [79] La Laurencie, *Bretagne*, p. 7.

which the royal court was to be transported across the Seine to Saint-Germain-des-Près in a large float dragged by other boats made to look like sea creatures, with musicians inside. The 'animals', however, refused to budge, and the disappointed King Henry had to go by coach. He volunteered the remark that it was obviously animals who gave orders to other animals.[80]

Not all political music was official state music, nor was it invariably complimentary to the persons or groups mentioned in the literary texts. Musicians occcasionally got themselves in trouble for becoming involved with controversial political subjects, and certain songs were prohibited by law, although such rulings were difficult to enforce. Already in 1395, Charles VI forbade the singing of chansons on the subject of the pope, the king, and the lords.[81] In 1413, Parisian children were punished for having sung *Duc de Bourgogne, Dieu te ramaint a joye*. At the same time another ballad against the Parisians was sung here and there. A harpist from Melun was arrested because he was circulating it. At the peace of Arras in 1414, all songs of a political nature were forbidden. In 1419, however, a group of peasants had a quarrel over a 'chanson des Bourguignons', and one of them was killed in the brawl. After the assassination of John the Fearless in the same year, Jacquinot Petit, one of Charles VI's musicians, was imprisoned at Meaux, where he was trying to buy wheat, because he had been in the service of the alleged murderer, the duke of Orléans.[82]

Louis le Jeune, lord of Contay, was sent on a mission to the court of Louis XI by Charles the Bold in March 1476, shortly after the battle of Granson. 'But however splendidly the lord of Contay was entertained by the king, he could not help but hear himself ridiculed by the townspeople; for chansons were sung publicly, praising the conquerors [the French] and shaming the conquered [the Burgundians].'[83] In 1516, at Hesdin, a man on patrol duty wounded his companion who had offended him by singing ballads of a political nature.[84]

---

[80] Yates, *Magnificences*, p. 262.   [81] Breton, *Chanson*, p. 61.
[82] Pirro, *Charles VI*, pp. 31–32.
[83] Commynes, *Mémoires*, II: p. 109.
[84] Pirro, *Histoire*, p. 315.

The musician Barthélemy Le Bel, master of the choirboys at the Sainte-Chapelle in Dijon, suggested, after Francis I's defeat at Pavia in 1525, that Burgundy be reunited to the Holy Roman Empire, by stating publicly that, as far as he was concerned, Charles V would be most welcome in Dijon. The authorities did not agree. Our articulate musician was arrested and sent before the municipal court, which washed its hands of the matter by turning him over to his chapter court. What decision was made we do not know, but Le Bel eventually moved to Geneva, where he died in 1553.[85]

A *chanson du printemps retourné*, printed in 1586, is a contra-factum on Ronsard's *Quand ce beau printemps je voy*—— sung perhaps to La Grotte's music. It reads: 'Quand ce dur printemps je voy/ Je cognois/ Toute malheurté au monde . . .'[86] The hard times in question have to do with the problem of the succession of the crown and the troubles between the League, organized by the Catholic Guises, who did not want to see Henry of Navarre on the French throne, and the Protestants.

Songs were also written about current events of a more frivolous nature, in which everyone, including nobility, took an interest. When Jeanne du Boys, a middle class Parisienne, whose claim to fame had been her erring way of life, decided to return to the fold and to her husband, a chanson was composed to celebrate the occasion: 'Jehanne du Boys est retournée/ Mardi bien tard sur la vesprée.' It appears in the Cardinal de Rohan's manuscript (Berlin: Kupferstichkabinett, *78 B 17*).[87]

Charles de Bourbon, constable of France under Francis I, turned against his king, owing to a controversy in a matter of inheritance, and passed over to the enemy. Charles V had him besiege Marseille, and the results were disastrous for him. This led to the composition of a song against the faithless constable: 'Quand Bourbon vit Marseille/ Il dit à ses gens/ Vrai Dieu, quel capitaine/ Trouverons-nous dedans?'[88]

A visit from Charles V to Francis I in Paris prompted an

---

[85] Lesure, *Minor*, p. 542, and Pidoux, *Psautier*, pp. 243–244.
[86] Barbier, *Histoire*, I: pp. 105–108.
[87] Droz, *Poètes*, p. 6.
[88] Barbier, *op. cit.*, I: pp. 59–60.

irreverent chanson, *Dedans Paris, la bonne ville, l'empereur est arrivé*, to be written about Charles's amatory exploits in the French capital. The piece was quoted in the farce *La Reformeresse*, about 1544.[89] A small composition in the same spirit was made for the death of Francis I. Its reference to the alleged cause of death rules it out as a state piece: 'L'an quinze cent quarante-sept/ François mourut à Rambouillet/ De la verolle qu'il avait.'[90]

Royal mistresses were not spared. The rivalry between Diane de Poitiers and Anne de Pisseleu, when Francis I was alive, was mentioned in the song 'Chasseresse Diane/ Avec son carquois/ Fait la chasse à l'âne . . .' The word âne (donkey) is of course a pun on Mme d'Etampe's Christian name. When she had to leave court after Francis I's death, another song was made for the occasion; *Qu'est devenu le temps où j'étais estimée?* The fact that Diane was some twenty years older than Henry II was not forgotten by the *chansonniers*, who wrote: 'Malgré son grand âge/ Diane ce soir à Blois/ Est en chasse, je crois . . .' She was also reproached by the Huguenots for her part in the religious conflict: 'O pauvres, pauvres protestants/ Que l'on mène au bûcher ardent/ C'est Diane qui vous fait brûler.' Another satirical chanson was written on the subject of Diane's jealousy when Henry II took a temporary interest in Lady Fleming, the young governess of Mary Stuart.[91] Its refrain, 'O le joli jonc/ Bon, bon, mon compère/ O le joli jonc/ Le joli jonc', suggests a juxtaposition of fragments from two chansons of Passereau: *Sur le joly jonc*, and *Il est bel et bon, bon, bon, commere, mon mary*. Marie Touchet, mistress of Charles IX, was a Huguenot, but remained with the king even after the massacre of Saint Bartholomew's day in 1572. This her fellow Protestants found hard to forgive, and they sang: 'Que vous importe nos malheurs/ Vous qui n'entendez ni cris ni pleurs. . . .'[92]

[89] Breton, *Chanson*, pp. 66–67, Saulnier, *Charles Quint*, pp. 211–212, and Brown, *Theater*, p. 204. A visit of the emperor to Cambrai was celebrated with more dignity. Jean Courtois, the cathedral's music director at the time, composed the motet *Venite populi* expressly for the occasion. Other motets performed were *O vera unitas*, by an unknown composer, and *Praeter rerum seriem*, probably by Josquin (Bridgman, *Charles Quint*, pp. 242–243).

[90] Breton, *Chanson*, p. 70.

[91] *Ibid.*, pp. 66–73.

[92] *Ibid.*, pp. 85–86.

Henry III and his *mignons* were denigrated in a song of the
time: 'Que ce sont de beaux compagnons/ Que le roi et tous
ces mignons./ Ils ont le visage un peu pale,/ Mais sont-ils
femelles ou mâles?' Another piece went so far as to praise
Henry III's assassin, the Jacobin monk Jacques Clément, for
stabbing 'Henry le vaurien' in the abdomen. Henry IV fared
no better than his predecessor in the undercover chanson
repertoire. As late as 1593, not everyone was happy that he was
king of France since 1589. A *chanson nouvelle sur l'opiniatreté de
certaines dames de Lyon qui ne voulaient pas abjurer* informs us that
one of these ladies would rather die a hundred times than obey
this king from Navarre, and call him 'prince, roy des
Françoys'. *Les Commandements d'Henry* (1597) is a parody on the
Ten Commandments, which reflects a Catholic point of view.
Although Henry IV had converted to Catholicism, he was not
strict enough for certain people's taste. The song enjoins him
to lead a more holy life, to convert his sister, who had
remained an ardent Calvinist, to dismiss all Huguenots from
important posts, and to take back his wife, Marguerite de
Valois.[93]

These are but a few examples of the impetus which royalty
and nobility gave to French musicians of the Renaissance, who
performed and wrote for them, or who composed pieces
about current events in which they took part or had an
interest. That some of the unofficial and anonymous chansons
were not always as respectful of the ruling class as might have
been proper—and even sporadic prohibition of their
performance did not seem to be particularly effective—shows
a trend which has maintained itself in France to this day. It is
evident that, as far as popular song-writers are concerned,
'plus ça change, plus c'est la même chose.'

[93] Barbier, *Histoire*, I: pp. 123–125.

4

Music's influence:
language, mores, morals

Music was not restricted to performance for its own sake. It was used as a spiritual agent to ask God for a favor, or to thank Him for one, or as a therapeutic agent to obtain a cure for illness, or perhaps a happy death. It is associated with various aspects of culture—formal education, theater, and competitions, as well as with less intellectual pursuits—outdoor manifestations, such as processions and *entrées*, work in the street or in the fields, hunting, and warfare. Music was very much a part of the existence of people from all walks of life. It even permeated their everyday language.

Many expressions in current French usage are derived from musical terms. One need only leaf through Georges Kastner's gigantic compilation, *Parémiologie musicale de la langue française*, to be convinced that this was already true more than a century ago. And we can find some examples in the writings of fifteenth- and sixteenth-century chroniclers and other authors, which surely reflect the musical terminology of their time. Charles d'Orléans writes of 'faulx bourdon de maleur.'[1] 'Accorder ses vielles' or 'accorder ses flûtes' (to tune one's *vielles*, or one's flutes) was used in the sense of coming to an agreement. Commynes, in reference to the league that was being formed in Venice against King Charles VIII of France, remarks that 'tant de vielles ne se peuvent accorder en peu de temps'[2] (so many discords cannot be settled in a short time, or, literally: so many *vielles* cannot be tuned in a short time). Bénigne Poissenot writes: 'Before going on, I beg you to tune these flutes [i.e., come to an understanding], for the dissonance is quite great.'[3] The expression 'sans trompette.'

---

[1] *Rondeau* 404; quoted in Defaux, *Charles*, p. 195.

[2] Commynes, *Mémoires*, III: p. 119.

[3] Poissenot, *Traité paradoxique*, Paris: C. Nicard, 1583, quoted in Kastner, *Parémiologie*, p. 318.

which is still used today in the slightly altered version 'sans tambour ni trompette' (without attracting attention; literally, without drum or trumpet) is found several times in Molinet.[4] The same author gives an account, in his *Chroniques*, of the assault of the castle of Bailleul by the French, in 1478. When a herald of the king of France summoned the inhabitants to surrender, they fired their harquebuses. This prompted the herald to remark: 'I did not think that in such a small chapel was such a large organ.'[5]

King Louis XII's confessor, Petit, used music in a simile, when he delivered the funeral oration for Queen Anne of Brittany at Notre-Dame de Paris, in 1514, and compared the city of Paris to a four-part musical choir—the Church, Justice, the University, and the People—in each part of which only sorrow could be heard.[6] On a less lofty level, terms referring to individual vocal parts, such as *basse-contre, teneur, dessus*, etc., to written or improvised polyphony, such as *note contre note*, or *gringoter*, and to other musical subjects are sometimes used in an equivocal sense in secular drama and the *timbres* accompanying it, or in other poems and chansons of a cheerful sort.[7] Clément Marot's second *Epistre du coq à l'asne* (1535) illustrates the use of the first type of term, in reference to Pierre Vermont the elder, a musician of the Sainte-Chapelle:

> Dieu pardoint au povre Vermont;
> Il chantait bien la basse contre,
> Et les marys la malencontre,
> Quand les femmes font le dessus.[8]

This brief passage from what amounts to a poetic hodge-podge is a deploration of a sort on the singer's death, but it is hardly a lament of the usual solemn type.

Claudin de Sermisy's *Une bergerotte* combines references to more than one musical manifestation, in the figurative sense:

[4] Linden, *Molinet*, p. 175.   [5] *Ibid.*, p. 171.
[6] La Laurencie, *Bretagne*, pp. 12–13.
[7] *See* Brown, *Theater*, pp. 101–105, for an elaboration of the subject and for many examples.
[8] C. Marot, *Œuvres*, I: p. 197.

Une bergerotte
Prinse en ung buisson,
Gardant brebiotte
Avec son mignon,
Et qui dit en bas son, et hon,
Une chansonnette :
'A l'ombre d'ung buisson.'

Adonc la fillette
De teneur print son,
Et Robin gringotte
Ung dessus tant bon,
En disant a bas ton, et hon,
Notte contre notte :
'Et l'amy Baudichon.'[9]

Jean Daniel, who uses this chanson as a *timbre* for a religious contrafactum, in his *Les grans nouelz nouveaux*, keeps some references to music:

Toute ame devote
Par bonne raison,
Chante haulte note
En ceste saison . . .

Here, however, allusions to music are used more literally than in the original.

Solmization syllables are sometimes used for puns. The first two words of the chanson *My larrez-vous tousjours languir*, which was set for five voices by Josquin and Certon, and for four voices by Roquelay and an anonymous composer of Attaingnant's repertoire, are a play on the hexachord degrees *mi, la,* and *ré*. This is confirmed by the musical settings which

[9] The first strophe given here is the only one that appears with Claudin's music in Attaingnant's *Trente et huyt chansons* (1530[5]). A variant version of that stanza and two additional ones are found in *La fleur des chansons*, a purely literary collection. The three strophes in that source have as their final line: 'Et l'amy Baudichon,' which is the title of a pre-existent chanson. The last line of the version in Attaingnant, 'A l'ombre d'ung buisson,' is also undoubtedly a reference to a chanson, 'A l'ombre d'ung buissonnet,' although it would make sense even if it were not a musical reminiscence.

assign these particular notes to these words. As was already
noted by Gustave Reese, Josquin used these degrees as initial
notes in four of the five voices.[10] Roquelay does the same in all
of his four voices, but divides them into two hexachords
(natural for all voices except the tenor, where the motif lies in
the hard hexachord), whereas Josquin uses the soft hexachord
for all pertinent parts. The incipit of Roquelay's setting
follows:[11]

The composer of the anonymous setting from Attaingnant's
Trente chansons (ca. 1528[4]) also shows an interest in the punning
possibilities of the text—but less obviously than the preceding.
The initial notes of the piece can be interpreted as *mi, la,* and *ré*
in all voices (except in the bassus, where the third note, by
virtue of its position, could only be a *mi*), assuming that
mutations are made from hexachord to hexachord. In the
example, I have transposed the music down a fourth, to avoid
the b-flat in the signature and to make the hexachord clearer. I
do not think this is tantamount to heresy, because
contemporary manuscripts and prints often give transposed
versions of pieces, when not more than one or two flats are
involved. There seems to have been nothing sacred about
absolute pitch, and singers undoubtedly transposed at sight.
The first three notes of the superius and contratenor represent
the previously mentioned solmization syllables in the soft,
natural, and soft hexachords. The same order applies to the

[10] Reese, *Renaissance*, p. 234.
[11] Du Chemin, *Quart livre*, 1551[7], fol. x[vo]; first appeared in Attaingnant,
33 chansons, 1532[12].

first two notes of the bassus. The three *a*'s in the tenor also form *mi-la-ré* in all three hexachords, progressing from soft, to natural, to hard, and exhaust the possibilities of the note *a*, which at the time was properly designated as *Alamire*.[12] The following example is from 1528[4]:

Whether a pun was also intended in Mouton's *La, la, la, l'oysillon du boys, ma dame* is not entirely clear, but it does not seem impossible that it was, at least in part, because the musical incipit in all four voices consists of the notes *a, c, a,* and *a* is of course *la* in the natural hexachord. It would be convenient if the second note could be passed off as *la* in a mutation to some other hexachord; we could then consider this piece parallel to Ockeghem's well-known *Missa Mi-mi*, which uses a similar procedure for its incipit, but on a different syllable. (The *Missa Mi-mi* has its secular counterpart in the chanson *My, my, my, my, mon doulx enfant*, from the *Bayeux manuscript*, in which the opening syllables are set to the notes *e* and *b*; these were sung as *mi* in the natural and hard hexachords respectively.)[13] In the song *La, la, la,* however, the note *c* could only be *sol, fa,* or *ut*, at the time, and certainly not *la*. Therefore we do not have three musical *la*'s to correspond to the initial syllables of the literary text, but we do have two

[12] The scribe Peter van der Hofe, who called himself Pierre Alamire, and whose manuscripts are being studied by Herbert Kellman in his work on illuminated music manuscripts from the Hapsburg-Burgundy court, was obviously attracted to puns on musical notes and their literary counterparts.—Cf. Kellman's lecture on *Fifty imperial choirbooks*, at the University of Pennsylvania, 12 October 1970.

[13] Gérold, *Bayeux*, music, p. 110.

out of three, which suggests that a play on words may have
been in the mind of the poet or the composer, or both.

Works in which the notes of the hexachord are used as a
unifying structural element for a musical composition, such as
Josquin's *Missa L'homme armé super voces musicales*, do not quite
belong in this category, because the play on syllables is of a
more purely musical nature than the other examples
mentioned, and do not depend upon a play on words for their
effectiveness.

Composers whose names contained some sound which by
some stretch of the imagination could be interpreted as
forming a solmization syllable could hardly resist the
temptation to have their names appear in rebus form in their
manuscripts. Dufay, for example, often appears as Du 𝄢 ■ y,
and Arnold de Lantins as A. de [♭] ntins, the note *d* being
la in the hard hexachord. Among the lesser-known musicians
who resorted to this practice was the Jewish exegete, geo-
grapher, and scribe Abraham Farissol, born in Avignon *ca.*
1450–51. He was a singer in Ferrara for some fifty years, and
signed his name on the title-page of a Hebrew illuminated
manuscript by means of the notes *fa-ré-sol*.[14]

Fictitious saints, such as Saint Frappe Cul and Saint
Andouille, appear in *sermons joyeux*, a type of comic theater
with some, though not many, musical references.[15] One of
these lively saints found his way into the current earthy
language of the Renaissance, for it seems that some people
used to swear 'par le corps de sainct Jambon.'[16]

Music and musicians seem to have influenced not only the
language, but also some of the customs of the time. Absence of
music sometimes denoted mourning. Alain Chartier, in *Le
Livre des quatre dames* (1416) mentions a lady who gave up
playing harp, organ, *douçaine*, lute, and *échiquier*, so as better to
mourn her lover, who had been captured by the English at the
battle of Agincourt.[17] For several weeks after the death of Anne
of Brittany, all dances, theatrical plays, and other musical

[14] Adler, *Pratique*, p. 48.
[15] Brown, *Theater*, pp. 11–12.
[16] Huguet, *Dictionnaire*, t. II: p. 560.
[17] Rokseth, *Orgue*, p. 27.

manifestations were forbidden by order of Louis XII.[18]

Tipping of musicians other than those from one's own household was not only permitted, but inevitable, among royalty and aristocracy, and it must have been a very old practice, judging from the many extant accounts of gratuities given by rulers to musicians of visiting dignitaries who came to their coronation, or who participated in some political meeting with them, or who came to pay a social call. In 1493, Anne of Brittany had money distributed to the musicians of the queen of Sicily, who had played before her, so that they might buy wine, and to five musicians from Paris, as well as to a cornettist, who had played for her at the castle of Plessis-lès-Tours. The latter belonged to her husband, Charles VIII, and was therefore on the king's payroll rather than on hers; he was given a token of recognition for service beyond the call of regular duty. At the time of the peace negotiations between Francis I and Emperor Charles V, at Nice, in 1538, in which Pope Paul III and others participated, the French king gave money to numerous musicians, including the queen of Hungary's cornets, the duke of Mantua's oboes, and the pope's band of trumpets and oboes.[19] That the custom of tipping musicians was not exclusively French, but was expected of Frenchmen abroad, is attested to by Philippe de Commynes in his recollection of one of his diplomatic missions to Italy in 1494 on behalf of Charles VIII. The memorialist, who was ever conscious of the high cost of living, reports that in his capacity as a royal ambassador, he was well treated and had his expenses defrayed by his hosts. 'But,' he adds somewhat ruefully, 'if one were to count carefully what must be given to the trumpeters and drummers, one hardly gains anything from this defrayal; but the treatment is honorable.'[20]

Musicians were not always employed for exclusively musical purposes. Trumpeters in particular served in a variety of functions, such as messengers. Indoors, they occasionally served as waiters. One of them waited on Charles the Bold, in 1465, at the house in Conflans where he had taken temporary

---

[18] Fouché, *Grandioses*, pp. 249–268.
[19] Prunières, *Chambre*, p. 238.
[20] Commynes, *Mémoires*, III: p. 107.

lodgings during the final stages of the War for the Public Good; and the trumpeter lost his life in the process.[21]

At some time in the Middle Ages, instead of a bell, a horn was sounded in manors to call people to meals.[22] Although some musicians are listed as *valets de chambre* or as squire carvers in the royal household, they did not perform domestic duties. During the reign of Francis I, the highest category of the king's chamber musicians, which included lutenists of the caliber of Albert de Rippe, were classified as domestic officials—an honor which they shared with artists and men of letters such as François Clouet and Clément Marot.[23] Titles do not always mean what they seem to indicate, and just as an honorary position as *valet de chambre* was not awarded on the basis of how well one could manipulate a broom, and did not indicate that one ever had to come near one, the title of *maître* of the royal chapel did not imply that the incumbent was necessarily a musician, or that he directed the singers. For example, the high-ranking statesman and political figure Cardinal François de Tournon, a poet at odd moments, a patron of the arts, and a close friend of Francis I, was also the king's *maître de chapelle*, at an honorarium of 1,200 *livres tournois* per annum, though he had no stated duties and was director in name only. The actual work was left to the chapel's *soubz-maistre*, Claudin de Sermisy, whose annual salary was only 400 *l. t.*[24] No tears need be shed on Claudin's economic situation, however, for he was no pauper by sixteenth-century standards. (A court poet under the reign of Francis I was considered well paid if he received 200 *l. t.*; and with two *l. t.* one could buy two sheep or a barrel of wine containing 200 litres.)[25] And

[21] *Ibid.*, I: p. 61. 'As he was having dinner [the artillery] fired two shots across the room where the count of Charolais [i.e., Charles the Bold of Burgundy] was staying, and killed a trumpeter on the stairs as he was bringing up a dish of meat.'

[22] Kling, *Cor*, pp. 99–100. This process was called 'corner l'eau' and apparently referred to the advisability of washing one's hands before and after meals, since fingers were used in lieu of forks. Whether the custom was strictly observed I cannot presume to say. The author also suggests that the horn may have served occasionally to convoke the faithful to church.

[23] Prunières, *Chambre*, p. 219.

[24] Cazeaux, *Sermisy*, I: p. 10.

[25] Saulnier, *Littérature*, pp. 13–14.

Claudin had other emoluments from his canonry at the Sainte-Chapelle in Paris. As for Cardinal de Tournon, he was relieved of his honorary musical directorship at the same time as his seat on the royal council by Henry II, a few days after his father's death on 31 March 1547.[26] The cause was purely political and had no apparent connection with the cardinal's musicality or lack of it.

Musicians were sometimes relied upon to give eye-witness accounts of historical happenings. Brantôme tells us that he received some of his information about Charles de Bourbon, constable of France, and about the siege of Rome at which the duke was killed in 1527 from 'an old French trumpeter who had been in the service of the late lord of Bourbon at the time; and he was employed by the emperor and the vice-roy. This trumpeter was sixty years old or more, and he had seen all the action.'[27] The fact that this musician was taken on by the emperor after the constable's death may imply that French trumpeters were held in high esteem abroad. Since trumpeters were men of many talents, musical and other, however, we cannot be sure that the reminiscing trumpeter's playing was solely responsible for his position in the imperial household.

Renaissance music was meant to do many more things than simply give pleasure. Most writers on music—*littérateurs* as well as theorists—mention the supposed effects of music, and frequently give standard examples from biblical, classical, and mediaeval antiquity. Molinet, in his *Chroniques*, Chapter 9, offers a beautiful tribute to the power of music in his definition of that art: 'For music is the resonance of the heavens, the voice of the angels, the joy of paradise, the spirit of the air, the organ of the church, the song of the birds, the recreation of all sad and desolate hearts,[28] the persecution and expulsion of devils.'[29] The proem to the anonymous treatise, *L'Art, science et practique de plaine musique*, reflects similar ideas:

[26] François, *Tournon*, p. 229.   [27] Brantôme, *Œuvres*, I: p. 321.

[28] This expression seems to have been the source of inspiration for the anonymous volume of poetry entitled *La Recreation et passetemps des tristes* (Paris: L'Huillier, 1573). The title may denote a connection with music, which the volume has, in the sense that several of its pieces were set to music elsewhere.

[29] Quoted in MacClintock, *Molinet*, p. 120.

Music is therefore the praise of God, the joy of paradise, the Office of the angels, the resonance of the air, the voice of the church, the appeasement of the children, the solace of the soul, and the torment of devils, and as it is written in the book *L'Echiquier amoureux* [i.e., *Les Echecs amoureux*, ca. 1370–80], music, according to Macrobius, is that by which all creatures are taken and conquered: the unicorns by the song of the maiden, the serpents by the sound of the enchanter, the dolphins by the sound of the chalumeau, the birds by the sound of men's whistling, the mariners by the voice of the mermaid, and the enemy by the sound of the harp. Music, according to Boethius, soothes the furor of tyrants. It animates men-at-arms in battle.[30]

Eustache Deschamps, in his *L'Art de dictier* considers music the medicine of the seven liberal arts, for when tired creatures are lacking in courage and low in spirit, pleasant music can cure and revive their hearts and spirits.[31] A treatise by Gilles Carlier, theologian and master of arts of the University of Paris (1403), attributes three qualities to music: it can chase demons and it is endowed with curative and moral powers. Pontus de Tyard, in his *Solitaire second* (1552), claims that music can impart consolation in disappointment, appeasement in anger, temperance in desire, and cure in pain. Calvin, like Saint Augustine, believed that music could inflame the heart to pray more ardently (*Institution Chrétienne*, Bk. 3, ch. 20); unlike the author of the *Confessions*, however, he thought that the first step in achieving this was to eliminate papist songs (*fringots et fredons*).[32]

Ronsard, too, believed that the minds of men reflect the status of music, and that well-ordered music leads to a good life. In order to achieve this, he and his fellow poets from the *Pléiade* tried to unify music and verse. The members of Baïf's *Académie* went further and used homorhythmic procedures on quantitative meters, along with other experiments, in order to produce an art which would improve men and make for a better state.[33] Humanists who tried to have Greek genera

---

[30] Brenet, *Méthode*, p. 8.   [31] Carpenter, *Universities*, p. 74.
[32] Pirro, *Enseignement*, pp. 32, 51–52.
[33] Lesure, *Musicians*, p. 93, and Walker, *Humanism*, p. 9.

adapted to French music considered them important for the effects which the resultant music could achieve. Tyard was one of them, and unlike Baïf and his confrères, he favored monody over polyphony for the revival of the Greek ideal, as the Florentine circles were to do later.[34]

French writers have occasionally given examples of effects of music, not only in ancient times but in their own. In his description of the siege of Neuss (1474–75) Molinet mentions a soporific effect of contemporary music, but cannot resist a comparision with mythology: 'As Orpheus opened the door of hell with the sound of his harp, the modulation of these musical instruments mitigated the bitterness of the savage Saxon hearts, and lulled the enemies to sleep by its mild consonance.'[35] Pontus de Tyard mentions a feat accomplished by Francesco da Milano, who enchanted all those who heard him play the lute. On one occasion, in Milan, when a listener dropped his chin to his chest and lost all his senses except his hearing, Francesco played more vigorously, and the sensitive man was immediately revived. Pierre Le Loyer, in his *Discours des spectres, ou, Vision et apparitions d'esprits* (2d ed., Paris, 1608) refers to curative effects of music in connection with Saint Vitus's dance, 'a sort of demoniac mania which is still today cured by the Germans to the sound of their lute,' and with the aphrodisiac effect of the Spanish sarabande, which is 'ordinarily played on the cittern' and at the audition of which people cannot help but dance and 'sometimes do worse.' Nicolas Bergier, in his *La musique spéculative* (Paris: Bibl. nat., *MS. fr. 1359*), written in the early seventeenth century, tells of a young man from Lorraine who was in such a furor that he tore the string of his hat to pieces with his teeth and blasphemed in addition. When the author played a 'passamezzo in the Phrygian mode composed of double spondees' on his lute for him, the maniac immediately returned to normal.[36] This interest in the healing power of music may have come to French authors through the influence of Ficino and his writings on the effects of music—including astrological music—to which theories many of them were exposed.[37]

[34] Yates, *Academies*, pp. 47, 58.
[35] Pirro, *Histoire*, p. 117.
[36] Walker, *Humanism*, pp. 112–113.   [37] Yates, *Academies*, p. 40.

Several practical applications of music for therapeutic ends seem to have been made. Philippe de Mézières, who was for a time in the service of the French king of Cyprus, and at the court of Charles V, used to recommend the sound of instruments for 'the good digestion of the royal person.' During one of Charles VI's illnesses, processions were made in all of France. On 1 August 1414, a Mass with deacon, sub-deacon, singers, and organ was celebrated for the king's health.[38] In 1424, Binchois was asked to set to music the rondel *Ainsy qu'a la fois m'en souvient*, at the price of two ells of scarlet material, for the benefit of the duke of Suffolk. The duke, who was the husband of Chaucer's granddaughter and a friend of Charles d'Orléans, had met with an accident and had to be transported to Paris, where he was confined to his room.[39] On Friday 24 July 1461, the members of the royal counting house met at the Sainte-Chapelle with the intention of making a procession (presumably with music), bare-footed and bearing candles, in order to ask God to save Charles VII during his fatal illness. They were informed, however, that the king had died two days earlier, at Mehun-sur-Yevre in Berry; and so they changed their plans and had Requiem Masses celebrated at the Sainte-Chapelle instead.[40]

According to Robert Gaguin's chronicles, Louis XI, who was close to death, returned to Tours, where he expected to be cured by means of the 'harmony of music.' For this reason he ordered that players of all musical instruments be called, and it is considered certain that up to one hundred and twenty of them were assembled.'[41] Another time when the king thought he was dying (1481), at Tours, he founded a Mass with music in honor of Saint John, at the Sainte-Chapelle in Paris, to be celebrated daily at seven o'clock in the morning.[42]

At Laon, where there was an epidemic of the plague, Bishop Charles of Luxembourg celebrated a solemn Office (19 July 1504) in which he sang the initial verse of the *Veni Creator*, to be continued by the singers and the organ.[43]

[38] Rokseth, *Orgue*, pp. 6, 31.
[39] Marix, *Musiciens*, pp. xv, xviii.
[40] Brenet, *Sainte-Chapelle*, p. 32.
[41] Brenet, *France*, p. 45.
[42] Brenet, *Sainte-Chapelle*, p. 37.   [43] Rokseth, *Orgue*, p. 167.

After the death of Anne of Brittany in 1514, Louis XII became ill and requested that the hymn to the Blessed Sacrament, *O salutaris hostia*, be sung in the churches throughout the realm. Gaguin, who relates this in *La mer des chroniques* (1518) adds that he believes the Blessed Sacrament and the precious body of Christ to have helped him greatly.[44] The improvement, however, proved to be of short duration.

After the massacre of Saint Bartholomew's day, when Charles IX suffered from consumption and felt depressed, he called for music and poetry in an effort to be cured.[45]

Music was performed in the rooms of women in childbed. As early as 1373, Burgundian instrumentalists played for the duchess, who had given birth to her second son. The custom was eventually transmitted to lower strata of society, and in 1534, Gratien du Pont describes a similar musical offering to a young mother of middle estate.[46]

There have been instances of persons dying (or almost dying) to music, accidentally or on request. Shortly before her projected marriage to Henry IV, his mistress Gabrielle d'Estrées, duchess of Beaufort, attended a *Tenebrae* concert directed by Jacques Mauduit, on Holy Wednesday, 7 April 1599, at the chapel of 'Petit Saint-Antoine.' There she felt uncomfortable, because of the heat, and after the service she had herself conducted to her aunt's house near Saint-Germain-l'Auxerrois, where she died shortly thereafter, on the night of Good Friday.[47] When Isabeau de la Tour d'Auvergne, demoiselle de Limeuil, one of Catherine de' Medici's maids of honour, felt death coming upon her, she had her violinist-valet play for her Janequin's *La Guerre*, according to Brantôme.[48]

Music apparently helped one not only to die properly, but to ascend to heaven, provided, of course, that one was worthy of going there. Guillaume Telin reports, in *La Louenge de musique* (1533) that Saint Martin of Tours and other martyrs and confessors had their spirits transported to the celestial

---

[44] Lowinsky, *Medici* (edition), III: p. 43.
[45] Yates, *Academies*, p. 211.   [46] Rokseth, *Orgue*, p. 19.
[47] Brenet, *France*, p. 235.   [48] Brenet, *Militaire*, p. 37.

realm to the accompaniment of angelic singing; as for Christ, his ascension was made with great jubilation and to the sound of trumpets.[49]

It was believed that music could bring about not only physical cures, but spiritual ones as well; and so there was expiatory music. In order to have his sins forgiven, Louis d'Orléans, brother of Charles VI and father of Charles d'Orléans, founded several Masses with music, for 'Messes a note' were more effective than low Masses in gaining indulgences.[50] Music was sometimes performed in expiation of sins other than one's own. On 11 June 1528, the musicians of Francis I sang an *Ave Regina caelorum* in a procession because of a sacrilege committed by a Huguenot.[51] Brenet has suggested that Josquin's *Miserere* was sung in one of the processions that were termed 'black, sad, and penitential' because they were meant to appease God's wrath and to avert famine, plague, and war.

Music was used to ask for special graces, both temporal and spiritual, and to attract beneficial forces from above, or in gratitude for favors received. Between Easter and Pentecost, 'white and joyful' processions were held. On 25 April of every year, at Rouen, a 'major litany' containing the respond *Christus resurgens* was sung in order to obtain good crops. Richafort's motet *Christus resurgens* may have been performed on one of these occasions.[52] A procession was organized on Saint John's day 1426, so that the rain would stop, and another in 1427, so that the overflowing rivers would subside.[53]

Richafort's *Exaudiat te Dominus* requests protection in time of war and may have been composed for Louis XII or Francis I.[54] The latter ordered a procession to be held on 21 January 1535 to ask God to 'keep all good and true Catholics in their good and holy faith, and to amend and redress those who have erred from the right path.' Among the participants were the canons of Notre-Dame, the dignitaries of the University of

---

[49] Brenet, *Méthode*, p. 27.
[50] Rokseth, *Orgue*, p. 23.
[51] Brenet, *Processions*, p. 8.
[52] *Ibid.*, p. 10.
[53] Rokseth, *Orgue*, p. 31.
[54] Kellman, *Links* (lecture).

Paris, the singers of the king's chapel and of the Sainte-Chapelle, the Swiss royal guards, with their fifes and drums, and the king's oboes, violins, trumpets, and cornets. A similar procession was ordered by Henry II on 4 July 1549, for the 'extirpation of heresies.'[55]

The religious processions of Henry III and Louise of Lorraine were held in part to obtain a male heir. Not all supplicatory or thanksgiving music was sacred, however, and Miss Yates has aptly demonstrated that it often borders on Neoplatonic occultism. The *magnificences* of 1581, in which Claude Le Jeune participated, were not merely wedding spectacles. The music, some of which was *mesurée*, was intended to attract the good influences from the stars in order to avert war and otherwise help the court. At the end of the *Balet comique*, the queen presents to the king a gold medal with the image of a dolphin, which symbolized the Dauphin that everyone hoped for. The plot of this ballet suggests that Mercury and Jupiter are 'drawn down by the powerful music of the *voute dorée* acting as a kind of musical astrological talisman in favour of the French royal house.'[56] An example of astrological prayer is Le Jeune's air *O Reine d'honneur*, which calls upon the heavens to bless Henry IV. The refrain, *Astres heureux tournez, tournez cieux, tourne le destin* has been compared to an incantation to the heavenly bodies to bring beneficial influences upon France and its king.[57] Costeley's *O mignonnes de Jupiter* has been called 'a sort of secular prayer for the king's recovery from a fever.'[58]

Thanksgiving music has often been performed spontaneously. After an Italian victory of Louis XII, his chaplains sang a *Te Deum* right on the battlefield.[59] Agricola's motet *Transit Anna timor* (1505) was composed for Louis XII's recovery from an illness.[60] In honor of the reconquest of Paris in 1437, an annual feast was instituted on the first Friday after Easter, at which the councilors, provosts, and aldermen of

---

[55] Brenet, *Sainte-Chapelle*, pp. 88, 97.
[56] Yates, *Processions*, pp. 235, 254–256, and *Magnificences*, p. 248.
[57] Yates, *Magnificences*, pp. 247–248.
[58] Godt, *Costeley*, I: p. 70.
[59] Thoinan, *Origines*, p. 88.
[60] Kellman, *Links* (lecture).

Paris marched to Notre-Dame to hear a High Mass with organ, called the Mass of the reduction of Paris. All the bells of Paris were rung, and a *Te Deum* was sung. This custom lasted for some one hundred years at least.[61]

That music was not considered beneficial for all situations is shown by a ruling made in 1390 by Pierre d'Ailly, chancellor of the University of Paris before he became bishop of Cambrai. It forbids the students of the Collège de Marmoutier from playing on musical instruments in the dormitory, for fear that it might disrupt their studies.[62]

[61] Rokseth, *Orgue*, p. 33.
[62] Pirro, *Enseignement*, p. 31.

5

Education and music: personal teaching, didactic writings

Music was part of the educational process of those who could afford to be cultured, and it was taught in establishments such as churches, universities, and colleges, as well as in academies, schools of *ménétriers*, and private homes. Various centers specialized in different branches of music. Theorists were formed at the university; church performers and composers were trained at the *maîtrises* and occasionally studied privately. Itinerant musicians and other secular instrumentalists learned from their colleagues in locations that changed from year to year. Though the disciplines were not merged in any one place, there frequently was cooperation between institutions— and occasionally rivalry. Choirboys were encouraged to study at the university when their voice changed, and royal scholarships were provided for the most worthy. Pierre Vermond and Antoine Mornable, from the Sainte-Chapelle were among those scholars, in 1513 and 1530 respectively.[1] In 1548, when he was in his early sixties, the composer Janequin enrolled as a student at the University of Angers.[2] Other persons associated with music who had studied at provincial universities include Eustache Deschamps, author of *L'Art de dictier et de fere chansons*, who was trained at the University of Orléans, and Jean le Bègue, master of the choirboys at Chartres, who had been enrolled at the University of Poitiers in 1469.[3]

When Baïf tried to have the royal letters patent and statutes for his *Académie* approved by the court of Parlement, in 1570, this body turned the whole matter over to the university authorities. On 30 December 1570, the University of Paris

[1] Brenet, *Sainte-Chapelle*, pp. 64, 87, and Pirro, *Enseignement*, p. 49.

[2] Lesure (in Honegger, *Dictionnaire* I: p. 537) suspects that Janequin, who complained about his poverty to his dying day, did this in order to obtain more lucrative prebends, but I like to think that he took this step out of respect for academic pursuits, and as a firm believer in adult education.

[3] Carpenter, *Universities*, p. 74, and Pirro, *Enseignement*, p. 45.

decided to consult each faculty and to ask Baïf whether he
wished to be separate from the university or to adhere to its
laws. There was obvious mistrust of the proposed institution,
and it took royal intervention to force the university to accept
the rival *Académie*.[4]

Whereas the term 'musician' in earlier times was reserved
for music theorists, it came to be used also for composers,
during the Renaissance. Performers were usually assigned
designations derived from the name of their instrument or
their voice.[5] One hears of 'joueurs de hautbois,' or simply
'hautbois,' or 'basse-contre', for example. Although the
generic term for singers was *chantres*, and for instrumentalists
joueurs d'instruments (Guillaume Telin, in his music book,
addresses an epistle to all musicians and *joueurs d'instruments*),
the word *musiciens* was occasionally employed in the meaning
of 'performers.' When Jean Marot writes of 'musiciens en leurs
voix argentines',[6] for example, he is clearly referring to
singers. So is the anonymous poet of Jean Guyon's chanson,
Musiciens qui chantez a plaisir (Paris, Du Chemin, 1550[9]).[7] Of
course, an individual could practice more than one discipline,
as did Tinctoris, who was theorist, composer, and singer. Most
of the ecclesiastic and royal singers were also composers. The
majority of the instrumentalists, with the exception of solo
virtuosi, were not, or at least they did not leave us written
compositions; they probably improvised, however. The term
sçavant musicien seems to have been applied to a person
conversant with more than one branch of music, as in the case
of Etienne du Tertre, who was organist, composer, and
arranger of music.[8]

A musical education was valued by those who wanted
success in their positions or in society. Francis I decreed, in
1531, that in order to become a chaplain at the cathedral of
Rouen, it would be necessary to show proof of musical
knowledge.[9] An anonymous poem from the fifteenth century

[4] Yates, *Academies*, pp. 26–27.
[5] Van, *Pédagogie*, p. 78.
[6] J. Marot, *Œuvres*, p. 160.
[7] Transcribed in Cunningham, *Chanson*, II: pp. 13–15.
[8] Cunningham, *Du Tertre*, p. 127.
[9] Rokseth, *Orgue*, p. 106.

shows a favorable attitude toward musically proficient clerics, at the expense of pure theologians: 'Ung clerc mixte qui scet lire et chanter/ Jouer du leu, des orgues, et harper/ Tousjours sera partout bien venu/ Plus tost congneu, de ce ne doubtez mie/ Que ne sera ung maistre en theologie.'[10]

Practical music was often taught the young with the help of sticks and other instruments of punishment, in order to observe the pedagogical principle that an error should be corrected as soon as it is made. Other educational materials were also used, however, such as slates for composition. Josquin is reported to have transmitted to his students the practice of using a blackboard to make rough drafts of compositions, but he was by no means the only musician of his time to do so, as Guillaume Cretin tells us in his *Plainte sur le trepas de feu maistre Jehan Braconnier, dit Lourdault, chantre*: 'Nostre bon pere et maistre Prioris/ Prenez l'ardoyse et de vostre faczon/ Composez cy un "ne recorderis." '[11] There were music instruction books for choirboys in the *maîtrises*, though we do not know their titles.[12] It has been suggested that the beautiful Chantilly *Codex 564 (olim 1047)* with its highly intricate notation, in which the difficulties seem to have been accumulated on purpose, was essentially a mensural notation manual, a pedagogical collection to train not only the voice but the intellectual faculties of the young singers. Guillaume de Van points out that 'the object of the *ars mensurabilis* was not simply to communicate a musical work to the performer, but also to surround the science with effective protection against the illicit curiosity of the uninitiated.'[13]

Much importance was attached to a good voice. A music master was expected to have one. In order that choirboys preserve their voice as long as possible, Jean Gerson, who assumed that voices are lost through overeating, recommended, in the *Doctrina pro pueris ecclesiae parisiensis* attributed to him, that the boys of Notre-Dame de Paris not eat too much.[14]

[10] Pirro, *Enseignement*, p. 45.
[11] Clercx, *Ardoise*, pp. 162–164, and Van, *Pédagogie*, p. 94.
[12] Becker, *Maîtrise*, p. 126.
[13] Van, *Pédagogie*, p. 82, and Bridgman, *Quattrocento*, p. 71.
[14] Becker, *Maîtrise*, p. 158. We should add, in all fairness to the chancellor

Josquin's teaching approach, as described by Adrian Petit Coclico, was a bit intuitive. He tried to make the students sing in tune, with good declamation, proper ornamentation and text underlay, and then taught consonances and the rules of counterpoint. Only after they had mastered these essentials did he decide whether they were by nature sufficiently gifted to undertake composition. If they were not endowed with innate musical talent, they were not considered worthy of studying that discipline. The chosen ones learned how to write in three, four, five, and six parts, and the master taught chiefly by giving numerous examples.[15]

Perhaps the most important center of music education was the choir school, or *maîtrise*, whose aim was to train boys in sight-reading and improvised discant and *fauxbourdon*, written notation, plainchant, polyphony, and grammar (which included reading, writing, and literature) so that they would serve their chapel well. Though it was not its main function, the *maîtrise* served as a preparatory school for the universities. It often supplied singers for papal, royal, and ducal chapels, in addition to its own church. It was hoped that the young men, after their training period was over, would eventually become churchmen, and most of them, including some of the best-known composers of the Renaissance, did. Cathedral schools occasionally accepted persons other than resident choirboys as students. Young laymen came for literary, and sometimes musical studies—as did older churchmen. Obrecht, during his stay at Cambrai, taught music not only to the choirboys, but to various ecclesiastics and canons who were in need of further instruction.[16]

The canons who recruited a master of music and a master of grammar expected them to be qualified not only educationally, but morally, for they were firm believers in preaching by example. Music masters sometimes had to prove that they could play the organ, improvise, and compose, as

of the University of Paris, that he did not put the children on a starvation diet, nor did he mistreat them. He specifically stated in another passage that they should be provided with good food, and he believed that gentleness and love could accomplish more than fear in educational practice.

[15] Roketh, *Josquin*, p. 204.   [16] Becker, *Maîtrise*, pp. 156–157.

well as sing. Vacancies for positions as choirboys occurred frequently enough owing to the illness or unruliness of the singers, and particularly to their change of voice. In order to find replacements, the position was announced at Mass in the parish churches, and occasionally musicians from neighboring cathedrals were consulted. Boys from all classes of society were admitted to the *maîtrise*, but those who were retained and eventually received promotions in the ecclesiastical ranks were generally from the middle estate at least; many were nephews of canons. The admissions policy of various *maîtrises* were not uniform—some institutions were particularly interested in the quality of candidates' voices, others in their ear, or in their memory—but a rough pattern emerges of what they were looking for. They generally obtained it by auditioning the boys and having their parents prove or affirm that they were lawfully married.[17] In 1575, the master of the children at the Sainte-Chapelle, named Bareau, was called to task for admitting practically anyone as a choirboy, as a favor to his acquaintances. Henceforth he was not to select any boy who had not been 'previously heard singing, in order to find out whether he had a voice and a mind to understand the art of music and reading, and if he is without bodily flaw.' At Chartres, if a candidate did not seem to be in good health, he was made to sing in the presence of a physician.[18]

Although the program of studies varied from cathedral to cathedral and from time to time—some *maîtrises* stressed academic studies more than musical ones, and vice versa—music and grammar were always taught.[19] In principle, Latin was both read and spoken. The Psalter and Antiphonary were generally learned by heart—either because it was considered meritorious, or because it saved light if Matins could be sung without music books. Furthermore, young clerics who had not yet learned to read music could be trained by rote.[20]

[17] *Ibid.*, pp. 93, 137–142.

[18] Brenet, *Saint-Chapelle*, p. 127, and Becker, *Maîtrise*, p. 140.

[19] Education at Chartres during the fifteenth century was more literary than musical, but in the following century, the position of master of grammar was left vacant for sixty years (Becker, *Maîtrise*, p. 84).

[20] Goldine, *Chartres*, pp. 168–169.

Classrooms were not always the most pleasant places. They could be located at the chapter house, or at the children's house. Classes were often held in a space in the cathedral instead of in a separate room. On 29 May 1449, the chapter of Rouen decided that the classes might be floored, so that the boys could work more comfortably there.[21] Hours for study were arranged between Offices and Masses, and left the students little free time. The masters of music and of grammar occasionally seemed to resent the time spent by the boys in their colleague's discipline. The Sainte-Chapelle provided recourse to the 'maître chapelain' in case of disagreement between the two masters. In the morning, the music master was not to take the students away from their grammar lesson unless they had to learn something at the last moment, to sing before the king. After Vespers, they might rehearse three or four motets, but not many more, because they had been singing most of the day for the services, and the master of grammar should have some time with them after dinner, so that they would not forget what they had learned in the morning. Choirboys were not taught only religious music. They were expected to know *ballades* and other secular music too, which they sang for official occasions outside their chapel. When Charlotte of Savoy, second wife of Louis XI, arrived in Paris by boat on the Seine, 1 September 1467, local dignitaries came also by the same means to meet her. In the boats were the 'little choirboys of the Sainte-Chapelle, who sang pretty *virelais* and chansons, as well as *bergerettes*, most melodiously.'[22] Gerson's rules stipulated that 'proper discants' might be taught, but not lewd songs.[23] Strangers were permitted to come to rehearsals, once in a while, so that the children might benefit from their presence, but they should not consort with them too often, because the boys might be disturbed as a result, and might learn from them 'things that are not profitable to them.'[24]

The children were not always well treated by their masters. The oldest choirboy of the Sainte-Chapelle was absent on 21

[21] Becker, *Maîtrise*, pp. 72–76.
[22] Brenet, *Sainte-Chapelle*, pp. 16–17, 34.
[23] Pirro, *Charles VI*, p. 19.
[24] Brenet, *Sainte-Chapelle*, p. 18.

December 1575, because his master, the above-named Bareau, had punched him and kicked him the previous day, during Compline. It should be noted, however, that such behaviour was not condoned by the authorities. On 8 November 1598, the Treasurer reprimanded the music master Jacques Renvoyré, because of the poor quality of meat, bread, wine, linen, and heat that he was providing, as well as the casual attitude he manifested in his teaching; he apparently spent more time on his domestic affairs and the promotion of his own profit than on instructing the boys in the art of music.[25]

Outside of the church service and classroom, other aspects of life at the *maîtrise* (also called *manécanterie*, or *psallette* at various times and places) were also strictly regulated. The boys' quarters sometimes gave its name to the street on which it was located—rue des Bons-Enfants at Dijon, for example. In certain places, the oldest choirboy, called the *spe*, intoned the *Veni Creator* to wake the rest, who responded sleepily at the unison. They then proceeded to church in double file to sing Matins, after which they returned for breakfast. During meals, they were treated to readings from the Scriptures, the lives of Saints, or other edifying material. Grace was sung after dinner and supper. Gerson recommended that the boys speak little or not at all during meals. The official language at most *maîtrises* was Latin. If the children spoke French, they were liable to punishment, such as being put on a diet of dry bread, or being sent to bed for the day; there they were probably lonely, for Gerson had stipulated that no beast or injurious bird might be lodged with them.[26]

At the Sainte-Chapelle, the boys were to have a valet and a chambermaid old enough to serve them properly. (This is not the only religious establishment where younger maids were frowned upon.) Parents sometimes had to contribute a present for the maid and other personnel, such as the barber, as well as for their son's colleagues. It was expected at Rouen. Most *maîtrises* allowed the children a short recreation period in the afternoon. The boys of the Sainte-Chapelle might play in the yard, in front of their house, but they had to be visible at all times, and were not to 'pass the brook or the corner, or to go

---

[25] *Ibid.*, pp. 127, 148.   [26] Becker, *Maîtrise*, pp. 157–158, 184, 294–296.

towards the Seine.'[27] Sometimes they had a short vacation
period. At Rouen, for example, they were given a few free days
in summer, in compensation for the abolishment in 1452 of the
mock ceremony of the Holy Innocents. At that feast, the boys
used to sing in the stalls usually reserved for the canons, who
prepared a banquet for them afterwards. Owing to excesses on
the part of the youngsters, the festivities, which had been
popular from the twelfth century to the sixteenth, were
gradually stopped everywhere.

The choirboys were issued new clothes twice a year, one set
for Easter, and the other for All Saints' Day or Christmas.
They wore a cassock, which was usually white, and an alb or
surplice over it. (It was on account of this garment that the
choirboys of Autun and Cambrai were called *enfants d'aube*.)
For their heads they had hoods or caps. In winter, the boys'
clothes were lined with white lamb's wool. The masters wore
more elegant fur-trimmed robes. At the Sainte-Chapelle, their
hoods were lined with grey squirrel. Some colorful habits
could be seen at Saint-Amé, in Douai, where the singers wore
a scarlet cassock with matching sash, skull cap and square
bonnet ornamented with a green silk tassel, a black hood for
winter, blue or red stockings, and shoes with silver buckles.
Inside the *maîtrise*, the uniform consisted of blue vest and
trousers, and a square bonnet with green wool tassel. At Saint-
Pierre, in the same town, the robes and headgear were violet
and the stockings red; the shoes had brass buckles. At Dijon in
1563, the boy who was chosen 'bishop' for the day, at the feast
of the Holy Innocents, wore a small hood of green satin.[28]

Music had its place at the universities, where it was part of
the liberal arts curriculum, as a branch of mathematics, and
later of physics. Jean de Muris, theorist of the *Ars Nova*,
mathematician, astronomer, and musician, had taught at the
Sorbonne. A former master of the choirboys at Notre-Dame
de Paris, Johannes Comitis, was listed as a teacher *in arte musica*
at the University of Paris, shortly after Gerson's tenure as
chancellor. Jean Dorat, of the Collège de Coqueret, though
not   a   music   teacher—he   was   professor   of   Greek

[27] *Ibid.*, p. 144, and Brenet, *Sainte-Chapelle*, pp. 11–19.
[28] Becker, *Maîtrise*, pp. 146–152. A fifteenth-century medal of the bishop
of the Innocents was found in the north of France.

literature—was very fond of music and may have influenced his students Baïf and Ronsard in their humanistic ideas on music.

Although the academic courses in music were undoubtedly speculative rather than practical, there was also music performed in connection with university life. In 1403, Guillermus Burgundi was listed as *cantor* at the University of Paris. In the various colleges where they were housed, students took part in the sacred services. At one of these places, they were expected to learn plainchant. By a ruling of 1380, the Collège de Dainville established the daily singing of an antiphon to the Blessed Virgin, and the celebration of a Mass with music on Sundays and holidays. The four 'nations' which formed the University of Paris also had music for various special occasions, such as the celebration of the feast of their patron saint.[29]

Baïf's *Académie de poésie et de musique* is often regarded as a center of music performance and composition in a certain style—which indeed it was—but it was also a center of learning. Its operation was guided by strict rules. Musicians and poets were to present their *vers* and *musique mesurés* every Sunday for two hours, at Baïf's house, for the benefit of auditors, who paid their subscriptions twice a year and were admitted to the concerts by showing an identification medallion. The auditors, of whom the king was the principal one, had to be on their best behaviour. They were not to talk, whisper, or make noise during a performance, nor were they allowed to enter in the middle of a number, or mingle with the musicians. The latter owed obedience in matters musical to Baïf and Thibaut de Courville. They rehearsed together after having learned individual parts separately, and were forbidden to give copies of their music to unauthorized persons. If a quarrel arose among auditors or musicians, they were not to attack each other in word or deed within one hundred feet of their meeting place. Although the statutes make no mention of

[29] Carpenter, *Universities,* pp. 64, 74, 115, 140–146, and Pirro, *Enseignement,* pp. 30–31. The cheerful students at the colleges surely did not limit their performances to religious music. G. Thibault has suggested that certain compositions which lie in a low tessitura were intended for men's colleges.

the *Acadé*mie's educational function, Mersenne, who obtained his information from one of its members, the aging composer Jacques Mauduit, reports on it in his *Quaestiones* (1623), and we gather from his account that music in the narrow sense was only one of many disciplines studied there:

> They appointed to this Academy men most skilled in every kind of natural sciences, and instituted a prefect of it who should be called the head teacher. I leave out the other masters, of sciences, of tongues especially, of music, of poetry, of geography, of the various parts of mathematics, and of painting, who promoted the good of the mind, and the military prefects who taught all those things which are useful for military disciplines and for the good of the body. . . .[30]

Educational institutions of an entirely different nature were the so-called schools of *menestrels*, which were not schools in the conventional sense, nor did they teach the practice of one's instrument. They were essentially annual reunions of *ménétriers* in certain towns, during Lent, since that was the time when most of them were unemployed. There they learned the latest popular songs from each other. When their means did not allow them to attend, they asked their more fortunate colleagues to teach them the new tunes on their return. Occasionally a patron of the arts paid their expenses to the musicians' congress—as did a magistrate from Lille who sent several *menestrels* to the school of Cambrai 'to learn the new chansons.' The most important and regularly-held 'schools' were in the Northern provinces, and seem to have lasted from 1313 to 1441. Lesure has found the following dates for certain centers. Ypres, 1313–1432; Beauvais, 1398–1436; Cambrai, 1427–40; St. Omer, 1424–41.[31] Lute schools for children existed in several towns. In 1545, the town council of Marseille established one in a house which they rented to the lutenist Barthélemy de la Croix for the purpose.[32] Jean Tapissier, who was music master of the choirboys at the Burgundian court

[30] Yates, *Academies*, pp. 21–25.
[31] Marix, *Histoire*, pp. 97–98, and Lesure, *Sociologie*, pp. 340–341.
[32] Reese, *Renaissance*, pp. 553–554.

between 1406 and 1408 also directed his own school of singing in Paris. The composer Thomas Fabri was proud to call himself 'scolaris Tapissier.'[33]

Musicians were often educated by a private teacher. Gifted students of a *maîtrise* were sometimes sent to a master at another cathedral, in order to perfect their art.[34] Children of kings and noblemen were instructed at home by resident teachers. Persons of lower estate sometimes signed contracts with musicians so as to learn music. In 1405, two brothers, both carpenters, formed an association with the *ménétrier* Jacot Lécrivain, who promised to teach them music and give them a third of their joint earnings.[35] Anthonius Girardi, a student at the University of Avignon, obtained by contract, on 4 November 1449, that the Jew Mosse of Lisbon would teach him to play several pieces, including *Joyeux espoir, Rostit bollit*, and *La bonne volonté que j'ay* on the zither or harp.[36]

For those who wished to be self-taught, a variety of books could be had. These include writings in praise of music, which try to define it and explain its aims. Of course, not all works of this type were instruction books. Poets and other authors who were not primarily musicians had much to say about various aspects of music in works devoted to other subjects, and composers sometimes had something to say about music in the preface to a collection of music. Anthoine de Bertrand, for example, explains, in the introduction to his *Amours* (1578) that the aim of music is to satisfy the ear; and in order to recreate the 'perfection' of Greek music, and to please, he uses the diatonic, chromatic, and enharmonic genera.[37] Some theory books, such as Guillaume Guerson's *Utilissime musicales regule* combine speculation and practice. Another type of didactic work is the dance tutor, such as Michel de Toulouze's *L'Art et instruction de bien dancer* (148–?), or Thoinot Arbeau (anagram of Jehan Tabourot)'s *Orchésographie* (1589) with choreography and music, or the manual to learn one or more

---

[33] Wright, *Tapissier*, pp. 184–185.
[34] Becker, *Maîtrise*, pp. 121, 170–172.
[35] Marix, *Histoire*, p. 96.   [36] Pirro, *Enseignement*, p. 45.
[37] Carruth, *Bertrand*, pp. 55–57. Bertrand's attitude seems to foreshadow by several centuries Debussy's remark that his music followed the rules of his own pleasure.

instruments, which often contained practical examples of music, and occasionally included rudiments of music.

Mediaeval texts on music were written in Latin, since that was the language of the church and the schools—with the exception of a small set of thirteenth-century discant rules in French.[38] It was in the Renaissance, and particularly in the sixteenth century that some educational works came to be written in French—and even in Hebrew. Occasionally, older books on music were translated into French. Such was *Le livre de la proprieté des choses*, Jean Corbichon's translation of an encyclopedic compilation by a thirteenth-century English Franciscan, 'Barthélemy l'Anglais' (Glanville), based on Isidore of Seville and other authors. This book is concerned only partially with music; other subjects treated include God, the angels, man, illnesses, metals, plants, animals, and colors, to name only a few. The treatise is preserved in the illustrated fifteenth-century *MS. fr. 22532* of the Bibliothèque nationale, Paris, and was also printed in the sixteenth century.[39]

On the whole, it was the predominantly theoretical works that were written in Latin, and the 'do it yourself' general rudiments books as well as practical instruction books for instrumentalists that were in French. There were exceptions to this generalization, of course. Oronce Finé's *Epithoma musice instrumentalis* (Paris: Attaingnant, 1530), an eight-folio lute teaching book, was in Latin. But then its author was among other things a royal professor of mathematics, and not a lute virtuoso; although he includes several diagrams, he does not give complete compositions as musical examples. Most of the other compilers of instrumental methods were practicing musicians rather than scholars, and probably had pity on their middle-class readers, who understood French better than Latin. Such may also have been the considerations of those who wrote theory books in French.

Most fifteenth-century treatises were in Latin. Gilles Carlier,

[38] Brenet, *Méthode*, p. 7. The anonymous treatise from the Saint-Victor manuscript (Paris: Bibl. nat., *MS. lat. 15139*) which is reprinted in Coussemaker, *Histoire*, pp. 244–246, was written in the margins of two folios of the manuscript (269vo–270ro) in a different hand from the rest of the volume.

[39] *See* Bibliothèque nationale, *Livre*, pp. 182–183.

who is listed as Master of Arts at the University of Paris in 1403 and who became dean of the chapter at Cambrai, wrote a theoretical treatise (Paris: Bibl. nat., *MS. lat. 7212*) in which he praises music and tries to show its usefulness. It has been suggested that, as in the case of many writings on music, the manuscript may be essentially a compilation of the author's class notes. At any rate, he places vocal music above all other, 'maxime si vox et cor sunt consona.'[40] Although the one-time existence of a theoretical work by Busnois has been hinted at, there is no tangible proof that it was ever written.[41] It is a bit difficult to claim the twelve treatises of one of the most outstanding theorists of his time, the Brabant-born Johannes Tinctoris, as French products, because most of them were probably not written in France, and because the author, though he was for brief periods at Cambrai and Chartres, and came to the Burgundian and French courts on recruiting trips for the Aragonese court of Naples, spent most of his time outside of France. I shall therefore not attempt to bestow French (or any other) nationality upon Tinctoris. Still, the omission of his name from this list would seem to be inexcusable, because his works, from the *Terminorum musicae deffinitorium*—the first known dictionary of musical terms—to the *Liber de arte contrapunti* and *De inventione et usu musicae* reflect the thinking of the Burgundian and early Franco-Flemish musicians whom he knew so well—many of them are mentioned by name and some received the dedication of his books—and are our best source of fifteenth-century French theory and performance practice.

Among the early printed Latin treatises was the *Elementa musicalia* of the theologian and humanist Jacques Lefèvre d'Etaples (Paris: Higman et Hopyl, 1496), which he dedicated to Nicolas d'Hacqueville, president of the Parlement and brother of Jacqueline, for whom Busnois wrote several chansons. Here Lefèvre presents Greek and mediaeval musical theories as they were taught in the *quadrivium*. He was used as an authority in an argument against Bartolomé Ramos de Pareja.[42] Guillaume Guerson's *Utilissime musicales regule*, first

---

[40] Pirro, *Enseignement*, p. 32.

[41] Bethel, *Burgundian*, p. 171. Fétis mentions this in his *Biographie universelle*, t. 2, p. 127.   [42] Riemann, *History*, p. 283.

published in Paris about 1500 by Michel Tholoze (or Michel de Toulouze), who had earlier issued the above-mentioned dance manual, is the first printed book in France that deals with counterpoint. Ferand finds that this work, which stresses the practical aspects of counterpoint, contains independent thoughts not encountered in the theoretical literature of the fifteenth-century—including the treatises of Tinctoris and Gafori. It enjoyed at least eight re-editions, and was known to Hawkins, who mentions it in his history (III: 239 ff).[43]

It probably influenced the work of Nicolas Wollick, professor at the University of Paris and later historiographer and secretary to Antoine, duke of Lorraine, the *Opus aureum* (Cologne, 1501), which seems to be the first book on music education printed in Germany, and its substantially enlarged version, the *Enchiridion musices* (Paris, 1509, 1512).[44] Wollick, born near Bar-le-Duc, studied at the University of Cologne, but underscored the fact that he was French by signing a letter to a former professor 'Nicolas Gallus.' He seems to have originated the term *sortisatio*, which appears in both of his treatises in the sense of improvised singing, in consonant intervals, of parts added to a plainchant melody. The term is otherwise found almost exclusively in German literature. Wollick was quoted as an authority by Italian theorists such as Lanfranco (*Scintille di musica*, 1533), who calls him Nicolo Vuolico, and Berardi (*Ragionamenti musicali*, 1681), who refers to him as Nicola Bolico Baroducense. His works seem to have had a certain influence on such theorists as Ornithoparchus, Coclico, and Claudio Sebastiani.[45] The latter author, who was from Metz, was one of the rare persons who could write a theoretical treatise on music with fantasy. His *Bellum musicale* (1563) represents plainchant and mensural music as rival provinces, the kings of which are brothers. The soldiers are musical notes, arranged in order of battle. Mensural music

[43] Ferand, *Guerson*, pp. 253–254. Hawkins states that 'the science of counterpoint had been cultivated to some degree before [Josquin's] time; one Guillaume Guerson . . . was the author of a treatise. . . . It is conjectured to be as ancient as the time of Franchinus [Gafurius].'

[44] A copy of the *Enchiridion* was in the collection of Jean de Badonvilliers, notary and secretary to Francis I (Lesure, *Badonvilliers*, pp. 79–80).

[45] Ferand, *Sodaine*, pp. 11–18.

eventually emerges the winner, and the two brothers become reconciled. Sebastiani gives praise to several French musicians, including Courtois, Consilium, and Claudin de Sermisy.[46]

A lost treatise by Alanus Varenius, *Dialogus de harmonia et de harmonia elementis*, was printed in 1503 by the Parisian Robert Estienne. In 1510 appeared Jean Mauburne's *Rosetum exercitorium* (Paris: Scabeler). A master of law at the University of Orléans, Pyrrhus d'Angleberme, wrote comments about music in his *Sermo de musica et saltatione ex Luciano* (1517) and his *Scholia in libros quatuor Floridorum* of Apuleius (1518).[47] An anonymous treatise, *Utilissimum gregoriane psalmodie enchiridion tonorum artem et regulas aperte demonstrans*, was published by Didier Maheu (Paris, 1530).

Glarean's *Dodecachordon* was not a French publication, nor was it written by a Frenchman, but its name seems to belong here because of its author's close relationship with France. This is hardly the place to review Glarean's significance to the history of music by his addition of four modes to the existing eight, his innovation of musical biography, and his contributions to the history of musical criticism by his evaluation of the music of his time and his establishment of critical standards of musical judgment. Although the *Dodecachordon* was not published until 1547, most of it was completed about ten years earlier, and much of the material that went into it may have been gathered while Glarean was at the court of Francis I, between 1517 and 1522—where he met humanists such as Guillaume Budé, and musicians such as Jean Mouton. He founded a private school in Paris, where he taught Greek and Latin.[48] He apparently never felt the need to learn French—a language which he thought stammers more than it speaks. With other humanists he could speak Latin or Greek, and with more simple souls he used an interpreter. It is reported that he had recourse to one in his conversations with Mouton.[49] It is somewhat amazing that the *Maîtrise*-trained

[46] Sebastiani, *Bellum*, fol. R4[vo].
[47] Pirro, *Enseignement*, p. 49.
[48] Miller, *Dodecachordon*, pp. 158–161, and Glarean, *Dodecachordon*, I: pp. 7–17. A full study of this theorist is given by Miller in his edition of the *Dodecachordon* and his article about it.
[49] Brenet, *Méthode*, p. 3, and Clinksdale, *Josquin*, p. 67.

Mouton did not speak Latin, since choirboys, in principle, learned that language. In practice, however, some students of the Renaissance may have been as poorly gifted in languages as many are today; perhaps, too, the rule that Latin must be spoken to the exclusion of French in the boys' house was not strictly enforced.

The composer Claude Martin wrote an *Elementorum musices practicae* (Paris: Du Chemin, 1550), which he dedicated to the humanist Jean de Brinon; it contains two motets for four voices on the same text.[50] Guillaume Postell, professor of mathematics and Oriental languages in Paris, was the author of a treatise in which he combines music and mathematics— *Tabulae in astronomiam in arithmeticam theoricam et in musicam theoricam* (Paris, 1552).[51]

Among the Latin works on music, we should mention translations of classical treatises by French university men, such as a Latin version of Psellus, *Ex mathematico Pselli . . . breviario, arithmetica, musica, geometria . . .* (Bordeaux, 1553?) by Elie Vinet, principal of the Collège de Guyenne, who had had Montaigne as a student,[52] and two translations of Euclid's writings on music by professors at the Collège de France, Jean Pena (1557) and Pierre Forcadel (1565).[53]

An anonymous Hebrew manuscript from the mid-fifteenth century, of probable Provençal origin, is a translation of class notes taken by a student at a music school in Paris, which may have been the private school of Jean Vaillant. It contains passages on intervals, proportions, etc. Three Hebrew texts on music are found in Paris: Bibl. nat., *MS. Heb. 1037*. One, by Jehuda ben Isaac, who probably lived in one of the Jewish colonies of Southern France in the fifteenth century, is not merely a translation, but an adaptation of Latin mediaeval sources, mostly on plainchant, with a small passage on mensural notation. In a burst of religious fervor, the author points out that Christians are wrong in believing that they have a monopoly on the science of music, 'for indeed their chant has been stolen from our ancestors, the Levites of the Temple.

[50] Lesure, *Du Chemin*, p. 293.
[51] Carpenter, *Universities*, p. 151.
[52] Bibliothèque nationale, *Musique*, p. 38.
[53] Pirro, *Enseignement*, p. 49.

It is simple justice to bring back musical science to its Jewish fold.' The manuscript seems to have been compiled in the middle of the sixteenth century and to have served as a manual for the training of Jewish musicians in the north of Italy.[54]

It was during the sixteenth century and shortly before, that concurrently with Latin treatises, theory books and practical music manuals began to be written in French, which most Frenchmen surely understood better. Becker has suggested that a book which a canon of Cambrai left by will to the library of the cathedral in 1433, *Le livre de l'art de musique pour les enfants d'autel*, may have been a teaching book in French, judging from its title.[55] The book, however, has not been found, and we cannot be certain that its listing in the will represents its title or its description. If the latter was intended, it could have been a French paraphrase of a Latin work.

The book which is probably the first music treatise printed in French, the anonymous *L'Art, science et practique de plaine musique* (1502?) is not an abstract philosophical and mathematical work for academic milieus, but a sight-singing manual for self-education, as the continuation of the title indicates: 'by means of which everyone will be able to understand, practice and learn by himself, and achieve great knowledge and perfection in the said science of music.' The author had intended to eventually write a second section on counterpoint, and a third on 'choses faites' (*res facta*, which probably means mensural music, as it does in Guerson and Wollick).[56]

Guillaume Telin's *La Louenge de musique* (Paris: Galliot du Pré, 1533) is only one section of a more encyclopaedic work, *Bref sommaire des sept vertus, sept ars liberaut, sept ars de poesie, sept ars mechaniques, des philosophies . . .*, which includes discussions of the 'fifteen magic arts' and 'several good reasons to confound the Jews who deny the advent of Our Lord Jesus Christ'

[54] Adler, *Musique*, p. 649, *Traité*, pp. 1–47, and *Pratique*, p. 48. Jehuda's thesis about Jewish origins of Christian plainchant has been borne out by such works as Solange Corbin's *L'Eglise à la conquête de sa musique*, and especially Eric Werner's *The Sacred Bridge*.

[55] Becker, *Maîtrise*, p. 126.

[56] Brenet, *Methode*, pp. 1–7, and Ferand, *Guerson*, p. 254.

—an academically-oriented book, published by one of the *libraires-jurés*, or university associated printers. Emery Bernhard's *Brieve et facile méthode pour apprendre à chanter en musique* (Paris: Jean Petit, 1541) is no longer extant. The use of the vernacular was evidently permeating all sorts of circles—even scholarly ones. A lost treatise, *Brieve introduction en la musique tant au plain chant que choses faites* (Paris: Attaingnant, 1545), was written by the composer and royal chapel singer Jean Le Gendre, who was praised by the poet François Gentillet (*Discours de la court*, 1558) for his motets and for his scholarly mind.[57]

Another practical didactic work is *Le droict chemin de musique* (Geneva, 1550) by the Parisian Loys Bourgeois, who contributed to the Huguenot Psalter, and was closely associated with Calvin's Genevan liturgy. His treatise is often cited by those who wish to perform sixteenth-century music with *notes inégales*, because it not only condones the practice in the case of equally notated semi-minims and *fusae*, but suggests it as more esthetically pleasing than assigning the same rhythmic value to each note.[58]

Maximilian Guilliaud, a graduate of the Collège de Navarre, theologian, composer, and singer, had his *Rudiments de musique practique, reduits en deux briefs traictez, le premier contenant les preceptes de la plaine, l'autre de la figurée*, published in Paris by Du Chemin in 1554, but its dedicatory epistle to Claudin de Sermisy is dated 15 September 1552.[59] In it he compares the musical director of the king's chapel not merely to Alexander the Great, but to Apollo. Whereas this sort of statement is hardly unexpected in a Renaissance dedication, another, to the effect that Claudin replanted music in France, is somewhat more difficult to explain. It may, of course, be simply one more laudatory expression, but on the other hand, it could also mean that French music of the immediate past was considered non-existent, or was not appreciated, at least

[57] Heartz, *Attaingnant*, p. 337.

[58] Geoffroy-Dechaume, *Secrets*, pp. 13–14, and G. Thibault, in Roland-Manuel, *Histoire*, I: pp. 1314–1315. Whether this reflects the theorist's personal taste, a limited practice, or a general practice cannot be decided here.

[59] Lesure, *Du Chemin*, pp. 281, 309–310.

by the author—at a time when almost everyone turned to the remote past for inspiration.

Claude Martin made an eight-folio condensation of the first part of his Latin treatise mentioned earlier, which he entitled *Institution musicale, non moins breve que facile, suffisante pour apprendre a chanter ce qui ha cours au iour-d'huy entre les musiciens* (Paris: Du Chemin, 1556). This French treatise was not written for a humanist, but for the benefit of two 'naively beautiful,' rich, and virtuous young ladies (according to the dedication), Mesdemoiselles Charlotte and Claude de Villemar, daughters of the bailiff of Touraine, who probably needed to learn sight-singing, but not the intricacies of mensural notation.[60]

Michel de Menehou, composer and choirmaster at Saint-Maur-des Fossés, dedicated another book of rudiments, his *Nouvelle instruction familiere, en laquelle sont contenus les difficultés de la musique* (Paris: Du Chemin, 1558; reprinted by H. Expert, 1900) to his patron, Cardinal Jean du Bellay. He includes a chanson for four voices of his own composition, *Le souvenir de ma dame joliette*. A similar work by the same author, *Nouvelle instruction contenant en brief les preceptes ou fondemens de musique tant pleine que figurée* (Du Chemin, 1571), which is lost, may have been a modified re-edition of his earlier method. Pierre Julien's *Le vrai chemin pour apprendre a chanter toute sorte de musique* (Lyon, 1570) is no longer extant. Another lost work on music, whose anonymous author may have been influenced by Ficino's neo-Platonic theories, is *La Main harmonique, ou, les Principes de musique antique et moderne: et les propriétés que la moderne reçoit des sept planettes*, printed by Du Chemin on one large folio in 1571.[61] It is most regrettable that we are deprived of this essay, which may have contained a concrete example of French astrological music.

Among the extant rudiment books may be mentioned an *Instruction de musique* by Corneille de Montfort, called de Blockland (Lyon: J. de Tournes, 1581) and a *Traité de la musique pratique* by Jean Yssandon (Paris: Le Roy et Ballard, 1582), the title-page of which unashamedly states that all the material has been extracted from several Latin authors. The compiler and translator, a native of the county of Foix, dedicates this manual to the music-loving Cardinal d'Armagnac 'from your

[60] *Ibid.*, pp. 282, 315.   [61] *Ibid.*, pp. 325, 345, 346.

palace at Avignon.' Not to be outdone, Adrian Le Roy wrote a rudiments book of his own, *Traicté de musique contenant une theorie succinte pour methodiquement pratiquer la composition* (1583).[62] Martin Basanier's *Plusieurs beaux secrets touchant la théorie et pratique de musique* (Paris, 1584) is lost.

The Protestant composer Philibert Jambe de Fer, whose picturesque name is a genuine surname and not a sobriquet, is the author of an *Epitome musical* (Lyon: M. du Bois, 1556, and re-edited by François Lesure [*Epitome*]), which is a combination of a music rudiments book and a treatise and instruction book for transverse flutes, recorders, violas da gamba, and violins. It is one of our best sources for the history of these instruments in France. An anonymous work on the fretting of instruments, a chapter of a *Discours non plus melancolique* (Poitiers: Marnef, 1556; re-edited by Weckerlin in 1890) has been variously attributed to Bonaventure des Périers, Elie Vinet, and Pelletier du Mans. It gives much information on the vogue of certain instruments in France.[63]

Several books on how to play a single instrument were published in the sixteenth century. The instructions sometimes consisted of introductory pages to a volume of pieces. Most of the extant methods are for lute. The first is Attaingnant's *Tres breve et familiere introduction pour apprendre par soy mesmes a jouer toutes chansons reduictes en la tabulature du Lutz . . .* (1529); the chansons are partly for voice and lute, and partly for lute alone. Albert de Rippe's *Quart livre de tabulature de luth* (Paris: Le Roy et Ballard, 1553) contains some diagrams for lute tuning, but not much more, by way of instruction. A lute method by Adrian Le Roy, first published in 1557 (or 1567) by his firm, under the title *Instruction de partir toute musique des huit divers tons en tablature de luth* is lost, as are several re-editions, from 1567, 1570, and 1583. The 1567 edition has the variant title: *Instruction d'asseoir toute musique facilement en tablature de luth.* Le Roy's instruction book, though not available in French, is known by two English translations, *A Briefe and easye instruction to learne the tablature . . .* Englished by J. Alford

---

[62] Bibliothèque nationale, *Musique*, p. 39, and Lesure, *Le Roy*, pp. 20, 43, 208, 213. *See* Davidsson, *Drucke*, and Seay, *Yssandon*, for lists of theoretical works.

[63] Lesure, *Guitare*, p. 187, and Heartz, *Parisian*, pp. 459–460.

Londenor (London: Printed by J. Kyngston for J. Roubothum, 1568) and a more complete one, *A briefe and plaine Instruction to set all musicke of eight divers tunes in tableture* . . . translated by I. Ki. Gentelman (London: Rowbothome, 1574). Giovanni Paladino's *Premier livre de tablature de luth*, published under the Gallicized form of his name, Jean Paul Paladin (Lyon: Gorlier, 1560) contains a 'brieve instruction de la tablature . . . de nouveau adjoutée.'

Le Roy's guitar method, *Briefve et facile instruction* (1551) and a later edition (1578) are lost, as well as his cittern method. It may have been translated into English (*The breffe and playne instruction to lerne to play on the gyttron and also the cetterne* (London: Rowbotham, 1568), but we will probably never know, because the English work is not extant either. It has been suggested that the instructions published by Phalese in his *Selectissima elegantissimaque gallica, Italica et latina in guiterna ludenda carmina* (Louvain, 1570) could have been a Latin translation of Le Roy's method.[64] Le Roy's *Premier livre de tabulature de guiterre* (1551) contains a diagram for tuning the guitar, which is instructive, but hardly a full-fledged method. An instruction book for mandora by Le Roy (1585) mentioned in Trichet's seventeenth-century treatise on instruments has not been found. We are more fortunate with his cittern method (*Breve et facile instruction pour* . . . *le cistre*, 1565), which has survived—as well as the instructions included in his *Second livre de cistre, contenant les commandmens de Dieu* . . . (1564).

A lost volume by Claude Gervaise, his *Premier livre de violle* (Paris: Veuve Attaingnant, 1556) contained instructions on tuning and playing the viola da gamba. Three other lost works are also presumed to have contained instructions for the harpsichord and the transverse flute: Guillaume de Brayssingar's *Tablature d'epinette* (Lyon: Moderne, 1536), Simon Gorlier's *Premier livre de tabulature d'espinette* (Lyon: Gorlier, 1560) and his *Livre de tabulature de flutes d'Allemand* (1558).[65]

---

[64] Heartz, *Parisian*, p. 457. That method is extant and has been translated into English by Heartz (*Galpin Society Journal*, XVI (1963).

[65] *See* Brown, *Instrumental,* and Lesure, *Le Roy*, for details on instrumental methods.

6

Music and other aspects of culture: book production, contests, theater

An important aspect of culture in France was the production of manuscript and printed music collections. French music books of the fifteenth and sixteenth centuries have been notated in a variety of ways. Vocal notation for liturgical books was of course in plainchant, which did not undergo much development at this time, but mensural notation for polyphony went through many changes—from black to white, from the complex proportional type of the late *Ars nova*, which Apel calls mannered notation, to the simpler type which is still in use today, and from writing in parts to writing in score. Non-vocal notations appear chiefly in printed tablatures for lute, guitar, and cittern. Exceptional notations found in manuscripts include a purely rhythmic one in the form of filled and unfilled squares, in Hardouin de Fontaines-Guérin's hunting manual, *Le tresor de la venerie* (1394), and a violin tablature from the south of France, written at the beginning of the seventeenth century (Paris: Bibl. nat., *Rés. Vmb. MS.* 5), in a system of numbers from 0 to 3 on four lines representing the strings of the instrument. The system resembles the Italian tablatures more than the French, because the latter generally uses letters instead of numbers.[1]

As is well known, accidentals that were meant to be performed were not always written in vocal notation. (Tablatures were more precise in the sense that they had symbols for every half step.) Mensural music books showed accidentals in the signature—and some pieces had partial signatures, such as one flat on one staff and none on the other; they occasionally had a flat or a sharp inserted within the text, presumably to call the attention of the singer to a change that was not perfectly obvious to them according to the rules of *musica ficta*—or for some other reason. In French music, a

[1] Lesure, *Orchestres*, pp. 53–54.

sharp sign usually cancelled a flat and made it into a natural. The natural sign seems to have been used for the first time for that purpose—as it is today—in a print by Le Roy et Ballard. It was used in Costeley's chromatic chanson *Seigneur Dieu*, and the composer himself seemed proud of this graphic innovation, for he states in the preface to this piece: 'Until now most musicians and singers have interchanged sharps for naturals and naturals for sharps. These will be found, however, marked in the above-mentioned chanson.'[2]

It may have been also Le Roy et Ballard who put bar-lines for the first time in French vocal mensural notation, in Planson's *Airs* (1587). They do not indicate regular measures, but simply the end of the line of poetry, and they show that the piece consists of irregular meters.[3]

Although it is not possible to say that text underlay becomes progressively better—certain contemporary manuscripts and prints are clearer than others in this respect—it has been noted that 'one of the most striking features of musical manuscripts written after 1400 is the gradual increase in compositions which have a text or partial text in their lower voices.' This happens chiefly in manuscripts with Latin texts.[4] Polytextual music, of course, required words in every voice. Although this genre was not as prevalent as in the Middle Ages—the polytextual and polyglot motet was giving way to the monotextual Latin motet—there were examples in the fifteenth and sixteenth centuries of bitextual motets, motet-chansons, double chansons, and *fricassées* (a term introduced in music by Attaingnant). Fifteenth-century *rondeaux*, on the other hand, usually did not have all of their words in more than one voice, and then it was only the refrain that appeared under the notes of the upper voice. The rest of the text, with the incipit of the refrain, appeared at the end of the music of the *cantus* or *superius*—either alongside of it if the three voices appeared successively on the same page, as in the *MS. Canonici 213* of the Bodleian Library at Oxford, or underneath it, if the upper voice was placed alone on the *verso* of one folio, and the other voices on the *recto* of the following folio, as in the *Laborde*

[2] Levy, *Costeley*, p. 227.
[3] Levy, *Vaudeville*, p. 192.
[4] Reaney, *Underlay*, p. 245.

Chansonnier (Washington: Library of Congress, *MS. M. 2.1 L. 25 Case*) and most other *chansonniers* of the period. (This, of course, does not apply to exceptional monophonic *chansonniers*, such as Paris: Bibl. nat., *MSS. fr. 9346 (Bayeux)* and *12744*.) The remaining voices had no words, or showed simply the incipit of the refrain.[5]

In French prints of the sixteenth century, music was issued in separate part-books, or in two volumes for four voices (superius and tenor on opposite pages of one volume, and contratenor and bassus on opposite pages of the other), or in one volume (superius and tenor not in score, but following each other on one page, and contratenor and bassus on the other). A particularly ingenious arrangement by Jacques Moderne has the music of two voices on the lower half of two opposite pages, and that of two other voices on the upper half, but facing in the opposite direction, so that one volume could be read by performers sitting across the table from each other.[6] Since the voices facing in one direction were superius-bassus, and in the other tenor-altus, the page arrangement made it necessary for a lady and a gentleman to sit next to each other, rather than two persons of the same sex. Perhaps Moderne was a matchmaker at heart. . . .

In these prints, the words were given in each voice, for one stanza. Additional strophes, if they existed, did not appear with the music in the earlier part of the century. We must look for them in purely literary collections. Brown has suggested that some of these anthologies served as word books of popular poetry to be sung to well-known tunes, and were intended for people too poor to buy music books.[7] Printers are not always more helpful than scribes in the way in which they underlay the text. In manuscripts and prints, the words are sometimes distributed haphazardly, wherever there is space, and so the modern editor often has difficulties in determining under which note a given syllable should be placed. Whether Renaissance singers had the same trouble we

[5] Borren, *Etudes*, p. 253.

[6] Pogue (*Moderne*, pp. 46–47) points out that this format was intended for amateur performers. More difficult music, such as *Le difficile des chansons*, Moderne printed in four part-books.

[7] Brown, *Theater*, p. 113.

do not know. Perhaps they all knew the rules of text underlay as well as they were supposed to know the principles of *musica ficta*—assuming that uniform rules existed everywhere. Perhaps they had a certain amount of choice about how they sang. Manuscripts sometimes have a final syllable placed under the penultimate note, although it might seem to us to belong with the final note. As Reaney explains,

> this surely does not mean, as we in the mid-twentieth century are too prone to believe, that there was a pre-scribed way of making the alignment. It is much more likely that the performers lined up final notes and syllables in whatever way suited them best, though it seems clear that where the syllables fall on main beats, they were intended to do so.[8]

Sixteenth-century prints are on the whole clearer than fifteenth-century manuscripts, not so much because printers were more careful of text placement than were scribes—though Du Chemin has been particularly commendable in that respect[9]—but because there is more syllabic music in the sixteenth century than there was in the fifteenth. It is, of course, easier to fit one syllable to one note than to several notes, and it is often the melismas which cause the difficulties in text underlay.[10]

Poets were rarely named in fifteenth-century music manu-scripts and in early prints. An exception was 'Bourbon,' who has been identified as Duke John II of Bourbon (d. 1488) and is mentioned in Paris: Bibl. nat. *MS. fr. 2245* as the author of *Allez regret*, with music by Hayne de Ghizeghem, and *Vous me faictes mourir d'envie*, with music by Compère.[11] Among the first music prints to give credit to poets were collections of psalms in French, with music by Mornable, Janequin, and others, published by Attaingnant and Du Chemin, which

[8] Reaney, *Underlay*, pp. 249–250.
[9] Alexander, *Moduli*, p. 119.
[10] I have encountered sixteenth-century prints with more syllables than notes.
[11] Droz, *Poètes*, p. 9.

mention Clément Marot as the translator.[12] Ronsard was mentioned in the musical supplement to his *Amours* (1552) and in complete volumes devoted to musical settings of his works, such as Pierre Clereau's *Premier livre d'odes de Ronsard* (Paris: Le Roy et Ballard, 1566) and Nicolas de la Grotte's setting of his chansons as well as of texts by Desportes (Le Roy et Ballard, 1569).

Early music books were usually collections by several composers, not all of whom were identified; fifteenth-century manuscripts sometimes brought together music in several genres, religious and secular. Although most prints are collective works, one finds more and more books devoted to a single composer in the course of the sixteenth century. Attaingnant seems to have started this practice in France by printing volumes entirely by Janequin or by some other composer. In an exceptional volume devoted to two composers, also by Attaingnant (*Tiers livre*, 1536[6]) Janequin shared honors with his lively contemporary Passereau. Other French printers including Du Chemin (who not only printed anthologies by single composers, but individual Masses in large folios) and Le Roy et Ballard promoted the practice of printing works by single composers, while continuing to produce collective prints. On the whole, printed works kept sacred and secular music separate. Certon's *Melanges* (Du Chemin, 1570) include cheerful chansons and spiritual songs in French, but no Latin liturgical works. Attaingnant's lost volume, *Chansons et motets en canon* (1528) is another exception. Le Roy et Ballard's *Musique* of Guillaume Costeley includes motets as well as chansons.[13]

France had been an important contributor of fifteenth-century prints containing music—chiefly plainchant notation—with separately reproduced notes (usually black) and staves (red). Some books contain vertical bars to separate musical and textual phrases; unlike modern bar-lines they do not imply metrically equal divisions. French printing equalled the German output and was second only to the Italian production. Kathi Meyer-Baer finds that nineteen books with music had been printed in Paris during the incunable period;

[12] It was Attaingnant who published the first musical setting of Marot's psalms, in 1546, by Mornable or Certon, and not Beringen at Lyon, in Bourgeois's setting (1547).   [13] Godt, *Costeley*, p. 123.

only Venice surpassed it, with thirty-six. Among the leading printers during the latter part of the fifteenth century were Higman, who produced most of the books containing music, Jean Dupré, who printed the earliest known French book with musical notes (a Missal), Gering, from Constance, who had printed for the Sorbonne, and Marnial, who may have been English, and also printed for Caxton.

The other French centers of musical incunabula were Lyon, with a strong Italian influence, and Rouen, which had belonged to England until 1449. The naturalized Englishman Pynson, who printed the Sarum Missal (London, 1500), the only known English incunable with all staves and notes completely printed, was a native of Rouen. Since several liturgical books for English use were printed at Rouen, Mrs. Meyer-Baer suggests that the music of this missal may have been added by some printer in that city. Two books for local use were printed at Vienne in Dauphiné.[14]

The main centers of mensural music printing were Paris and Lyon, with an occasional contribution to the history of printing from other cities, such as Avignon. The earliest French examples of mensural music in print occur in two publications of Michel de Toulouze, which were mentioned earlier. He also printed a *Processionarium* with music, whose present whereabouts are not known. His dance manual is quite similar to the beautiful Brussels manuscript of basses-danses, Bibl. royale, *MS. 9085*, which contains undifferentiated breves that in themselves indicate pitch but not rhythm—and which may have belonged to Margaret of Austria. The printer's mensural types appear in addition to the square black basse-danse notation, and were executed from movable type on separately printed staves. His publication of Guerson's music rules also contains musical illustrations by plainchant notes and by mensural notes of the type that was first used in Franciscus Niger's *Grammatica* (Venice, 1480) to illustrate poetic meters. The re-edition of Guerson by Regnault and Marnef in 1514 also contained musical examples. In addition to being the first specimens of mensural music in France, Michel de Toulouze's prints represent the last known use of

[14] Meyer-Baer, *Incunabula*, pp. xxv, xxxiii, xxxv.

mensural types before the end of the incunable period.[15]

A lost collection entitled *Se ensuyvent les Nouelz nouvaulx* (Le Mans, 1512) contained four two-voiced pieces, which Heartz believes were woodcuts. He also suggests that another woodcut print appeared at Lyon in 1530 or earlier, and that it could have been cut by Andrea Antico. A woodcut collection, Cavazzoni's *Recerchari, Motetti Canzoni* (Venice: Vercelli, 1523) has a papal privilege that forbids the subjects of the French king to print the music under pain of confiscation, censure, and excommunication. To Heartz this implies that the French may have been interested in printing woodcut music.

The *Contrapunctus seu figurata musica*, published by Estienne Guaynard in Lyon, 1528, which contains music of the Mass Propers, partly by François de Layolle (The Italian Francesco dell'Aiolla, who taught music to Benvenuto Cellini, and eventually became the corrector of the printer Jacques Moderne), has both plainchant and mensural notation. It is the first publication of religious polyphonic music in France produced by multiple impression from type—one for the staves and another for the notes. It was in the same year that Attaingnant, who was to become the first royal printer for music, began to print from a single impression, with a short vertical fragment of the staff attached to the note on the same piece of type. Both staff and notes were printed in black, in contrast to the two colors of earlier double-process prints—which Attaingnant kept for his two books containing plainchant—a Missal (1541) and a Ritual (1546) for Noyon. Whether he or the type-cutter Pierre Haultin deserves the credit for introducing the new music characters in France has been debated, but it was from his presses that they first came out.[16]

Attaingnant published more than one hundred and fifty volumes of sacred and secular music. His son-in-law Hubert Jullet joined him in his enterprise, and his widow continued to print music books after his death. The pieces in collections were mostly in Latin and French, and occasionally in Italian, such as Sermisy's *Altro non e'l mio amor,* and in French regional

---

[15] Reese, *Renaissance*, p. 37, King, *Printing*, pp. 13–14, Heartz, *Attaingnant*, pp. 44–45, and Meyer-Baer, *Incunabula*, p. xxxiv.

[16] Lesure, *Religieusse*, p. 64, Heartz, *Attaingnant*, pp. 145–146, and Chapman, *Antico*, pp. 102–103.

dialect, such as the same composer's *Hari, bouriquet*. Attaingnant's volumes of instrumental music for flutes, lute, and keyboard were the first prints of their kind in France. Since he was closely associated with the French court and the neighboring Sainte-Chapelle, and did not have much serious competition in the publishing world, one might say that he was largely responsible for the wide dissemination of French music of his time, at home and abroad. Well over one thousand pieces which he printed are chansons. He did not compose any, as far as we know, but had it not been for his efforts in their propagation, there may not have been the same incentive for so many composers to write such quantities of chansons in the same locality and at the same time. If one wished to follow the practice of some popularizers of music history who bestow symbolic paternity upon someone or other for practically every musical genre—we hear of the father of the symphony, or of the string quartet—one might call Attaingnant the father of the Parisian chanson of the second quarter of the sixteenth century.

The next important Parisian music publisher was Nicolas Du Chemin, who printed more than one hundred music books between 1549 and 1576. He employed music consultants, the most famous of whom was Claude Goudimel. The others were Nicole Regnes, Loys Bisson, and Henry Chandor. In addition to Parisians, composers represented included provincials, such as Cadéac and Clereau, and foreigners, such as the Spaniard Guerrero. The expression *Missa ad imitationem moduli* (or *cantionis*, or *moteta*) followed by the name of the borrowed material to designate a Mass was first used by Du Chemin in 1552 as the title of a work by Goudimel: *Missa ad imitationem cantionis Il ne se treuve en amitié*. Earlier printers, such as Attaingnant and Moderne in France, and Petrucci and Antico in Italy, had used simply the term *Missa*, followed by the name of the model, such as *Missa Ung jour Robin*, or *Missa super*, or *sur*, such as *Missa sur fantasie*. Du Chemin's practice was continued by Le Roy et Ballard. The term 'parody' for what is called today a parody Mass was not used in French prints. There is an isolated instance of its use in Germany in 1587: *Missa: parodia mottettae Domine da nobis auxilium, Thomas Crequilonis,* and Lockwood believes that it is simply a Greek translation of Du

Chemin's expression 'ad imitationem' following the humanistic practice of substituting a classical Greek word for a Latin one.[17]

Adrian Le Roy and his cousin Robert Ballard became royal printers after Attaingnant's death. They began to print in 1551 and continued to the end of the century, after which the descendants of Ballard kept up the business of the firm until the end of the eighteenth century. It is assumed that Robert Ballard took care of the commercial aspects of the partnership, while Le Roy, a lutenist and composer, friend of musicians and poets and musical adviser to Charles IX, was artistic director. It was Le Roy who presented Lassus to the French court and published many of his works. Other important prints from the presses of Le Roy et Ballard include *airs de cour*, collections on texts by Ronsard, and the *Balet comique de la royne*, which contains the first extant music printed for violin. In Le Roy et Ballard's publications we can observe the transition from four-voiced chansons, which had been the norm in Attaingnant's time, to pieces from five to eight voices.[18] This transition to a thicker, more Flemish-sounding texture may not have been brought about entirely for musical reasons. Le Roy states in the dedication of Arcadelt's *Missae tres* (1557) that the powerful Charles de Lorraine, duke of Guise, had requested that he print the Masses of his household composer. We have no doubt that the publisher was honored to oblige. At the same time, one did not refuse a Guise's request, regardless of one's personal taste. The public seemed satisfied with whatever came out from the royal presses, which did not have too much competition. And so they accepted music by Flemings along with the French fare.

Michel Fezandat, a minor mid sixteenth-century Parisian music printer, who issued two books of chansons and two of spiritual songs in French, is significant chiefly for his instrumental music books—tablatures for lute and guitar by Gorlier, Morlaye, and the latter's teacher Albert de Rippe (published posthumously). Fezandat had been briefly in partnership with Robert Granjon, whose most significant contributions to music printing, however, were made in Lyon.

[17] Lockwood, *Parody*, pp. 562–565.
[18] Lesure, *Du Chemin,* and *Le Roy,* and Boyden, *Violin,* p. 3.

The Lyon circle was dominated by Attaingnant's most important competitor outside of Paris, the Istrian Jacques Moderne, who printed some fifty music books from 1532 to 1557. Included in his prints are works by many foreigners—Germans, Spaniards, and particularly Italians. Layolle, Janequin, and Villiers had songs with Italian texts published at Moderne's presses. The latter composer also wrote a chanson in Lyonnais dialect. Many of the composers represented in Moderne's prints belonged to the papal chapel.[19] Others who printed music in Lyon included the Beringen brothers, who received a privilege to print psalms, chansons, and motets in 1547 from Henry II, the composer Simon Gorlier, whose collections, which he began to publish in 1558, are chiefly instrumental, and Robert Granjon, who printed four collections in 1559, including two *Trophées*, in special types which he had invented, and to which we shall return shortly.

The white mensural notation produced at the above-mentioned presses was of the usual type—*breves* and *longas* square-shaped, and lesser note-values diamond-shaped. This was the dominant pattern, although there were brief experiments in rounded notes, somewhat similar to those in use today. They were abandoned, however, and printers went on producing diamond-shaped notes all during the sixteenth century and later.

The first French printer to use slightly rounded notes was Jean de Channey, in the four books of sacred works by Elzéar Genet, called Carpentras, between 1532 and 1537 at Avignon.[20] The music was produced by double impression from types cut by Etienne Briard. They may have been modelled after rounded notes used in manuscripts, which can be written faster than lozenges.[21]

Several years later, Robert Granjon, who had printed non-music books in a cursive rounded type of his invention, *lettres d'art de main*, or *lettres françaises*, later called *caractères de civilité*,

---

[19] *See* Pogue, *Moderne*.

[20] It has recently been discovered that Carpentras's illness during his stay at the papal court in Rome was attributable to overwork (Miller, *Cardan*, pp. 417–419).

[21] Heartz, *Attaingnant*, pp. 110–117.

applied the same idea to music in 1558–59, in his four books with rounded notes. They were reminiscent of Channey's prints, but much smaller. And the letters of the words under the music were in *civilité*, whereas Channey's were gothic. Granjon's music was printed from movable type in a single impression.[22]

Granjon's types were imitated by Richard Breton in Paris, for his only musical publication, *Quelques odes d'Anacreon,* by Richard Renvoysy (1559). The notes are lighter and more elegant than Granjon's and the space between the notes is greater. The composer, a gifted lutenist, who was also choirmaster and canon at the Sainte-Chapelle of Dijon, and was burned for sodomy in 1586, added an entertaining and flippant preface to his odes.[23] A re-edition of this music (in normal diamond-shaped notation) by Le Roy et Ballard in 1573, omits the preface. Royal printers must have found it beneath their dignity to print frivolities as introductions, although they did not object to trivial texts under the music.

Breton's music types may have been borrowed by Claude Micard, publisher of Jehan Chardavoine's *Recueil des plus belles et excellentes chansons en forme de voix de ville* (Paris, 1576), the only print of monophonic chansons which comes to us from the sixteenth century. The literary text is in Roman type; only the music is in *civilité*—although Micard published two other works with *lettres en civilité,* but without music. Chardavoine may have composed some of the tunes, but he otherwise compiled or adapted the music of the 'chant commun' or popular melodies whether by well-known composers or by unknown ones, which had passed into the 'timbre' repertoire.[24]

We do not know how many copies of music books were issued at one time, except in a few instances which Lesure has discovered: 500 copies of Genet's works in Channey's prints (1532–35), the same number of Beaulaigue's *Chansons nouvelles* (Granjon, 1558–59), and 1,200 copies of Albert de Rippe's tablatures (1552–58, edited by Morlaye at the press of Fezandat).[25] The statistics are too few to permit us to draw

---

[22] Dalbanne, *Granjon,* pp. 226–232.

[23] Thibault, *Breton,* pp. 302–308.

[24] Frissard, *Chardavoine,* pp. 58–75, and Verchaly, *Chardavoine,* pp. 205–212.   [25] Lesure, *Sociologie,* pp. 341–342.

conclusions, but it seems that prints of instrumental music were expected to be in demand.

In order to encourage the creation of first-rate poetry and music and to maintain high standards of composition, competitions were organized in various cities, and prizes were awarded in several categories. The *jeux floraux*, founded in Toulouse in 1323, were contests for poets and musicians who wrote in Provençal and Catalan. From 1356, the *joya principal*, or *violette d'or*, was the prize for the best chanson, *vers*, or *descort*, the *souci d'argent* for the best *dansa*, and the *eglantine* for the best *sirventes* or *pastourelle*.[26]

Religious associations founded *puys*, or annual contests of a literary nature, sometimes accompanied by plays and music, in many French towns, including Beauvais, Amiens, Caen, Dieppe, and Béthune. Some of these *puys* were in existence as early as the twelfth or thirteenth centuries. By the time of the Renaissance, they were more concerned with lyric poetry than with theater, but some plays with music were still performed occasionally in connection with these festivals.

The *Puy de l'Immaculée Conception de la tres saincte Vierge*, or *Puy des palinods*, was instituted in Rouen in 1486, and gave prizes for various types of poetry. A palm and a lily were awarded for the two winning *chants royaux*; a laurel and a gold star went to the authors of the best Latin epigrams; a rose was for the best *ballade*, and a gold seal for the best *rondeau*.[27] It is in a manuscript of *chants royaux* on the Immaculate Conception, which were crowned at Rouen (1519–1528, Paris: Bibl. nat., *MS. fr. 1527*) that the well-known posthumous miniature of Ockeghem wearing eyeglasses is found.[28]

The contests were called 'puys' because the poems were read on a platform or podium (from which the word *puy* is derived–cf. *Dictionnaire Robert*). The poems—*chants royaux* and *ballades*—ended with a verse which was repeated as a sort of refrain, and was called 'palinod.' In the Rouen poems, the Blessed Virgin was often compared to symbols derived from the Scriptures, or to recent events. In 1523, the palm-winning *chant royal* of Nicolle Le Vestu, preceded by a poetic

[26] Apel, *Fourteenth*, p. 15.
[27] Brown, *Theater*, p. 35.
[28] Bibliothèque nationale, *Musique*, p. 52.

'argument,' attempted to compare the Immaculate Conception to a musical conception—Ockeghem's thirty-six voice motet.[29]

One of the best-known *puys* was that established in 1575 by the Confraternity of Saint Cecilia, at Evreux. The society had been founded in 1570, with Guillaume Costeley as its leader, to honor 'Madame Sainte Cécille,' the patron saint of music, on her feast day, its eve, and the following day (21–23 November), by means of musical services at the cathedral. The Vespers for the eve were to include a Magnificat sung in *fauxbourdon*, with organ. During the festivities, the people were to be called to church by the sounding of three carillons. On the third day, a High Requiem Mass was celebrated for the repose of the souls of all the faithful deceased, and particularly the founders of the society. One of the founders was elected 'prince,' or leader, for the year, and another treasurer for a term of three years. The first 'prince' was Costeley. It was his duty to have the church and 'the image of Madame Sainte Cécille' decorated for the festivities and to provide candles for the singers, the organist, and his blowers, by means of common funds. After the High Mass, he was to provide a decent place for the annual meeting of the founders, and a table for dinner—which should take place 'without any scandal, insolence, or excess.' He was not expected to supply food for the meal unless he wished to, because each founder was to provide his own food—probably so as not to place too much of a financial burden on a poor 'prince.' The confraternity seemed to accept people from many walks of life; it included at some time or other lawyers, priests, and titled noblemen. One of them, Charles de Lorraine, duke of Aumale, joined the association in 1578, but sent his wife to the meeting in his place (presumably with her picnic basket delivered beforehand).

After the contest, or *puy de musique*, was established, the 'prince' in charge was to give two months' notice to the jeweler, so that he could make the prize medallions, and have about two hundred notices printed by Le Roy et Ballard, three months before the *puy*, so that musicians could be invited to

[29] Plamenac, *Autour*, pp. 30–39.

send their works in time. Once the judges had made their decision, members of the association and singers marched to Notre-Dame, to give thanks to God, 'singing with full voice' the two prize motets of the contest.

The deliberations were normally held at the house of the choirmaster, who was expected to furnish clean table linen and utensils. Once again the considerate founders had their own food brought in 'so as not to be a burden to the master of the children.' We have no record of whose duty it was to clear the table and wash the dishes; perhaps it was the middle-aged maid of the *maîtrise* who attended to that. Occasionally, a well-to-do 'prince' had the *puy* deliberations held at his own house instead of at the music master's. Such was the case in 1581, during the tenure of Jehan La Biche, lawyer, who invited everyone concerned to his castle and kept the guests there for a full seven days. He was assisted by the singers of the king's chapel and chamber, who came to Evreux for the celebration. He paid the expenses incurred by all those who came from Paris, including their servants and horses. In 1583, it was Cardinal de Guise who lent his singers for the *puy*; among them was Pierre Guedron, who was to become a leading composer of *airs de cour*. His voice was changing at the time, 'but nevertheless he sang *hautecontre* very well.'

Prizes were given for several categories of composition. The jewels were oval-shaped, with an image on one side and the name of the 'prince' on the other. Latin devices were engraved on the borders. The prize for the best motet was the image of an organ, and the second best, a harp. A lute and a lyre were awarded for the two winning five-voiced chansons 'on a text of the composer's choice, except that it must not be scandalous,' a cornet for an air in four parts, and a flute for a light and facetious four-voiced chanson. All the above-mentioned prizes were of silver. The most coveted prize, 'the triumph of Cecilia,' was made of gold and was given for the best Christian sonnet in French. Among the best-known laureates were Eustache du Caurroy (cornet, organ, and lute prizes), Jacques Mauduit (organ), Jehan Planson (harp), Pascal de l'Estocart (harp), Fabrice Caietain (cornet), and Orlande de Lassus (organ). Jehan de Maletty, from Provence, one of Ronsard's musicians, obtained the lute. Jean Planson, who set to music quatrains by Pibrac, obtained the harp and the triumph in the same year (1578).[30]

Another cultural manifestation of which music formed a part was the theater. We have seen how it was sometimes connected with *puys*. There were relationships between church musicians and the theater—even when the plays presented were not specifically religious. So-called liturgical dramas were of mediaeval origin. They were not limited to the inside of the church. The clerical participants occasionally continued their acting beyond the church and eventually were joined by professional companies of actors and sometimes by hundreds of townspeople at the market place. At the annual feast of fools, the minor clergy elected a sham bishop or pope, dressed up as women, played dice, sang lewd songs to the accompaniment of instruments, performed unedifying plays, and otherwise behaved badly in and out of church. Although frowned upon by the authorities, the feast continued well into the fifteenth and sixteenth centuries.

Religious drama included Biblical and hagiographic mystery and miracle plays, such as the Passions that were performed in several towns, and they often contained many a secular element. Emperor Nero, in one mystery play, sang *L'ami Baudichon*.[31] It is therefore difficult to establish a line of demarcation between sacred and secular. Allegorical moralities and comic farces, *soties*, *sermons joyeux*, and monologues are predominantly secular, though they are not always devoid of references to religion. *Sermons joyeux*, which parody church sermons, are an example of this. As Brown expresses it, 'if the boundary line between sacred and secular is exceedingly vague, that between theatrical and nontheatrical simply does not exist.'[32] It is true that acting, often to the accompaniment of some music or dancing, could take place during banquets, with *entremets* and *momeries*, or in the open air, as for the *entrée* of a king or other high-ranking dignitary, with pageants and *tableaux vivants*. Even street cries of peddlers have been considered to a certain extent theatrical.

[30] *See* Bonnin, *Puy*, and Godt, *Costeley*, pp. 85–87.
[31] Lebègue, in discussion of Lesure, *Eléments*, p. 180.
[32] Brown, *Theater*, p. 3.

Church musicians took an important part in performances of mysteries, moralities, and even farces. This is attested to by documents from *maîtrises*, which periodically admonish choirboys not to participate in non-ecclesiastical activities. The composers Jean Cornuel and Pierre Regnault, called Sandrin, acted in plays.[33] The latter may have acquired his sobriquet from the name of a character in the musical farce *Le Savetier qui ne respont que chansons*, in which the cobbler answers his wife by singing chanson incipits.

The music of most of the plays was not continuous, and it is not shown in the manuscripts or prints. The rubrics, however, often call for instruments to accompany certain situations, and some characters are required to sing particular songs, either with the original words or with new ones adapted to older tunes, or *timbres*, which are mentioned by name.[34] The music may have been sung monophonically or polyphonically. Some Protestant tragedies had choruses in the form of psalms.[35] Other incidental music for plays included dance tunes, fanfares, preludes, and interludes.

A mid fifteenth-century *Mystère du siège d'Orléans*, about Joan of Arc, requires trumpets and clarions for the entrance of lords and soldiers, and an organ for Joan's vision of Saint Michael.[36] On 21 January 1534, the streets of Paris were decorated for a procession and lined with scaffolds on which mystery plays were represented; the most conspicuous one was that of the Holy Host and the Jew. While that was being acted, the ecclesiastics and singers from the Sainte-Chapelle and royal chapel sang antiphons and responds of the Blessed Sacrament, in the street, and royal instrumentalists played.[37]

[33] Lesure, *Brown*, p. 235.

[34] Brian Jeffery (*Comedy*, p. 90) informs us that *La fidélité nuptiale*, a comedy by Gérard de Vivre, a Ghent schoolmaster (Antwerp, 1577), incorporates several French popular songs, including *Susanne un jour, Bon jour mon coeur, Mon coeur se recommande à vous*, and *Changeons propos*. We have no way of knowing whose musical versions were used—especially for *Susanne*, which was set by practically every French-speaking composer of the second half of the sixteenth century. The first name that comes to mind in connection with the initial three titles, however, is Lassus, and with the fourth, Sermisy.

[35] Lesure, *Musicians*, p. 102.

[36] Rokseth, *Orgue*, p. 53.   [37] Brenet, *Processions*, p. 8.

The languages sung were not always meant to be understood. In the *Mystère des trois doms*, which was put on at Romans in 1509 in thanksgiving for the end of the plague of 1507—the townspeople's means did not allow them to put it on earlier—pagans were made to sing in a fanciful language, as they had in an Incarnation mystery at Rouen in 1474. Jews also sang nonsense syllables.[38] A comic dialogue placed within the Incarnation play includes musical definitions, and its author refers to Jean de Muris in the margin, thereby showing that the theorist was still being studied in France in the latter half of the fifteenth century.[39]

Georges Chastellain was one of the well-known literary men who organized dramatic entertainments at the court of Burgundy. Other authors of literary value who wrote plays for the king and the municipal theater include André de la Vigne, Pierre Gringore, and Jean Bouchet. Etienne Jodelle wrote comedies in the Italian style; in the prologue to one of them he apologizes for the fact that the entr'acte music has little relationship to that of Antiquity.[40] Jean-Antoine de Baïf's *Le Brave* (1568) contained 'chantz recitez entre les actes de la comédie.'[41]

Most of the playwrights belonged to the middle class, socially. An exception is Marguerite of Navarre, who wrote comedies—moralities and farces. Some of the authors were also actors and belonged to professional acting societies, such as the *Basoche* and *Enfants-sans-souci*. Noblemen probably took some part in private indoor entertainments, but hardly in moralities, farces, and *soties*. The *Enfants-sans-souci* are

[38] Brown, *Theater*, pp. 20, 47. Passion plays, which were normally annual affairs, were sometimes postponed for lack of funds. Rouen, for example, in 1530, had not had one for forty years. On the other hand, after a Passion play was fianally produced, it could last for a long time. The one given at Issoudun in 1535 lasted a full month, attracted many tourists, and provided profit for the inhabitants (*ibid.*, p. 21).

[39] Pirro, *Enseignement*, p. 46.

[40] Lesure, *Musicians*, p. 103.

[41] Jeffery (*Comedy*, p. 110) remarks that 'in view of Baïf's known interest in music, "recitez" may well mean "sung." It is only surprising that Baïf, who even founded the Académie de Musique et de Poésie precisely in order to re-create the practice of the ancients in writing poetry and music, was not also interested (as far as we know) in uniting forms of drama.'

mentioned in one version of the chanson *Le cueur est bon*, and in *Nous sommes de l'ordre de Saint Babouin*. They are pictured as cheerful people who live without sorrow or melancholy. Many of the laymen's societies for entertainment, the *societés joyeuses*, were formed at the end of the fifteenth and in the early sixteenth centuries; the members gave plays, danced, wore masks about town, and at times tried to correct abuses. Dijon's society, for example, had its merry activities led by a 'mère folle' and sometimes punished men who beat their wives. (The practice of wife beating was forbidden during the month of May in various towns, but in Dijon, it was prohibited all year.)

Certain individual musical compositions were shown to be political in nature; the same holds true for some plays. In 1451, the town of Troyes organized a morality play in honor of Charles VII's conquest of Guyenne; and in 1530, Paris, Le Puy, and Vienne put on plays to celebrate the return of Francis I's children from their Spanish captivity—the same occasion which had prompted the composition of Janequin's *Chantons, sonnons trompettes*. Not all political plays were respectful of their subjects. In 1515 and 1516, actors were punished for taking part in farces and other theatrical pieces against the king's mistress and his mother.[42]

[42] Brown, *Theater*, pp. 9, 20–41. Brown's study of music in the French secular theater must be consulted for a full treatment of the subject to 1550, and Jeffery's *Comedy* for the later period.

7

Music and the outdoors: street, cemetery, field; hunting, military

Many outdoor manifestations were a bit theatrical in nature, although they did not always require acting. Processions were organized for various reasons, as we have seen earlier—to ask for favors, to atone for sins, or to thank God for a happy event, for example. Music was an important part of these processions. Often the town and royal musicians participated, particularly if a king had organized the event. This was true of penitential marches established by Henry III. We know that during Holy Week of 1583, the king's singers and others, arranged into three distinct groups, sang the litany 'melodiously in fauxbourdon.' When they arrived at Notre-Dame, they knelt and sang the *Salve Regina* 'with very harmonious music.' At other times during the same period, the penitents carried a large figure of Christ attached to an enormous wooden cross, while the musicians sang the *Miserere*. The singers of the Sainte-Chapelle often joined the royal chapel. Towards the end of the sixteenth century these processions often included the singing of psalms in fauxbourdon, as well as a four-voiced form of the litany of Loreto, imported to France from Italy and printed in Paris in 1578.[1]

Various municipalities paid for town instrumentalists who played for processions, *entrées*, and other events of a public character. The town of Aix-en-Provence had a group of four trumpets and four drums, in 1480.[2] These bands consisted of high instruments.

The arrival of kings or other notable personages into a town was the occasion for much music-making. When Isabeau of Bavaria came to Paris in 1389, children representing angels, and young ladies, sang, while men played the organ along the

[1] Brenet, *Processions*, pp. 8–10.
[2] Rokseth, *Instruments*, p. 208.

way. At Notre-Dame, she was received by the clergy, singing loudly and clearly, and at the palace, plays derived from the Scriptures were enacted to the accompaniment of instruments.[3] Her husband Charles VI was given a more spontaneous welcome when he arrived in his capital on 13 October 1414; at about eight o'clock at night the good people of Paris began to make bonfires and to sound their horns 'more than had ever been seen for the past one hundred years.'[4] The duke of Bedford made a solemn entry into Paris in 1424, preceded by his four trumpeters. The Parisians, dressed in vermilion, came to meet him and sang the *Te Deum* and other praises to God; pageants were performed, and then everyone shouted: 'Noël!'[5]

After Charles VII reconquered Paris from the English in 1437, the townspeople welcomed him with celebrations that lasted for six days. *Tableaux vivants* were shown in the well decorated streets, where musicians sang and played. Instead of water, improvised fountains gave forth red and white wine and hypocras.[6]

Louis XI's cortège upon his return to Paris after his coronation in Rouen included fifty-four trumpets. Not all of them were sounded, however. As a mark of respect, only the trumpeters from the royal household played their instruments.[7]

During a visit to Rouen by Charles VIII in April 1485, the king was honored with several pageants. In one of them, the twenty-four Old Men of the Apocalypse played instruments. At Troyes, in May 1486, he saw a pageant of the Holy Trinity, with organ music, and heard a young lady singing a *Te Deum* to organ accompaniment.[8] Outside of his own country, he was also honored with music in the street, when he made his entry into Florence, 17 November 1494. Musicians played pipes and large drums, while gentlemen on floats sang: 'Welcome to the liberator and restorer of liberty.'[9] Louis XII, on one of his

---

[3] Pirro, *Charles VI*, p. 11.
[4] Kling, *Cor*, pp. 101–102.
[5] Tuetey, *Bourgeois*, p. 200, and Bowles, *Processions*, pp. 151–152.
[6] Bowles, *Processions*, p. 153.
[7] Brenet, *Militaire*, p. 27.
[8] Bowles, *Processions*, p. 155.   [9] Bridgman, *Quattrocento*, p. 57.

Italian expeditions, was also received with much outdoor music, in Venice.[10] In his own city of Paris, he was received on 2 July 1498, with 'trumpets, clarions and high instruments which made such beautiful sounds that it seemed to come from Paradise.'[11]

In 1550, during the entry of Henry II into Rouen, violinists disguised as muses played in his honor, and in 1565, during the festival offered to Catherine de' Medici at Bayonne, women wearing costumes from Burgundy and Champagne danced to the accompaniment of oboe, violin, and drum.[12]

Much music was performed for the newly converted Henry IV upon his entry into Paris, 22 March 1594. A procession was made to Notre-Dame. Participating were royal officials, the Parlement, in red robes, officers of the municipality, and the crowd. The clergy of the Sainte-Chapelle carried the relics. All the mendicant orders were represented, with the exception of the Jacobins, who had been excluded from the ceremonies because a member of their order, Jacques Clément, had murdered the previous king.[13] Claude Le Jeune composed a salute to Henry IV for this entry into Paris, in the form of a measured air, *Muze, honorons de ta chanson*, which departed from the earlier practice of its type because it was rhymed.[14]

Occasionally, persons of middle estate hired musicians to celebrate a royal *entrée*. In order to mark the arrival of the king and queen into Paris, in 1549, the printer Claude Chaudière engaged a fifer and a drummer to accompany him for two days, wherever he might go. Sometimes minor personages seemed to want to celebrate their own entry into one place or another. Two Parisian bourgeois who were going on a pilgrimage to Mont-Saint-Michel took with them a drummer who was to sound his instrument 'in all towns, villages, bridges, ports, and straits' along the way.[15]

Among musical sounds heard in the street were cries—such as 'Noël,' which at the time was a cry of joy for any circumstance and not reserved for the Christmas season, and the formulae of peddlers selling their wares. Street cries found their way into plays, some of which derived their title from a

[10] Jean Marot, *Œuvres*, pp. 158–160.   [11] Chaillon, *Louis XII*, pp. 64–65.

[12] Pincherle, *Violonistes*, p. 19.   [13] Brenet, *Sainte-Chapelle*, p. 145.

[14] Levy, *Le Jeune*, p. 14.   [15] Lesure, *Sociologie*, pp. 345–346.

given product or service advertised in the street. Examples of this are the *Farce du vendeur de livres* and the farce *Ramonneur de cheminées*. Certain cries are incorporated in chansons, and one, *Buerre frais*, is the title of a basse-danse.[16] The four-voiced chansons which contain the most street cries and are built entirely on them are Janequin's *Les cris de Paris* and Jean Servin's *La Fricassée des cris de Paris*. Hesdin's *Ramonnez-moy ma cheminée, ramonnez la moy hault et bas* is based on the chimney sweep's call; it has a double meaning, one of which has nothing to do with that honest man's profession. An earlier example of street cries which found their way into polyphony is the well-known *Frese nouvelle*, from the Montpellier *Codex H 196*. In modern times, street cries were once again incorporated into drama in Charpentier's *Louise*.[17]

Public proclamations, such as the announcement of peace, were made to the sound of the trumpet. Other outdoor activities accompanied by that instrument may have included executions, or public torture. It is reported that in 1365, in Cyprus, 'two Genoese seamen jumped ship after receiving their salaries. They were captured and their right ears were cut off "au son des trompettes, selon la coutume." '[18] Whether this custom also applied to France is not certain, but it does not seem impossible, since the kings of Cyprus were French at the time and may have introduced French customs to the island.

Although bells were often sounded throughout a city for joyful occasions, they could also be the signal for tragic events. The bells of Saint-Germain-l'Auxerrois, and of the palace, and then all those of Paris tolled to announce the massacre of Saint Bartholomew's day. Occasionally the bells of a city were removed, if they had served to call together seditious assemblies, or if the government wished to prevent a revolt. This punishment was inflicted on Bordeaux in 1552 and on Montpellier in 1574.[19] Fourmentin's *Quarillons* are polyphonic representations of bell sounds.

One place where one might be entertained and have some fresh air at the same time was the cemetery. Parisians of the

[16] Brown, *Theater*, pp. 84–85.
[17] Ringer, *Chasse*, p. 15, and Brenet, *France*, p. 172.
[18] Hoppin, *Cypriot* (article), p. 90.
[19] Kastner, *Militaire*, pp. 83–84, and *Danses*, p. 81.

early fifteenth century liked to go to the cemetery of the Innocents on a Sunday afternoon, where they could see the dance of death in paintings and performed as a play, probably with some musical accompaniment. These spectacles, in which Death was the principal character, were begun at the cemetery in 1424, on the occasion of a visit to Paris by Philip the Good. These representations were popular in nature. They began in August and lasted for about six months, until Lent of the following year.[20]

There was music in the fields, as we are told by Christine de Pisan in her *Dit de la pastoure* (1403), where she describes shepherds playing the *musette* and the drum.[21] And many years later, Du Fouilloux, the hunting expert, gives us concrete examples of how shepherdesses from his native Poitou sang to their sheep when they sheared them:[22]

or called each other to the pastures:

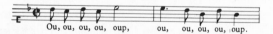

to which her companion responded:

These may be the only authentic specimens of 'music of the people' from the sixteenth century that has come down to us, though as Lesure points out, they can hardly be called songs, since they are merely calls, or cries.[23]

[20] Meyer-Baer, *Spheres*, pp. 307–308. One of the plays refers to a farce named *Danse de macabré* (Brown, *Theater*, p. 157).

[21] Pirro, *Charles VI*, p. 22.

[22] Du Fouilloux, *Venerie*, pp. 285–288.

[23] Lesure, *Eléments*, p. 170.

From time to time, writers refer to pastoral music. This interest in the subject surely stems from the mediaeval *pastourelle*. Eloy d'Amerval, master of the choirboys in Orléans, in his *Livre de la deablerie*, written between 1497 and 1507, states that shepherds like to sing and play instruments.[24] Jean Molinet, in his *L'Arbre de Bourgogne*, depicts shepherds celebrating the Burgundian dynasty by means of games, dances, and other entertainment, and 'according to the bucolic estate, [they] took musical instruments and blew into their *musettes*; *musette* players played their little chansons; singers sang their beautiful *rondeaux*. . . .'[25] Music of the fields was once used for therapeutic purposes, according to Robert Gaguin's chronicle. Some of the musicians whom King Louis XI called in his last illness were shepherds, who made music continually for several days, not far from the king's chamber, in order to console him, and so that he would not succumb to the sleep which was most harmful to him.[26] Since Louis XI was very fearful of death and did everything in his power to ward it off—he sought the help of monks, made costly gifts to churches,[27] asked for relics from various places in Europe, and even for the Holy Ampulla from Reims, so that he could be anointed once more with the oil with which he had been crowned—it is not impossible that he also resorted to pastoral music in the hope of prolonging his life.

Queen Eleanor of Portugal, upon her entrance in Bayonne, where she came to be married to Francis I in 1530, bringing with her his two sons who had been held captive in Spain, was welcomed by means of bonfires, a *Te Deum* sung at the cathedral, and a *bergerie*, or comedy of shepherds, written by a secretary of Cardinal de Tournon.[28] The comedy, which is unfortunately lost, probably included some musical sections. And we can thereby see that things pastoral were not considered too lowly to present before royalty.

Pastoral themes are reflected in art music, such as Josquin's

[24] Pirro, *Histoire*, p. 128.　　　[25] MacClintock, *Molinet*, p. 115.
[26] Gaguin, *Les grandes chroniques*, quoted in Brenet, *France*, p. 45.
[27] Commynes disapproved of money being distributed where it was least needed, and thought that King Louis would have done better to levy fewer taxes on his subjects.
[28] François, *Tournon*, pp. 86.

Bergerette savoysienne, Claudin's *Une bergerotte prinse en ung buisson,* Janequin's *Ung gay bergier prioit une bergiere,* or Passereau's *Je ne seray jamais bergiere;* most of these chansons can hardly be considered work songs, because on the whole they have little to do with tending one's sheep.[29] Shepherds and shepherdesses are found in the *air de cour* repertoire of the late sixteenth and early seventeenth centuries. By this time, they do not take much better care of their sheep than they did in the past, but they have become a bit more precious, and their language is considerably more delicate.

The calls of other field workers, such as plowmen, were sometimes incorporated into the polyphonic chanson. Certon's *Ung laboureur au premier chant du coq* contains the cry 'Hau, hure, hau,' the equivalent of *huhau,* which is used to make a horse advance or turn to the right, and Claudin's *Les dames se sont tailladés* has the refrain *Hari, bouriquet.* The term 'hari' is still in use today, and is the proper but often ineffective way to address a Southern French donkey, if one hopes that it will move along fast. (The animal, however, often responds by moving backwards.) Janequin's *La meusniere de Vernon* (Du Chemin, 1551) may be an example of art music inspired by a rustic occupation; it is only fair to add that the young lady's talents as a miller are not the subject of the chanson.

The aristocracy occasionally participated in country scenes with music. On the first of May, for example, young people made a procession to the country and gathered green branches. They were supposed to wear green, which was the color of May, or be told: 'Je vous prends sans vert,' which may be at the origin of the modern expression 'prendre sans vert' (to be taken by surprise). The illustration for May, from the calendar of the *Tres riches heures du duc de Berry,* shows elegantly dressed people attending the May procession to the accompaniment of wind instruments.[30]

The hunt was a favorite pastime among royalty and nobility.

[29] The setting of such pieces is usually a meadow with a bush or two that provide shade and privacy, as the initial verses of a three-part chanson by Revez (Antico, 1536[1]) suggest: 'Le bergier et la bergiere/ Sont assis pres d'ung buisson./ Ils sont si pres l'ung de l'autre/ Qu'a grand peine les voit-on.'   [30] *Tres riches,* fol. 5[vo] and explanatory text facing the illustration.

As Alexander Ringer points out in his excellent and full study of the hunt and its musical aspects, it was in the late Middle Ages that the war-like sport of earlier times was transformed into a splendid royal institution. French hunters became more concerned with the method of conducting the hunt than with the speedy death of the victim, which by now was a stag instead of a bear; and so 'hunting was turned into . . . a French art.'[31]

Under the influence of their royal patrons, undoubtedly, and as early as the fourteenth century, musicians too began to take an interest in the hunt, and composed canonic pieces which they called *chaces*. Guillaume de Machault, for example, not only wrote *chaces*, but participated in the hunt every day, at Crécy-en-Brie, in June 1363, with his 'sovereign lord' Charles, regent of France during the English captivity of his father John II the Good, and king of France in 1364 under the name of Charles V. They hunted with the help of dogs and birds. In his poem *Jugement du roi de Navarre*, Machaut represents himself as interested 'in nothing except what he hunts.' Among his favorite quarry was the hare.[32]

King Louis XI's interest in the hunt was second only to his passion for dogs, and prior to 1473, perhaps for ladies.[33] For

[31] Ringer, *Chasse*, p. 6.

[32] Machabey, *Machault*, I: pp. 58, 76.

[33] Commynes (*Mémoires*, II: pp. 325–326) tells us that he had given the latter up after 1473, because of a vow he had made to God, following the death of his infant son, the duke of Berry; he promised that from then on he would be faithful to his wife (Charlotte of Savoy). Although he concedes that 'this was no more than he should have done . . . according to the laws of matrimony,' the memorialist finds this feat particularly commendable 'considering that the queen was not the kind of person in whom one might take great pleasure, although she was a good lady.' As for dogs, Ringer (*Chasse*, p. 63) explains that 'the relationship between the men and their faithful companions and collaborators, the dogs, must indeed have been closer than the sportsman of today could possibly imagine. They shared not only the pleasures of the conquest, but also the many dangers that went with it, and there is nothing to tie together living beings, animal or human, like facing a common threat.' Louis XI collected animals, and especially dogs, particularly towards the end of his life, when, according to Commynes, he wanted to make expensive purchases so that people would think he was well. This strong attachment to animals—more than to most humans—has sometimes been interpreted to imply mental weakness on his part; but perhaps it is also explainable by his great interest in the hunt, of which dogs were such a vital part.

the statue which was to grace his tombstone, he wished to be represented in the costume of a hunter, with a horn at his side.[34] He went hunting continually when he was not involved in some war, and although he and Charles the Bold of Burgundy fought almost every summer, during the latter part of his life, they made truces during the winter. These reprieves sometimes lasted for six months out of a year or more, and one wonders whether their purpose could have been, at least in part, to leave free time for hunting. Louis XI certainly took the sport seriously. Commynes reports that

> when he went hunting, he had almost as much trouble as pleasure, for he took great pains in his enterprise. He pursued the stag energetically and got up early in the morning to do it; sometimes he rode very far and did not abandon the chase, regardless of what the weather might be. And so he often returned very tired, and he was almost always angry at someone, for it is a sport which is not always managed according to the pleasure of the leader. However, he was more of an expert on the subject than any man who lived in his time, in everyone's opinion.[35]

Francis I was so devoted to the sport that he spent as much as 150,000 *livres tournois* a year on it.[36] The cornettists from his household musicians kept him well supplied with hunting horns, for which he paid generously.[37] Charles IX is said to have written a treatise on the hunt,[38] and it is to him that Jacques du Fouilloux dedicated his *La Venerie* in 1560.

Hunting was not limited to men. Among the high-ranking women who took part in the sport were Catherine de' Medici and her cousin and rival Diane de Poitiers. In an attempt to regain the affection of her husband, the future Henry II, Catherine became a huntress and launched a new manner of riding on horseback, with the calf on the saddle-tree.[39] Diane,

[34] Hervé, *Chasse*, pp. 461–466.
[35] Commynes, *Mémoires*, II: p. 326.
[36] Ringer, *Chasse*, p. 50.
[37] Prunières, *Chambre*, p. 237.
[38] Hervé, *Chasse*, p. 461.
[39] Erlanger, *Diane*, p. 114.

the royal mistress, had been closely associated with hunting since childhood. She was barely six years old when her father took her to her first hunt. For the rest of her life she rose at dawn, took cold baths, and rode on horseback through the woods, where the ladies wore red boots and black velvet masks, in order to protect their faces from the branches and to keep their complexion fair.[40] Diane's husband and her lover had both enjoyed the hunt. Her emblem, which includes a stag, is the symbol not only of the goddess Diana, after whom she is named, but of her own exploits as a huntress.[41]

Musical symbols—vocal and instrumental—were devised as an inseparable part of the hunting ceremony. These calls seem to have been limited, at first, to a single pitch and a number of elementary rhythmic patterns. By the time of the Renaissance, the signals became slightly more tuneful and numerous, although they were by no means as elaborate as the eighteenth-century fanfares of the marquis of Dampierre, which not only include signals for each type of hunt, but special ones for particular occasions, such as 4 November, which is the name-day of Saint Hubert, patron of hunters. These are *bona fide* little musical pieces, whereas the Renaissance calls are not. Some of the earliest authors of French hunting manuals refer to the practice of calling or signalling. The anonymous *Le Dit de la chace dou cerf,* which dates from the end of the thirteenth century or the beginning of the fourteenth, mentions the terms *jupper* (to cry or call) and *corner* (to sound the horn). The anonymous *Le livre du Roy Modus* and the *Livre de chasse* of Gaston III Phébus, count of Foix, refer to *huer* and *corner,* or *crier* and *corner chasse.* To call the dogs, for example, one must *huer* or *corner* three long sounds (or *mots*). The count's book, incidentally, was still much read during the fifteenth century and later.[42] *Le Tresor de venerie* (1394) of Hardouin, lord of Fontaines-Guérin, mentions *jupper et corner* and *dire et corner,* whereas the treatise of Du Fouilloux

---

[40] *Ibid.,* p. 24.

[41] Lowinsky, *Medici* (article), p. 102.

[42] One of the most beautiful of some forty extant manuscript copies, Paris: Bibl. nat., *MS. fr. 616,* includes an illustration of a lesson in voice and horn calls, and is entitled: 'Comment on doit huer et corner.'—*See* Bibliothèque nationale, *Musique,* p. 32.

refers to *sonner et parler, sonner et hupper, forhuer et sonner, crier et hucher, crier et sonner,* and *sonner pour chiens en criant.*[43] The horn calls that later came to be known as fanfares used to be called *cornures.*[44]

Le Dit de la chasse dou cerf lists as many as nine signals. Fontaines-Guérin gives fifteen *cornures*; he is the first to do so in musical notation—and of a rather unusual sort. It is a purely rhythmic notation, which gives no indication of pitch, and in which the meters are expressed by means of conjunct and disjunct black and white squares. Since complicated notation was available at the time—this was the period of the so-called 'mannered notation'—and scribes seem to have had no problem in expressing pitches as well as the most intricate rhythm—whether singers had any difficulty in reading them is another matter—we can assume that the calls were indeed metrically simple, and that they were probably performed on a single tone. The meters alone apparently helped to distinguish one *cornure* from the other. Each one could consist of one, two, or three 'haleinées' (breaths, roughly corresponding to metrical patterns). The idea that a single pitch was implied by the notation has been explained by the belief that the horns of the time could produce only one sound. Ringer, however, points out that this was not true.[45] Du Fouilloux, whose signals are more melodious and varied than Hardouin's, used the normal white mensural notation of his time for his examples.[46]

Some of the *cornures* may have been local in character and later have come to be adopted in all of France. Maine, Anjou, and Poitou seem to have been the principal hunting-grounds of France, and Hardouin seems to make a difference between

[43] Taut, *Jagdmusik*, pp. 66–67, 76.

[44] J. des Airelles (in Boursier de la Roche, *Chasse*, p. 33) quotes the following verses apropos of this transformation: 'Lorque les fanfares parurent/ Les cornures/ En moururent.'

[45] Brenet, *France*, pp. 167–168, and Ringer, *Chasse*, p. 25.

[46] Many years later, Mersenne was still referring to the times of Du Fouilloux. (*See* Boursier de la Roche, *Chasse*, p. 33.) Du Fouilloux himself paid tribute to his predecessors such as Gaston Phébus and laments that 'there are few men today who know how to sound the horn [trompe] well and to speak to dogs in pleasant cries and words as the ancients used to do.' (*See* his *Venerie*, pp. 152–153.) There is no lack of nostalgia for the past on the part of hunting experts.

cornures of Anjou and *cornures* of France.[47] But of course hunting took place in many regions; Fontainebleau, for example, was often used by royal hunters of the Valois-Angoulême dynasty. At any rate, specific *cornures* could be used for corresponding aspects of the hunting ceremonial—calling people, calling dogs, etc. What was musically proper for the stag hunt was not necessarily acceptable for chasing the hare. *A cornure d'ayde* to call for help to finish off the stag was different from a *cornure de prise*, which signified that the animal was taken, or a *cornure de la cuirée*, which was sounded when a portion of the quarry was allotted to the hounds.[48] In a stag hunt, according to Du Fouilloux, a companion might be called by means of a horn call: 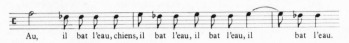 or a vocal call:

The sound of the horn is supposed to be thin rather than loud. When the stag is in the water or has crossed it, one must sing to the dogs:

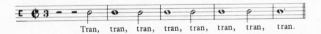

After the hunt is over, the dogs are to be taken back to the kennel to the horn sound of:

To call the dogs to the hare hunt, on the other hand, the signal is:[49]

Reflections of the royal sport soon found their way into poetry and art music. Already in 1359, Gace de la Buigne wrote some fanciful lines in which he describes the sounds of the hunt in musical terms, with dogs singing mediaeval motets and other complex contrapuntal pieces:

[47] Taut, *Jagdmusik*, p. 113.
[48] Ringer, *Chasse*, p. 15.
[49] Du fouilloux, *Venerie*, pp. 153–207.

Adoncques y a telle noise,
Qu'il n'est homs qui sur deux pieds voise
Qui onc oyst tel melodie;
Car n'est respons ne alleluye
Et feust chantée en la Chappelle
Du roi, qui la est bonne et belle,
Qui si tres grant plaisance face
Comme est ouïr une tel chace.
Les uns vont chantant le motet,
Les autres font double hoquet,
Les plus grans chantent la teneur,
Les autres la contre teneur;
Ceux qui ont la plus clere gueule,
Chantent la tresble sans demeure,
Et les plus petits le quadrouble,
En faisant la quinte surdouble.
Les uns font semithon mineur,
Les autres semithon majeur,
Diapenthe, diapazon,
Les autres diathessaron.
Adonc le roi met cor a bouche.[50]

The poet was King John the Good's chaplain and mentor to royalty in matters of falconry. Hunting horn calls are prescribed in the rubrics of several theater pieces of the Renaissance, such as the monologue *Le Franc archier de Bagnolet*, or the morality *L'Orgueil et presumption de l'empereur Jovinien*.[51]

Following the *chaces* of the *Ars nova*, only one French piece of the kind is known to exist in fifteenth-century sources—the three-part composition *Hahu ahu apres l'escoufle* (Hahu ahu, pursue the hawk) from *MS. 5-1-43* of the Biblioteca Colombina, Seville.[52] The piece has canonic and other imitative devices which are characteristic of hunting pieces of

[50] Quoted in Marix, *Histoire*, p. 15.
[51] Brown, *Theater*, p. 72.
[52] It was discovered and transcribed by Dragan Plamenac (*Colombina*, pp. 522–523, transcription, pp. 536–537). The superius is lacking in the Seville chansonnier, but the piece is musically complete in Bologna: Civico Museo Bibliographifico Musicale, *Cod. Q 16*, with the incipit given as *Han haula*.

the preceding century, but does not use the hoquet, which older *chaces* did. For this reason, and because there is no literary text except the few words listed above, Ringer suggests that it may have been performed instrumentally, and that it could have been a love song as well as a hunting song.[53]

Probably the best-known of the Renaissance hunting pieces is Janequin's programmatic chanson *La chasse* (1528), with its lively polyrhythmic, polytextual, and onomatopoetic effects, and its references to hunting practices of the time. For example, four whippers-in address four different dogs in a different manner.[54] Brenet finds an analogy between the following passage from *La Chasse*

Il   est temps de s'en re - tour - ner

and Hardouin's *cornure de mescroy*, which was sounded when one had made a mistake and had to retrace his steps; the first 'haleinée' consisted of two short notes followed by three long ones.[55] Whether or not she is correct in relation to Hardouin, it has been observed that Janequin's signals do not correspond exactly with those which Du Fouilloux was going to codify several years later. The syllable *tronc* in *La Chasse* is evidently reminiscent of a horn call. Du Fouilloux has it in his collection, but writes it (and probably pronounced it) *tran*. It is immaterial that the two words varied, because the syllable was simply a symbol for something that was not sung but played by a *trompe de chasse*—hence the onomatopoeia beginning with 'tr'. To this day there are people (not among the most cultured, perhaps) who pronounce *non* as if it were spelled *nan*. The poet of Janequin's piece was more imaginative than Du Fouilloux; he made a pun by spelling the sound as *tronc*, because the word means 'trunk.'[56] As for the musical variants between actual hunting motifs and polyphonic settings of them, they can perhaps be explained by the fact that it is not always easy to adapt pre-existent tunes to part-writing without

[53] Ringer, *Chasse*, pp. 39–41.

[54] *Ibid.*, p. 55. Ringer agrees with Brenet that an element of quodlibet exists there.   [55] Brenet, *France*, p. 168.

[56] In Janequin's *Vents hardis et legiers* (1552[4]), the sound of the hunting horn (this time spelled *tron*) is compared to a messenger of love. The punning possibilities of the word *trompe* are not neglected: 'Dictes-luy que ma trompe/ Son desir point ne trompe/ Et qu'y seray ce jour. . . .'

making some small changes. One can see that in parody technique, and in quodlibets, where material is not always quoted verbatim.

Be that as it may, it has been noted that sixteenth-century hunting pieces mention names of dogs that were current at the time, and employ typical expressions, such as *arriere, appelle,* etc., which were already part of the fourteenth-century vocabulary. 'All these calls, then, and many others were in use at least two centuries before the chansons were written, an eloquent confirmation of the relative stability of hunting symbols at the disposal of generations of composers.'[57]

The stag hunt was the most closely associated with royalty, and Janequin's *Chasse* belonged in that category. Hare-hunting could be a more plebeian sport, but it was not altogether disdained by gentlemen. Susato's *Dixiesme livre* (1545[17]) contains two *chasses de lièvre*—one by Gombert, predictably the more sober and Flemish-sounding of the two, and an anonymous one, which has been ascribed to Janequin on no particular grounds.[58] The latter is of the lively French chanson type and contains polytextual passages. Another descriptive hunting piece is Delafont's *Chasse à la perdrix*, called *Le vol de la perdrix* (*As-tu point veu quelque espervier prest a voller*) in Le Roy et Ballard's *Unziesme livre* (1559[11]). It depicts, again by onomatopoetic means, the partridge hunt with the help of hawks, and reproduces the cries of falconers as well as the names of their birds. This may be one of the last tributes to falconry, which seems to have gone out of style towards the end of the sixteenth century.[59]

Music was an important part of military operations, as is sometimes mentioned by music theorists, among others. Tinctoris states in *De inventione et usu musicae* (*ca.* 1485) that wind instruments could be heard day and night in the soldiers' camps and in the towns, and Zarlino (*Instituzione armoniche*,

---

[57] Ringer, *Chasse*, pp. 92–93.

[58] *Ibid.*, p. 82. Ringer points out that Franz Commer, in his *Collectio operum Batavorum*, XII: p. 104, though he does not state why he attributes the piece to Janequin, could be right on stylistic grounds, and because this is a royal hunt. The title 'Sire' is spoken, and it might refer to Janequin's patron, Francis I, who was 'an inveterate hunter of all quarry.' But he agrees that one needs more evidence than that to make meaningful attributions. [59] Brenet, *France*, pp. 170–171, and Ringer, *Chasse*, pp. 18–19.

1562) points out that one army would not attack another unless it were invited to do so by the sound of trumpets, drums, or some other instruments belonging to the adversary.[60] This custom was in force not only among the Italians but among the Germans, the Swiss, and the French. The various nations learned from each other, and that is how France eventually adopted the Swiss fifes and drums.

Chroniclers, poets, and other writers, such as Chastellain, Froissart, Jean Marot, and Thoinot Arbeau tell us that brass and percussion instruments were used whenever the army left camp, marched, or retired. The tune which the trumpet played for the departure of Charles VIII's army from Fornovo on 8 July 1495, one hour before dawn, was *Faictes bon guet*.[61]

At some time in the sixteenth century, high-ranking military men had private bands of violins, mostly to provide music for their meals and leisure; however, they had them follow in time of war. Brantôme tells us that they were once used by Bonnivet while he was being besieged by the forces of the duke of Alba. On the day of the expected assault, and as long as the alarm lasted, he had them play along with the drums and trumpets, with the result that none of the men appeared apprehensive. The war instruments described are usually trumpets, fifes, and drums (which are sometimes called *bedons*—e.g., in Jean Marot's *Le voyage de Venise*). Antoine of Navarre, father of Henry IV, used to march off to war with cymbals, when he was lieutenant general for Charles IX; the practice, according to Brantôme, was of German origin. He notes the presence of foreign mercenaries in the French army during the religious conflicts—each with his own customs and instruments—and surmises that the war would have been more noble if everyone had had the same standards, arms, drum rolls, trumpet calls, and order of battle.[62]

Chastellain tells us that the duke of Burgundy's forces used to sing and play the flute, as well as other instruments during the siege of Neuss.[63] Molinet, relating how Arras was taken in

[60] Reese, *Fourscore*, p. 35, and Kastner, *Militaire*, p. 92.
[61] Commynes, *Mémoires*, III: pp. 102–103. The memorialist adds that nothing else was played, nor was it necessary.
[62] Kastner, *Militaire*, pp. 93–101, and *Parémiologie*, p. 362.
[63] Pirro, *Histoire*, pp. 116–117.

1492 (by the Austrian forces), mentions that signals were arranged between the men-at-arms and others, by means of the song *Marchons la dureau, hault la durée*, which may be related to a chanson from Dijon, *MS. 517*, and to a *basse-danse*.[64] Jean Marot, in his *Epître à la Royne Claude*, reports on the French victory over the Swiss and mentions the heralds' announcement of the good news to the people, to the accompaniment of trumpets, clarions, and drums, while the populace shouted: 'France!'[65]

Commynes reports that the German mercenaries in the French army at Fornovo (6 July 1495) were on patrol and played their drums very well that night, after having received three hundred *écus* from the king. On 10 October of the same year, again during the Italian expedition, some dissatisfied Swiss mercenaries sounded their drums to call a nocturnal meeting, for the purpose of discussing the best means of obtaining the payment to which they considered themselves entitled. (One suggestion made was to capture the king and his wealthy friends, but it could not be carried out because Charles VIII was warned about it and moved to another town before they had come to any conclusion.)[66]

The most important military instrument was the trumpet. During the action, the trumpeter stood near the commander, ready to give signals, or near the standard-bearers. To the instrument was attached a pennon of damask or satin with gold embroidery, fringes, etc., in the colors of the leader. Account books of kings and princes classify military trumpeters differently from 'trompettes des ménestrels,' who played for balls and banquets.[67] In time of war, trumpeters were used not only to play their instrument, but to relay messages in diplomatic negotiations. They had to be strong men, ready to serve at any hour as musicians or messengers, and had to be discreet, particularly in the latter capacity. They were not to use any other terms except those agreed upon by

[64] Linden, *Molinet*, pp. 176–177.   [65] J. Marot, *Œuvres*, p. 160.
[66] Commynes, *Mémoires*, III: pp. 196, 243–244. A song from Paris: Bibl. nat., *MS. fr. 12744, Et que feront povres gendarmes*, mentions Duke Maximilian's losses at the battle of Fornovo: 'A la journée de Fourneuf/ Il luy mourut beaucoup de gens.' (Paris, *Chansons*, p. 126, 69.)
[67] Brenet, *Militaire*, p. 27.

their master, and were not to add advice or comments of their own, so that there would be no ambiguity in conferences and peace parleys.[68] The messenger-trumpeters had to be brave men indeed, although they did not fight. They were sometimes mistaken for combatants and fired upon by the enemy. Commynes, in one of his numerous ambassadorial missions, had trouble finding a trumpeter who was willing to go to the enemy camp, because nine of them had already been unwittingly killed in battle.[69]

Other sounds heard on the battlefield were war cries. Each company or battle corps had its own call, which could be a device, religious invocation, name of a state, city, or prince. Soldiers' valor was judged partly on the loudness and vigor with which they made their cries when they charged upon the enemy. These sounds made with conviction were supposed to frighten the adversaries, who took them for a mark of courage. Silence, on the other hand, was taken to signify fear. It is believed that some of the exclamations in the text of Janequin's *La Guerre*, such as 'Alarme,' 'Suivez François, le roi François,' and 'Suivez la couronne,' were actual battle cries which found their way into art music.[70]

Military institutions, or specific wars and victories, and occasional defeats, were often the subject of particular songs or motets. Perhaps the most popular song of the fifteenth and sixteenth centuries, judging from its numerous adaptations, was *L'Homme armé, l'homme armé doibt-on doubter*. It was used as a *cantus firmus* in more than thirty Masses from Dufay to Carissimi, and served for many chansons, simple and double. It was the tenor part of a quodlibet which appears in the *Proportionale* of Tinctoris, with *O rosa bella* as its cantus, and *Et Robinet* as its bassus, and was also the basis for numerous instrumental compositions. Judith Cohen gives the most complete list of its uses, which includes a *Phantasia super L'Homme armé* for organ by Johann Nepomuk David, written in 1930.[71]

We do not know as much as we would like about the origins

[68] Kastner, *Militaire*, pp. 106–107.
[69] Commynes, *Mémoires*, III: p. 197.
[70] Brenet, *France*, pp. 116–117, 137.
[71] Cohen, *L'Homme armé*, pp. 72–74.

of the *L'Homme armé* tune, which was sometimes attributed to Busnois because Pietro Aron seemed to suggest it in *Toscanello in musica*. The first known polyphonic source in which it appears is the *Mellon Chansonnier* (New Haven: Yale University). It is an anonymous three-part chanson, which seems to have served as as the model for Robert Morton's four-part setting. Just as we cannot tell who composed the tune, we also do not know exactly who *l'homme armé* was. The cantus of the piece in the *Mellon chansonnier* refers to 'le doubté turcq' (the feared Turk—i.e., the sultan) who may be beaten by maître Symon or Symonet le Breton (a friend of Dufay at the Burgundian court). Christendom had never entirely accepted the fall of Constantinople to the Turks, and always wanted to reconquer it. Ruth Hannas has therefore suggested that *L'Homme armé* was originally a call to arms for an attack on the Turk. Be that as it may, it has also been shown to refer to other persons at other times. The Mass on *L'Homme armé* by Regis associates the powerful man with Saint Michael, and a similar Mass by Morales links *l'homme armé* with Emperor Charles V.[72]

It is also possible that the song referred not just to one specific individual but to a representative group of military men who made their mark in fifteenth-century French history partly by making nuisances of themselves across the country—the men-at-arms of the king's army. They were usually called 'hommes d'armes' or 'gens d'armes', but occasionally also '[hommes, or gens] armez.'[73] Commynes describes them as

> . . . constantly quartered throughout the country, without paying for anything, and doing other evils and excesses which everyone of us knows about: for they are not content with their rations, and so they beat and abuse the poor people and force them to go and find bread, wine, and other food for them; and if the good man has a wife or daughter who is beautiful, he would be wise to keep her out of sight.[74]

[72] *Ibid.*, pp. 19–21.

[73] When Commynes (*Mémoires*, III: p. 74) mentions 'cinq cens arméz,' he obviously does not mean 'five hundred armies,' but five hundred armed men, or more properly, men-at-arms.

[74] *Ibid.*, II: p. 216.

One of the oldest streets of Paris, which was demolished about 1880 and whose original houses were said to date from the reign of Louis VII in the twelfth century, was the *rue de l'Homme armé*. It began at the *rue Sainte-Croix-de-la-Bretonnerie*, ended at the *rue des Blancs-Manteaux*, and formed part of what is now the *rue des Archives*. Historians have speculated that the *rue de l'Homme armé* may have derived its name from the sign of an inn with the image of a man in armor—which is said to have existed as early as 1432. A restaurant with an eighteenth-century sign representing a seemingly cheerful and harmless 'homme armé' on a cannon was located at 25 *rue des Blancs-Manteaux* in the early twentieth century.[75] Possibly the well-known song was at the origin of the name of the inn and of the street, rather than the other way around. Perhaps it was a chanson that came to be associated with taverns, although the words do not refer to drinking. There is also the possibility that both the chanson and the street derived their name from whoever the original 'homme armé' was.

Another type of soldier honored by song was the free-archer from the royal militia, whose main role was to maintain order and prevent pillage. The anonymous *Le franc archer a la guerre s'en va*, from Paris: Bibl. nat., *MS. fr. 12616*, and Compère's *Ung franc archier*, from Petrucci's *Odhecaton* are examples of this.

An anonymous motet, *Adoretur/ In ultimo/ Pacem*, was written to celebrate the surrender of Bordeaux to Charles VII on 30 June 1451.[76] Dufay's *Lamentations*, of which one is extant, were composed to mourn for the loss of Constantinople. The popular song *Gentils galans de France* pertains to the war of Brittany and the battle of Saint-Aubin du Cormier, when its duke, Francis II, was taken by the forces of Charles VIII in 1488; the French troops had their standards marked with white crosses and the Bretons with black crosses. White had been the color of the royal troops.[77]

The victory of Francis I over the Swiss mercenaries of the Milanese in September 1515 prompted the writing of a

[75] Plates and newspaper clippings from Paris: Bibl. nat., Dept. des estampes, *VA. 249d (Topographie)*.
[76] Ficker, in *New Oxford*, III; p. 164 (transcription in *DTÖ*, xl, p. 77).
[77] Paris, *Chansons*, pp. 127-128.

political motet by Jean Mouton, *Exalta Regina gallie, Jubila mater Ambasie*. It is presumably addressed to Louise of Savoy, who was regent of France in her son's absence. The work is a unicum in the *Codex Medici*.[78] The most famous piece about this battle, however, is Janequin's long programmatic chanson, *La Guerre* (sometimes called *La bataille de Marignan*), which was transcribed for instruments all over Europe. Verdelot added a fifth voice to the existing four in Susato's *Dixiesme livre* (1545[17]); it has been pointed out that Janequin must have been pleased with this tribute, since he included it in his own later editions of the piece.[79] We recall that Mlle. de Limeuil requested *La Guerre* on her deathbed, and had her valet, Julien, play it on his violin. The passage corresponding to 'Tout est perdu' in the vocal version she had Julien play four times. Then she turned to her lady attendant, saying: 'Tout est perdu à ce coup et a bon escient,' and died.[80] Noël du Faïl, in his *Contes d'Eutrapel* (1585), recalls that whenever the piece was sung before Francis I, all the men present checked whether their swords were in their sheaths and raised themselves on their toes, so as to look more elegant.[81] Almost a century after its composition, it was sung to the accompaniment of instruments, in connection with a pageant about Hercules and the Hydra, when Queen Marie de' Medici made her entry into Avignon, on 19 November 1600.[82] It was sung as far as Mexico under the title *La Batalla de Juaniquin*,[83] and may well be the most famous battle piece in music history. Its author wrote several other pieces of its type, such as *La Guerre de Renty, Le Siège de Metz, La Prinse de Boulongne*, and *La Reduction de Boulongne*. The latter piece contains a tribute to Henry II 'neuviesme des Valois,' his queen, and their children. Janequin almost seems to have been the official battle music

[78] Lowinsky, *Medici* (article), pp. 84–85.

[79] Levy, *Le Jeune*, p. 136. Janequin made a new version of the piece in 1555, for five voices instead of four, and somewhat longer than the first. The Swiss of Marignano are replaced by the soldiers from Hainault and the Burgundians. (*See* Dottin, *Janequin*, p. 134, and Merritt, *Janequin*, pp. 607–609.)

[80] Lesure, *Musicians*, p. 38, and Kastner, *Danses*, p. 5.

[81] Heartz, in Haar, *Chanson*, p. 112.

[82] Durand, *Avignon*, p. 77.

[83] Lesure, in Roland-Manuel, *Histoire*, I: p. 1049.

composer of France. A year after Francis I's victory at Marignano, Johannes Vannius composed an anti-French political motet, *Attendite popule*, in which he (or the author of the literary text) urged the Swiss not to make peace with the French king.[84]

Whereas victories are often celebrated with official music, defeats are usually glossed over, at least by musicians of the losing side. Janequin is supposed to have written a *Praelium ad Paviam*, which was printed possibly in 1545, in a collection of music which is now lost. It is most unlikely, however, that Janequin would have commemorated Francis I's worst defeat at Pavia, 24 February 1525, as Heartz rightly points out, and so the piece was probably written in honor of Marignano and wrongly interpreted by whoever composed the title.[85] The *Bataglia Taliana* by Matthias Herrmann Werrecore, on the other hand, was probably a glorification of the battle of Pavia from the point of view of the Milanese, since the composer was at the time *maestro di cappella* of the cathedral of Milan.[86] A popular song about one of the French commanders, La Palice, which is still sung today, mentions his death at the battle of Pavia. The well-known verses from that piece, to the effect that a quarter of an hour before his death he was still alive, may originally have been intended to show that he was fighting bravely until he was killed; they nevertheless gave rise to the expression 'vérité de la Palice,' which means 'truism.'[87]

Costeley wrote the battle pieces *La guerre de Calais*, which describes the capture of Calais from the English by the forces of the duke of Guise in January 1558, and *La prise du Havre*, which refers to the French victory over the English on August 1563. Since the Parlement of Rouen declared that King Charles IX had reached his majority, at the age of thirteen, on 17 August of that year, it has been suggested that the latter piece may have been written in honor of that event. Another chanson by Costeley, *Chanton de Dieu les merveilles*, is not a battle piece, properly speaking, but its allusions to Charles's

[84] Glarean, *Dodecachordon*, I: p. 31.
[85] Heartz, *Attaingnant*, pp. 337–338.
[86] Borren, in *New Oxford*, IV: pp. 6–7.
[87] One version of the song (from Paris: Bibl. nat., *MS. fr. 12666*) is given in Barbier, *Histoire*, I: pp. 60–61.

brother the duke of Anjou, who was to become Henry III, and to enemies of the king, have led to speculation that the work was written shortly after the battle of Jarnac (March 1569), when Henry fought successfully against the Huguenots.[88]

Battle pieces are not limited to describing exploits on land. In their *Unziesme livre* (1559[11]) Le Roy et Ballard published a *Guerre marine* (*Sus mathelots, voyci la guerre ouverte*) for four voices, by Desbordes, along with other descriptive music.

La Guerre is the subtitle of an air of Claude Le Jeune, 'Arm', arm',' published posthumously in 1608. Miss Yates thinks that it might be a rhymed and altered version of his war-like piece on *vers mesurés* by Baïf, which had caused an auditor at the *magnificences* for the wedding of the duke of Joyeuse to become agitated. It was a composition for a symbolic tournament—a combat against love, with love emerging triumphant.[89]

[88] Godt, *Costeley*, I: pp. 69–71; II: pp. 437–439.
[89] Yates, *Magnificences*, pp. 244–245.

PART TWO
Musical Manifestations

8

General trends and sources

France had been the most important European polyphonic center for several centuries before the Renaissance. (Whether canonic writing and *fauxbourdon* originated in the British Isles or on the Continent is immaterial at this point, although it has occupied musicologists for many years and probably will for many more.) And the majority of French composers maintained their interest in polyphony throughout the fifteenth and sixteenth centuries, while the more avant-garde group experimented with genres that were to lead to accompanied monody by the end of the sixteenth century in all of Europe. Lesure sums up the French musical art of the Renaissance in the following terms:

> Such art is characterized by a refusal to destroy the balance of the work by anything resembling excess, exaggerated emotion and immoderate indulgence in feeling; by a search for equilibrium within a judicious and intimate lyricism which, capable of suggestion, is averse to total self-surrender; finally, by a tendency to seek intellectual solutions for all problems, including those of musical art. If a continuity in the union of French poetry and French music exists at all, one must search for it along the lines indicated.[1]

Although Lesure was thinking of sixteenth-century music when he wrote this passage, much of it also applies to fifteenth-century works. The age of Busnois and Josquin displayed on the whole more sentimentality than the age of Janequin, to be sure, and the pieces were generally more serious. It was the culmination of heart pieces and 'regretz' pieces—*Allez regretz, Mille regretz,* etc., which on the surface may seem somewhat doleful. They were probably no more than a literary convention, however, and do not deserve to be performed like funeral music, as they sometimes are.

[1] Lesure, *Musicians*, pp. 122–123.

Furthermore, whatever sentimentality exists in fifteenth-century music is found chiefly in secular music. Most of the sacred works—and they are numerous—are models of moderation. The underlying emotion which is undeniably present is not allowed to overshadow the other traits of a given composition. In spite of the gaiety of much of the sixteenth-century repertoire, the slightly melancholic themes of the previous era maintain themselves as a minority current in part of the chansons, but always with some restraint. A particular feeling may be suggested, but not exaggerated.

Renaissance society did not become humanistic, enlightened, and scientific overnight. Certainly by the fifteenth century, feudal institutions were on their decline and sometimes almost meaningless to many people. Pierre de Vaissière maintains that the sixteenth-century had experienced the most intimate *rapprochement* between the common people and the upper classes that ever took place during the Old Regime, and Lesure believes that this might be a reason for the variety of chansons—courtly and vulgar—which one finds in the collections of the period.[2] Elsewhere he points out that sixteenth-century society 'knew nothing of mystical passion and had lost the serenity of a deep-seated faith.'[3] All this is perfectly true. It seems nevertheless that vestiges of mediaeval thought linger on in many aspects of French life in the fifteenth and sixteenth centuries—including music.

The intensity that one finds in some of the lyrical poems probably stems from courtly literature of an earlier age—as do the ideas of chivalry and the unattainable woman. This is expressed in the *Heptameron* of Marguerite of Navarre, in which one of the characters, a married woman, has a 'perfect lover' with the knowledge and consent of her husband, who also openly serves another lady—most honorably on the part of all concerned—and in such poems as Francis I's *Dictes sans peur*, with music by Sermisy. Kottick, however, sees the deterioration of *amour courtois* already in the texts of the fifteenth-century *chansonnier cordiforme*, owing to the violence and moral decadence of the society in which its owner lived.[4]

Whether or not Renaissance society still experienced

[2] Lesure, *Eléments*, p. 169.   [3] Lesure, in *New Oxford*, IV: p. 239.
[4] Kottick, *Cordiforme* (dissertation), p. 53.

mystical passion, many people acted outwardly as if they did. The numerous processions performed with great pomp, which were mentioned earlier, testify to this. The hooded penitents of the Counter-Reformation, though more sober than the flagellants of the Middle Ages, nevertheless walked the street for the same purpose. Protestants were very intense in their beliefs—so much so that many of them accepted torture and death rather than abjuration. And death was not made easy; victims were sometimes burned, or drawn and quartered. Catholics who could afford it made frequent pilgrimages to holy shrines. Many miracles were claimed, and they did not always occur at places of devotion, but almost anywhere. The kings of France were believed to have the power to cure the scrofulous, and so they periodically touched the sick, after having first gone to confession and to Mass.[5] Marvels could also happen in the market place. When a hanged man resuscitated there once, probably as a result of having been insufficiently strangled, the populace proclaimed that he had died and had been brought to life again by divine intercession.[6] Belief in the occult sciences seems to have been as intense as in organized religion. The most extreme superstition was rampant even among the best educated and humanistically oriented individuals. One must recognize that in many phases of French Renaissance life, there was a dualism—not important enough to upset unity of thought, perhaps, and not as conspicuous as in the so-called Baroque era, when several styles were consciously cultivated side by side—but present nevertheless. People then seemed to be able to compartmentalize various aspects of their lives and still keep their sanity. It is not really paradoxical that a person with a scientific mind believed in astrology and other divinatory practices. When he was engaged in scholarly pursuits, he used intellectual methods, and when he was concerned about his own future, or things that science could not explain, he turned to faith and intuition. Just as he did not try to explain belief

[5] A book of Hours (Amiens: Bibl. municipale, *fonds Lescalopier* no. 22) made for Henry II, which is shaped like a fleur de lys when open, contains prayers to Saint Marcoul which were 'said by the kings of France when they want to touch the scrofulous' (Bibliothèque nationale, *Livre*, p. 74).

[6] Bourilly, *Journal*, p. 313.

scientifically, he did not attempt to define scholarship supernaturally.

There had been a literary polemic, at the beginning of the fifteenth century, about the merits of the mediaeval *Roman de la rose*. It was the source of allegorical characters which appear in fifteenth- and sixteenth-century poems. Malebouche, for example, is mentioned in Binchois's *Nous vous verens bien*, and in *Mon seul espoir et toute ma liesse*, and *Ha, la doloreuse journée*, from Paris: Bibl. nat., *MS. fr. 12744*. Faux Semblant is found in the anonymous *Se Faux Semblant vous fait joieuse chiere*, from the Cypriot-French repertory of the early fifteenth century,[7] as well as in Sermisy's chansons *Amours partes, je vous donne la chasse,* and *Si vous m'aymez, donnez-moy asseurance*. Bel Acueil is most conspicuous in the piece of the same name by Busnois—the opening chanson of the *Mellon chansonnier*. It is also found in the third strophe of Clément Marot's *Secourez-moy, ma dame par amours*, with musical settings by Sermisy in 1528 and later by a group of Flemings, including Gombert, Lassus, Monte, and Pevernage, as late as 1590. Doux Accueil may be a variant of Bel Accueil, and it appears in Sermisy's *Rigueur me tient et Doux Accueil m'attire*.

The mediaeval hocket, or *ochetus*, as a complete piece—such as Machault's *Hoquetus David*—is not found in the Renaissance. As a technique or special effect (the rapid alternation of two or more vocal or instrumental parts breaking up a melody into single notes or short groups of notes by means of rests), it survives in small sections of a limited number of polyphonic compositions, such as Dufay's *Gloria ad modum tubae*, or Claudin's *Les dames se sont tailladés*:

---

[7] Hoppin, *Cypriot* (article), p. 95, and *Cypriot* (edition), IV: pp. 68–69.

In the latter piece, the *ochetus* (hocket) effect is connected with word painting on the syllable 'ha,' which is onomatopoeia for the braying of the donkey. It is also combined with paired imitation of the type used extensively by Josquin.

Another example of the survival of the *Ars nova* in a small part of renaissance music is the predilection for strict imitation or canonic writing—which is called *fuga* in the fifteenth century—and for the 'puzzle' canons, often with enigmatic formulae which, if resolved, allowed one to interpret a given melody notated once, in a variety of ways—in augmentation, diminution, retrograde, or strictly at a particular interval and at a given distance from its first statement. That the canons, or prescriptions, for the resolutions are not always clear to everyone is shown by different solutions of a given piece by various musicologists, all of whom are respectable. In fact, some pieces, such as Ockeghem's *Prenez sur moy*, which Isabella d'Este had inlaid in her *grotta*, and which Glarean quotes, without words, as an example of a *catholicon*—a composition that can be sung in more than one mode—were surely intended by their composers to be ambiguous. The use of the *catholicon*, incidentally, is another example of mediaeval influence in Renaissance music, since it has been traced back to the tenth-century treatise *Musica enchiriadis*.[8]

Enigmatic formulae, which were intellectual exercises, sometimes contained puns. The *Credo* of Josquin's *Missa De Beata Virgine* contains the following direction for the fifth canonic voice: 'Vous jeunéres les quatre temps.' The musical interpretation is that one must wait the equivalent of four *tempora* before starting, but the literal meaning is: 'You will fast during Ember Days.'

Perhaps the most complex canons of the French Renaissance were the thirty-six part canon, *Deo gratias*, attributed to Ockeghem (with as many as eighteen voices appearing simultaneously) and Josquin's twenty-four part psalm *Quis habitabit in adjutorio*, with all of its voices singing together. The thirty-six voices of the *Deo gratias*, arranged as four canons for nine parts, have been interpreted to symbolize nine angelic choirs which glorify God in a never-ending hymn of praise—i.e., the repeated canon, and an example of true

---

[8] Reese, *Renaissance*, p. 120.

mediaeval mysticism 'expressing the heroic humility of an
artist willing to undergo the most extreme difficulties in the
service of an idea, in an attempt to create in sound the effect of
a mystical vision.'[9]

Vestiges of the mediaeval concept of embellishing a piece of
liturgical music by adding something to it or substituting
something unrelated for part of it—i.e., tropes on a linear
plane—have been shown to be still alive in the Renaissance.
Not only did they survive as textual tropes in such pieces as
Dufay's *Sanctus papale* and in various polyphonic settings of
Gloria IX (*De Beata Virgine*) with the traditional interpolation
of Marian tropes, a practice which lasted until the Council of
Trent,[10] but they led to such genres as parody Mass, tenor-
motet, motet-chanson, and *motetti missales*. In relation to the
latter, which were peculiar to the Ambrosian service in the
Milanese diocese, and were written by some Franco-Flemings
in Milan, Finscher finds that

> the substitution of the traditional and inviolable Ordinary
> and Proper by liturgical and unliturgical texts obviously
> unrelated (except the Elevatio-motets) to the ritual meaning
> and the ritual texts they replace . . . adds an element of
> subjective interpretation to the objective ritual of the
> Mass.[11]

It is difficult to determine whether the French Renaissance
manifested more or less religious interest, musically speaking,
than the Middle Ages. In terms of numbers, there are certainly
more religious polyphonic compositions in the fifteenth
century than in the fourteenth. Towards the middle of the
century, the sacred motet becomes more and more often
monotextual—which seems to imply respect for the Biblical
text. French prints on the whole appear to show more interest

[9] Lowinsky, *Ockeghem*, pp. 157–158. The author points out that Josquin's
piece, the counterpart to Ockeghem's canon, may symbolize the twenty-
four Old Men of the Apocalypse. The psalm deals with the relationship
between God and man, with the angels as guardians of men. 'Ockeghem
sings of the angelic praises of God; Josquin of the human soul in search of
God and in need of the angels. Josquin's canon is a symbol of Christian
humanism; Ockeghem's of Christian mysticism' (pp. 179–180).

[10] Reese, *Renaissance*, p. 60.   [11] Compère, *Opera omnia*, II: p. *ii*.

in secular than in religious publication in the course of the sixteenth century, but this may not be entirely true. Although there may have been more chansons printed than Masses and motets, they are shorter and take less time to compose; they were not necessarily considered by publishers and public to be more important than religious music, and the two genres were probably equal in importance. It has been noted, however, that after the generation of Certon and Maillard, between 1570 and 1582, there were only about five or six new Catholic religious publications by Frenchmen. In 1583, Le Roy et Ballard were reprinting Masses by Claudin, who had been dead for more than twenty years.[12]

It is more difficult than ever, during the Renaissance, to separate secular from sacred elements. The motet-chansons and chanson-based Masses are examples of this. So are the Huguenot songs for private devotion, many of which are contrafacta on street and court songs. The mingling which was noticed between upper and lower social classes also took place between church personnel and laity. We have seen earlier how both cooperated in theatrical productions. Occasionally ecclesiastics were admonished not to fraternize too much with the outside world. In 1466, for example, the monks of Strasbourg were forbidden to disguise themselves and attend public dances. Another time, a preacher from the same city expressed disapproval because some priests who said their first Mass celebrated the event by dancing with ladies.[13] In 1499, the bishop of Troyes forbade the nuns of the Paraclete from attending the Rogations—ceremonies which take place during the three days preceding Ascension Day, at which time people pray to obtain divine help with their crops—because, after the responds, many of the villagers organized a ball, during which one could hear 'songs in French, sometimes improper.'[14] These statements merely show that the two worlds, secular and religious, were not far apart. Churchmen thought nothing of writing light and occasionally obscene poetry and music, which they published to everyone's knowledge. They were never censored for that, although they

---

[12] Lesure, in *New Oxford*, IV: p. 248.   [13] Pirro, *Histoire*, p. 149.
[14] Brenet, *Processions*, p. 7.

were sometimes reprimanded for various unworthy acts. It was political and religious writings which could bring upon them the wrath of the authorities. Love songs and drinking songs were not subject to official blame; they were in the category of harmless pastimes. High-ranking churchmen such as Cardinal d'Amboise, Cardinal de Tournon, and Cardinal de Lorraine often spent more time, or at least as much, in the service of the state as in the service of God, and they became important patrons of the arts. These are only a few examples of the dual aspects of Renaissance society and of its music, in spite of the undeniable blending of various elements.

The musical ideas of the French Renaissance hardly proceeded by revolution. Few new genres were invented, although some, such as the *ballade* and *virelai* were abandoned along the way—as were certain techniques, such as isorhythm. The existing genres, Mass, motet, and chanson were modified, to be sure, but not destroyed.

The idea of returning to the ancients for inspiration, which was enunciated by so many humanists, and of which Baïf's *Académie* was the principal spokesman in matters musical, may not always signify a complete break with the immediate past. In fact, the term 'ancients' is not always synonymous with the Greeks and Romans, and can be somewhat vague. It sometimes includes Egypt, Judea, and Gaul—and occasionally seems to be applied to the mediaeval troubadours, and the earlier sixteenth century. Vauquelin de la Fresnaye, in his *Art poétique*, written by command of Henry III, finds that the troubadours have revived the poetry and music of the Greeks and Romans. Ronsard, in his preface to the *Livre des Mélanges* (Le Roy et Ballard, 1560, repr. 1572) speaks of 'music of the ancients' in relation to the circle of composers around Clément Marot. And one must agree with Miss Yates that 'to the Academicians it seems that the "music of the ancients" is a continuous stream of melody, running through the ages, to be tapped at various points.'[15] Although many scholars think of the musical Renaissance as starting early in the fifteenth century, with the important rhythmic and textural changes which took place at the time, it should be noted that to many French musicologists, the Renaissance in France does not

[15] Yates, *Academies*, pp. 43–45.

begin until the middle of the sixteenth century, when the humanistic movement in philosophy, literature, and music, with the idea about returning to the past, was beginning to be felt strongly.

All poetic and musical humanists were in favor of close union between poetry and music, although not all agreed as to how it should be achieved, or whether one should try to imitate the music of the Greeks, and if so, to what degree. Pierre Le Loyer, in his *Discours des spectres*, is against it. For one thing, he states that harmony of the voices and concerted music with instruments do not derive so much from the Greeks as from the Hebrews and Syrians. He reports on the effects produced by contemporary music, and concludes that it is not necessary to revive ancient effects. Pontus de Tyard, on the other hand, wanted to recapture these effects by means of chromatic and enharmonic genera.[16] Between the two were theorists such as Glarean and Mersenne, who found ancient music superior to modern music only in certain respects, and often found contemporary pieces more advanced than earlier ones.[17]

It was generally agreed that the literary text should be of utmost importance in a musical setting, that it should be heard clearly, and that its meters should be respected.[18] In that case, perhaps one could consider some of the pronouncements of church chapters in favor of good Latin prosody and psalmody antecedents of musical humanism. At any rate, concrete statements in France about the union of poetry and music came from Joachim du Bellay in his *Deffence et illustration de la langue française* (1549) in which he advises that odes be sung to the lute. Barthélemy Aneau, in *Quintil Horatian*, recommends the submission of music to the literary text. Ronsard, in the musical supplement to his *Amours* (1552) accepts four pieces on which all sonnets might be sung.

Many of the poetic texts chosen were of noble quality and by

[16] Walker, *Humanism*, pp. 10, 111, 118.
[17] Carruth, *Bertrand*, pp. 114–115.
[18] Not everyone in the sixteenth century thought that French metrics were exemplary. Bruno and Basilius Ammerbach, who came to Paris from Basel, were warned in a letter from their father not to elongate short syllables 'as it is done in France' (Pirro, *Enseignement*, pp. 47–48).

classic poets, such as Goudimel's setting of Horatian odes
(1555, lost), Jambe de Fer's similar collection, also lost,
Renvoysy's *Odes d'Anacreon* (1559), and Arcadelt's settings of
poems by Virgil, Martial, and Horace—or by contemporary
poets in imitation of the ancients, such as Clereau's version of
Ronsard's odes (1559). The most suitable sort of music was
homophony, with the domination of the upper voice, since it
made the text more understandable, and did not call as much
attention to itself as polyphony. Many four-voiced chansons of
the Attaingnant repertoire, as well as lute songs and Huguenot
psalms, corresponded to this ideal, although no one claimed
any humanistic aims for them at the time. With the advent of
the *Académie*, which followed closely the aims of Ronsard and
the Pléiade, but went a bit further, we find the application of
quantitative meters to French poetry and music, with the
length of the notes limited to two values—long and short, the
long being worth twice the short. This often resulted in
irregular metrical patterns impossible to place between
regular bar-lines in transcription. The homorhythmic style
was the only one accepted, for the sake of textual clarity. All
these methods, and other techniques meant to bring out the
expressive content of the text by musical means, served to
illustrate the attempted revival of the remote past, which may
have been the most significant contribution of the
Renaissance.[19]

Among the principal sources for music of the late fourteenth
and earlier fifteenth-century music are the Chantilly *MS. 564
(olim 1047)*, with its repertoire almost entirely secular; the Apt:
Trésor de Ste. Anne, *MS. 16 bis IV*, which contains music from
the court of the Avignon popes; Modena: Bibl. Estense, *MS.
a. M. 5. 24,* from shortly after 400; Turin: Bibl. naz. *MS. J II 9,*
the Cypriot-French anonymous corpus of religious and secular
music from *ca.* 1413–34; Bologna: Civico Museo Bibliografico
Musicale, *MS. Q 15 (ca.* 1430); Aosta: Seminario, MS. of sacred
music; and Oxford: Bodleian Library, *MS. Canonici misc. 213*
(ca. 1450). The Trent Codices include works from the second
half of the century.

The manuscripts which were written in the last third of the
fifteenth century and early sixteenth century are too numerous

[19] *See* Verchaly, *Métrique*, pp. 67–69, Levy, *Vaudeville*, pp. 194–195,
Carruth, *Bertrand*, pp. 114–115, and Yates, *Academies*.

to attempt to list here.[20] Some of the best-known polyphonic ones are the *Cordiforme*, Dijon, Copenhagen,[21] and Wolfenbüttel *chansonniers*, the Escorial (*MS. iv. a. 24*) and Montecassino (*MS. 871 N*) manuscripts, the Pixérécourt (Paris: Bibl. nat., *MS. fr. 15123*), Nivelle de la Chaussée (Paris: Bibl. G. Thibault), Laborde, and Mellon *chansonniers*. The latter two are housed in American libraries, the first at the Library of Congress, and the second at Yale University. Two collections from the Bibliothèque nationale, Paris—*MSS. fr. 9343* (Bayeux) and *12744* are noteworthy because they are the only examples of secular monophonic manuscripts. *MS. Pepys 1760* of Cambridge: Magdalene College, and the British Museum's *MS. Harley 5242* are transition collections which bridge the gap between the end of the fifteenth century and Attaingnant's first prints, after which the number of music manuscripts declined sharply. Exceptionally colorful manuscripts from the sixteenth century which include pieces by French composers are Bologna *Q 16*, the *Codex Medici*, and Cambrai: Bibl. de la Ville, *MS. 125–128 (olim 124)*, from 1542, which has recently been studied by George Diehl (dissertation, University of Pennsylvania).

From 1501 on, French music is to be found in Italian prints, such as those of Petrucci and Antico, and after 1528 chiefly in the prints of Attaingnant, Moderne, Du Chemin, and Le Roy et Ballard, for which we are fortunate to have excellent and complete bibliographies. French works also appear in minor French publications and in major foreign ones, mostly Italian and Belgian.

The composers who wrote music from the death of Machault until about the end of the first quarter of the fifteenth century include Tapissier, Carmen (authors of religious music exclusively) and Cesaris, who are praised by Martin Le Franc in his *Le Champion des dames*, Baude Cordier, Senleches, Loqueville, and Grenon. Their music, and even that of later composers, exhibit some traits that were already

---

[20] Reese (*Renaissance*, pp. 97–98) lists some of the most important ones; a fuller list can be compiled from his index, under 'manuscripts.' E. Droz, in *Jardin de Plaisance*, lists over sixty manuscripts.

[21] Kongelige Bibl., *MS. Thott 291[8]*, not to be confused with the sixteenth-century music manuscript from the same library (*GKS 1873*) which contains chansons and sacred works.

found in the mid fourteenth century, particularly in the works of Machault, but these features frequently undergo some modification. Masses, motets, and the *formes-fixes* (*ballade, virelai*, and *rondeau*) were still being used, but not quite in the same manner as before, and some of the genres practically disappear by the end of the fifteenth century. *Ballade* texts, which had traditionally been love-oriented, became also political or commemorative in nature. The *ballades* of Trebor and Solage, mentioned earlier, written in honor of Gaston Phébus and the duke of Berry, are examples of this trend. The treble-dominated style characteristic of fourteenth-century *ballades* was retained (with some exceptions such as in the occasional use of two canonic upper voices over a textless contratenor) and was transferred to other genres. Turn of the century Mass movements, for example, were often written with solo cantus over textless tenors and contratenors. The *ballade* structure itself, however, became more and more complex. Its length was frequently doubled and the refrain treated separately. Not all *ballades* were lengthened, of course; Hasprois's *Se mes deux yeux*, for example, is short and simple. The *ballade* began to take on some of the features of the old motet, such as the adoption of Latin texts at times (Lebertoul's *O mortalis homo/ O vos multi/ O pastores quibus*, for example, which is cast in *ballade* structure but has three different texts), and the setting of words occasioned by special events. Coloratura writing is still prevalent in *ballades* by Grenon and Hasprois—the older unorganized melisma as well as the more sequential type, with repetition of characteristic motifs.

The ballade was eventually to disappear, along with the *virelai* in its older polystrophic form. The *virelai* was sometimes reduced to one stanza, as in Grenon's *La plus belle et doulce figure*. This monostrophic *virelai* came to be called *bergerette* and was in use until the early years of the sixteenth century.

The *rondeau*, which was soon to supplant the other *formes-fixes*, expands into the *rondeau quatrain*, with a refrain of four lines, and the *rondeau cinquain*, with five. Eventually the free, presumably monostrophic chanson, with an unspecified number of lines, displaced all of these.

The motet becomes once again a predominantly sacred work, and its main language is Latin. The change was a gradual one, to be sure. Sacred and secular motets continued to exist side by side throughout the Renaissance. The occasional motets that were mentioned earlier are but a few examples of non-liturgical pieces. French texts were abandoned more and more in favor of Latin ones, derived largely from the Proper of the Mass and from the Psalms. Bilingual motet-chansons, such as Compère's *Royne du ciel/ Regina caeli*, which flourished in Josquin's time, were still printed later in the sixteenth century—Mouton's *Antequam comedam suspiro*, with *Je ris et si ay la lerme a l'œil* in the second tenor, in Attaingnant's eleventh book of motets (1535[3]) or Agricola's *Belle sur toutes, ma doulce amye*, with *Tota pulchra es* in the bassus, reprinted from *Canti C* in Attaingnant's forty-two three-part chansons (1529[4]), are examples—but they are no longer the norm by this time. Isorhythm eventually disappears from the motet's structure, by about the middle of the fifteenth century, although an element of it, the *color*, or repeated melodic pattern, has been suggested as the prototype of the basic element of the cyclical Mass.[22] An early example of a pre-existent tenor used with free rhythm rather than rigid isorhythm is found in a *Credo* by Jean François de Gembloux, based on the melody of the Marian antiphon *Alma redemptoris mater*.[23] Some three-part Latin motets from *ca.* 1440 to *ca.* 1490 are treble-dominated. They are sometimes called song-motets for their simple style, reminiscent of the chanson. The tenor-motet, however, with more than one text and a borrowed tenor in larger note values than the upper parts, is still prevalent throughout the fifteenth century at least. It is during this century that the tenor will move up from its position at the base of a composition to become an inner voice, although isolated examples of this feature could be found earlier, such as in the *Roman de Fauvel*. Before this was established, one could frequently find voice crossings between the two lower voices of a motet—and the fabrication of a special part, the

[22] Borren, *Etudes*, p. 73. Ficker (in *New Oxford*, III: p. 164) points out that after *ca.* 1430 the talea in motets was often replaced by free melodic variation, and that this influenced the cyclical mass, 'for the different sections now became "coloured" arrangements of one and the same *canto fermo*. Each Mass was thus a cycle of large-scale variations.'

[23] Bukofzer, *Fauxbourdon*, pp. 46–47.

solus tenor, which consisted of the lowest notes of the composition, regardless of which of the two lower parts contained it; by means of this combination, a given piece could be sung with one real bass part instead of two competing ones. An exception to this practice is found in the Cypriot-French repertory of the Turin manuscript. There all pieces are for four real parts and contain no *solus tenor*.[24]

A work which encompasses old and new traits is Carmen's motet *Pontifici decori speculi*, from *MS. Canonici 213*, with the two upper parts in canon and the two lower ones free, and isorhythm pervading the whole work. Reaney describes it as 'a true transition work, a cross between the isorhythmic and the cantilena motet.' He adds that 'even the strictly isorhythmic motets of Carmen prove that he leads definitely into the Dufay period proper by their use of the *solus tenor*, which is a sure sign that the idea of a combination-bass is present.'[25]

The polyphonic Mass was not an important part of early fifteenth-century music. Machaut's example of a complete setting of the Ordinary was not immediately followed. Isolated movements were set polyphonically, and sometimes pairs of movements. The cyclical Mass, whose various sections are linked thematically, and was probably first used in England by Leonel Power and Dunstable, is not found in France before the time of Dufay. Opinion is divided as to whether the paired movements constitute a preliminary step to the cyclical Mass. Bukofzer believes that they do; Schrade, however, finds that they are parallel manifestations rather than successive ones. Early Mass movements are often written in a note-against-note syllabic style, particularly in *Gloria* and *Credo* movements, which have a long literary text—as well as in treble-dominated style. Isorhythm and canonic imitation are not rare. A type of declamatory melody similar to *recto tono* psalmody is found in certain Mass movements by Hugo de Lantins and Loqueville.[26]

[24] Hoppin, *Cypriot* (edition), II: pp. ii–iii.   [25] Reaney, *Fifteenth*, I: p. iii.

[26] The best summaries of the music of the period between Machaut and Dufay are found in Reese, *Renaissance*, pp. 10–33, Hoppin, *Mass, Christmas*, and *Cypriot*, Schrade, in Roland-Manuel, *Histoire*, I: pp. 868–887, and the introductions to Apel, *Fourteenth*, and Reaney, *Fifteenth*. Other useful collections of music include Borren, *Polyphonia*, Marix, *Musiciens*, Stainer, *Dufay and his contemporaries*, and Hoppin, *Cypriot* (edition).

Apparently the various genres, sacred or secular, to which we shall return shortly, borrowed from each other in their strictly musical aspects. It cannot be said, for example, that treble-dominated music belongs exclusively to the *ballade*, or that music constructed upon a tenor is an attribute of religious music alone, although Aegidius de Murino, at the beginning of the fifteenth century, recognizes that this is the general trend when he prescribes that in the composition of motets one should first write the tenor, and in the composition of *ballades*, *rondeaux*, and *virelais*, one should first write the *discantus*, or upper voice.[27]

Melodic lines of the French Renaissance become progressively less angular than those of the preceding era, and the phrases are shorter. By the second quarter of the sixteenth century, phrases are more dominated by the literary text than before; they are short because the settings are often syllabic, and they come to a cadence point where the poetic line ends, regardless of whether or not an *enjambement* is present. Certain melodic turns characteristic of the fourteenth century, such as

which occurs several times in Machault's Mass and has been interpreted by Machabey to be a conscious unifying device (and by Bukofzer to be an uncharacteristic and inconspicuously placed formula), or variants thereof, can be found in several religious and secular works of the fifteenth century, including motets from the Cypriot-French Turin manuscript. The use of melodic motifs as a principle of construction becomes established in the fifteenth century. It can already be found in works of Johannes de Lymburgia and Arnold de Lantins, and in anonymous paired movements of the Turin manuscript.[28] The placement of the head-motif or similar melodic fragment at the beginning of several movements of a Mass is of course one way in which fifteenth-century composers unified Masses. They also used recurring melodic fragments for the same purpose, such as in Josquin's Mass on the *soggetto cavato La, sol, fa, re, mi*. But these *ostinato*

[27] Bukofzer, *Fauxbourdon*, p. 38.

[28] Borren, *Etudes*, pp. 92, 110–113, Bukofzer, *Studies*, pp. 219–222, and Hoppin, *Cypriot* (article), pp. 117–118.

melodies remain a nordic trait and are not transmitted to the mainstream of French music.[29] Short melodic fragments will become characteristic of the non-lyrical sixteenth-century chanson.

The so-called Burgundian cadence, with its melodic approach to the final tone in the upper voice from the lower minor third, which was used throughout the fifteenth century, gives way to the more tonal approach by way of the lower second (raised by the rules of *musica ficta*). Other types of cadences were in use too, and a particularly beautiful one from the turn of the century is the one found in *L'Amour de moy* and several other pieces from *MS. Harley 5242* of the British Museum:[30]

It is perhaps in rhythm that French Renaissance music underwent some of its most noticeable changes, in the direction of simplification. The newer music of the fifteenth century avoids frequent syncopation, irregular groupings, and polyrhythms of the late fourteenth century. Proportional notation was not abandoned; *hemiola* is found in much music of Dufay's generation, and rhythmic intricacies are present in much of Busnois's music, as well as in such pieces as Ockeghem's *Missa prolationum*, a double mensuration canon. But none of these are as complex as specimens of mannered notation such as those of Chantilly *MS. 564*. Meters such as ☉ (transcribed as $\frac{9}{4}$ or $\frac{9}{8}$) and ₵ ($\frac{6}{4}$ or $\frac{6}{8}$) become less usual after the first third of the fifteenth century, when the preferred meters seem to have been O|($\frac{3}{2}$ or $\frac{6}{4}$) and C. Occasionally the latter two appeared in alternation in religious music particularly. Towards the end of the century chansons were often notated in ₡, which originally had the significance of *tempus imperfectum diminutum*, with the beat on the breve instead of on the semibreve, and therefore represented acceleration in relation to the section of music that preceded it. By the sixteenth century, ₡ became practically the only meter used and had lost its implication of diminution. Triple meter is

[29] This was clearly stated by René Lenaerts at the Josquin Congress, 1971.

[30] Chaillon, *Françoise*, p. 17.

sometimes used in alternation with the more prevalent duple, in the course of a chanson, but rarely throughout a composition—with the exception of dance music.[31] Thus ternary meter, which had dominated music for several centuries, gave way to the binary, and intricate rhythmic patterns gave way to simpler ones in fast-moving pieces. In *musique mesurée* of the late sixteenth century, incidentally, one could not speak of binary or ternary meter, because the irregular quantitative patterns often defy normal barring of measures. This special current could be considered in a sense more rigid than *musique non-mesurée*, because the patterns are arbitrarily imposed, and at the same time more free, because they are not limited to one or two metrical schemes.

The dactylic beginning that one finds in countless chansons of the Attaingnant period and later (♩ ♪ ♪ ♩) seems to have been used to a degree in the later fifteenth century. The Petrucci chanson prints and *MS. Harley 5242* of the British Museum contain a number of examples. It was used here and there in works of Busnois and Caron among others, and occasionally even in fourteenth-century music. Machault has a few isolated examples, and so does Chantilly *564*. The second section of the anonymous *ballade Ma dame m'a congié douné* begins with a dactylic pattern in the upper voice on the words 'N'arai jamais.' A combination of simple lively rhythms on repeated tones, a frequent trait of the declamatory Parisian chanson of the sixteenth century, is found already in Binchois's four-voiced chanson *Filles a marier, ne vous mariez ja*, although this was rare among composers of his generation.[32]

The practice of slowing down the tempo within a section of a composition by lengthening the notes, to set apart important words, invocations, etc.—such as Machault used in the *Credo* of his Mass on the expression 'ex Maria Virgine'—is followed by Dufay's generation and later composers. Compère's *Missa Galeazescha* has chordal passages in long notes in several of the substitution motets, such as at the beginning of the *Loco Sanctus,* on the words 'O Maria' and in the Elevation motet, on 'Adoramus te, Christe.' In the *Sanctus* of his Nativity Mass, the same procedure occurs on the words 'Verbum caro factum

[31] Borren, *Etudes*, pp. 126–128.
[32] *See* Chaillon, *Françoise*, pp. 17–18, and Pirro, *Histoire*, p. 92.

est.' One finds this also in secular music, such as in Gardane's
O doulx regard, and Janequin's *L'Amour, la mort et la vie*.

In matters of texture, the dominant tendency from the late
Middle Ages to the end of the sixteenth century was a gradual
simplification of complex polyphony with independent
individual lines towards homogeneity of writing, until almost
perfect homorhythmic composition and even accompanied
monody are achieved. Once more, it cannot be said that one
type displaced the other totally, or that one was a logical
outgrowth of the other—only that the emphasis was changed.
Both types, the motet principle and the conductus principle,
existed long before the Renaissance, and sometimes within the
same composition, such as Machault's Mass, in which
melismatic movements are set in the first manner, and the
syllabic ones (*Gloria* and *Credo*) in a note-against-note style.

Nicole Grenon's short piece, *La plus jolie et la plus belle*, is an
early example of fifteenth-century simple texture, with its
homophonic (or quasi-homophonic) passages in dance-like
rhythm. By the mid-sixteenth century, with Certon's *Premier
livre de chansons* (1552) in the style of *vaudevilles*, which contains
short strophic, homophonic and syllabic pieces, composers
are openly and manifestedly cultivating the homorhythmic
genre that leads to *musique mesurée* and the *air de cour*. This
style, however, was cultivated earlier in harmonizations of the
Huguenot psalter and in secular music. Arcadelt had
published two strophic pieces in the new manner at the presses
of Attaingnant (1547[12]).[33] But earlier in the century composers
wrote chansons that were mostly or fully homorhythmic, such
as Lourdault's *Amours me trocte par la pance,* from Petrucci's
Canti B, Janequin's *Ce moys de may*, and Claudin's *Je n'ay point
plus d'affection*, from Attaingnant's repertoire.

An important homophonic technique which has been the
subject of many musicological controversies as to its definition
and origins is *fauxbourdon*—a method of harmonizing
plainchant written out in the upper voice, with a notated lower
part or tenor at the lower sixth, or occasionally at the octave,
by singing the unwritten middle part (contratenor) a fourth
below the highest voice and parallel with it. According to
Besseler, the first piece to contain the direction 'fauxbourdon'

[33] *See* Levy, *Vaudeville*.

is the Communion *Vos qui secuti estis*, the last section of Dufay's *Missa Sancti Jacobi* (*ca.* 1428), although Bukofzer has suggested that other composers, such as Binchois or Johannes de Lymburgia might have used this procedure before Dufay.[34] At any rate it originated in France in the early fifteenth century and was used throughout the Renaissance. The term has been used loosely to designate a succession of what would be called in modern terminology parallel $^6_3$ chords, although it might be more appropriate to call it 'fauxbourdon-influenced,' since all parts are written out.

It was in the fifteenth century that the contratenor part became transformed into a real bass part. Some contratenors, which Besseler (in *Bourdon und Fauxbourdon*) calls the 'deep-clef' variety because they have a lower range than the tenor (although they usually remain above it at cadence points), have been found mostly in secular works by Pierre Fontaine, Cesaris, and Dufay. A few song-motets by Dufay and a *Gloria* by Grossin also show this trait—as do several anonymous pieces, sacred and secular, in Turin: Bibl. naz., *MS. J. II. 9.* These contratenors serve alternately as bass and middle voices, with triadic figures passing from the top to the bottom of the large range, and frequent fourths and fifths as bass progressions. A later type of contratenor (*ca.* 1430–40) exhibits the same features but participates as the lowest voice in a double octave cadence. Hoppin believes that the earliest example of the 'deep-clef' contratenor may be in four pieces of the Cypriot-French manuscript, a Mass movement, a motet, and two *rondeaux*.[35]

It is difficult to determine whether polyphony or homophony was the dominant current at any given time except at extreme points of the Renaissance. Not only were both types of works written during the same period, but a vast majority of compositions show a judicious mixture of both elements. It is sometimes believed that strict canonic writing was one of the most important traits of fifteenth-century French music—particularly that of Ockeghem—whereas it was not. Certainly canons were never abandoned during the Renaissance, but they represented an older style of writing.

[34] Bukofzer, *Fauxbourdon*, pp. 33–37.
[35] Hoppin, *Cypriot* (article), pp. 118–124.

Guillaume Faugues's Missa *L'Homme armé*, which treats the tune canonically at the lower fifth in all four-part passages, is one of the earliest examples of a canon Mass.[36] What came to be developed more and more was a freer use of counterpoint in which only a portion of a voice-part is imitated in the other voices. Traces of this are found increasingly in the fifteenth century. A *Gloria* by Gembloux contains motifs which are imitated in three parts. Dufay's *Missa Ecce ancilla* includes successive entrances in three parts on the word 'confiteor;' this passage has been interpreted as an important step in what was to become systematic imitation.[37] Busnois is perhaps one of the oldest composers to have used free imitation in three voices more than sporadically, and in a variety of ways. Many of his chansons form an almost (but not entirely) canonic duet in the upper voices over a freer contratenor. A few have all three voices involved in points of imitation at the beginning of each new line of text. Some four-part chansons exhibit paired imitation.[38] This came to be used extensively by Josquin and his successors. Points of imitation, or polyphonic sections in which a melodic fragment connected with a small phrase of the literary text is treated imitatively, are also a distinctive feature of Josquin's music (and Compère's), in conjunction with other types of counterpoint and with homophonic passages.

The Fleming Gombert went even further in the use of non-canonic imitation by employing throughout a composition a process which has been called through-imitation, or pervading imitation, which leaves little or no room for other types of writing; the voices, with their dovetailed entrances, are constantly active and afford little opportunity for breathing; neither is much relief from polyphony provided for the listener. Hermann Finck was among those who approved of this multiplication of points of imitation and avoidance of pauses and clear-cut cadences, for he praises Gombert on that account in his *Practica Musica* (1556). Gombert, however, cannot by any stretch of the imagination be considered a Frenchman, and the thick polyphony which he uses,

[36] Reese, *Renaissance*, p. 111.
[37] Borren, *Etudes*, pp. 108, 152.
[38] Brooks, *Busnois*, pp. 138–140.

particularly in his motets, but also in some of his French chansons, did not take root in France—except insofar as music by Flemings was circulated by the French presses, and particularly by Le Roy et Ballard. French composers on the whole did not follow this nordic current and kept the lightness of touch and variety of polyphony shown by Josquin and his disciples. If any element shows an increase in use, it is lightness rather than thickness. Heavy polychoral music is not firmly established in France much before the end of the sixteenth century, though it was composed earlier.

In contrast to the *cantus firmus* technique and the *Missa choralis*, in which the borrowed material consists of a single line of music (regardless of whether it is used in long notes in the tenor, or in paraphrase in the discantus), the process that has come to be called the parody technique, which can be found in chansons as well as Masses, makes use of entire polyphonic sections from pre-existent compositions, in a reworked version.[39] Although sporadic examples of this method have been noted in Italian music of the late *trecento*, it is in French music of the fifteenth century that it begins to be applied to entire sections of Masses, such as Faugues's (or Ockeghem's) *Missa Le serviteur*, based on all voices of Dufay's chanson of the same name, and in Ockeghem's *Missa Fors seulement,* based on his own *rondeau, Fors seulement l'attente.* Masses by Obrecht, such as *Rosa playsant,* based on a composition attributed to several composers including Caron, are important milestones in the history of parody technique; this work is essentially a *cantus firmus* Mass, however, with occasional use of parody.[40] Another user of the parody technique, which was to become so important in the sixteenth century that it practically displaced some of the earlier techniques, is Compère. His *Missa Alles regrets*, based on Hayne de Ghizeghem's popular chanson, has been described as a 'singular combination of very advanced parody technique with traditional cantus firmus treatment,'

[39] Some slightly anachronistic chansons for three voices by Claude Gervaise (Attaingnant, 1550) use a combination of *cantus firmus* and parody technique. It is chiefly the superius of a model that is borrowed; the parody is limited to beginnings and ends of lines (*see* Bernstein, *Chansons*, pp. 197, 228–229).

[40] Reese, *Renaissance*, p. 113, 127.

which places the composer 'side by side with Obrecht as one of the first forerunners of the parody-mass composers of the 16th century.'[41]

Dissonant passing tones in the harmonic texture, such as consecutive seconds, which occur frequently in fourteenth-century music, tend to disappear in Renaissance music, and perfect consonances (fifth and octave) are interspersed with imperfect ones (thirds and sixths). The purity of the modes had long been altered by the use of accidentals, written and unwritten, at cadence points and elsewhere. Partial signatures, or the use of accidentals (usually b-flat) in some but not all of the parts of a composition, were common before the sixteenth century. There have been conflicting views (chiefly by Hoppin and Lowinsky) on these conflicting signatures and their significance. Possibly they show the use of more than one mode within the same piece; or the several possible cadences, including the Burgundian cadence with double leading tone (raised fourth and seventh degrees) and others produced by various modes, made the indication of a b-flat in some voices unnecessary, because these parts were not going to require one. Canonic imitation at the upper fifth of a piece notated with one flat in the signature made the flat superfluous in the signature of the upper part for the same reason.[42]

How universally and strictly *musica ficta* was applied is another controversial question. And this is not the place to try to resolve it. Convincing summaries of theoretical recommendations on the matter have been made by such scholars as Geneviève Thibault, Helen Hewitt, Edward Lowinsky, and Gaston Allaire. These additions of accidentals in performance have undoubtedly contributed to a disintegration of the modal system and its gradual transformation into tonality. At what point this took place is not easy to determine. Pieces that date from the fifteenth century and even earlier have been found to sound tonal to modern ears. Works such as Sermisy's *Tant que vivray* (1528) seem to be unequivocally in a major tonality, with dominant-tonic progressions. Other works of the same period have bass lines which progress in fourths and fifths, and therefore

[41] Finscher, in Compère, *Opera omnia*, I: pp. i–ii.
[42] *See* Hoppin, *Conflicting*, and Lowinsky, *Conflicting*.

suggest a harmonic bass—at least to us. This or that piece by Busnois or Josquin has been shown to be a prefiguration of the major-minor tonal system. All of this is undoubtedly true, but one should realize that describing these traits by means of a vocabulary which was developed much later is anachronistic, and that in theory at least, composers thought polyphonically and modally rather than harmonically and tonally. The rejoinder to this is often: 'Yes, but it is not the terminology of the theorists that counts, but what the composers heard; and they heard chords and tonal progressions the same as we do.' Considering the different explanations of a given piece of music made by different scholars of the twentieth century, each of whom seems to be convinced that everyone hears (or should hear) the same thing as he does, I will not presume to make any speculation about the ears of Renaissance listeners and what they heard in their music.

At any rate, however firmly major and minor tonality had been established in practice if not in name, theorists continued to speak of the modes and their modifications. But French Renaissance theorists are more often retrospective than ahead of their time. Glarean, to whom this description does not apply, extended the modal system to include those pieces which sound major and minor to us under the Ionian, Hypoionian, Aeolian, and Hypoaeolian modes. By the last third of the sixteenth century, the Ionian mode had come to be placed as the first (as in Zarlino) instead of the eleventh (as in Glarean)—which may show the importance attached to the sound of the major mode. It is this system that Claude Le Jeune uses in his posthumous *Octonaires de la vanité et inconstance du monde*, settings of thirty-six eight-line Huguenot poems by Chandieu—three for each of the twelve modes, which Pascal de L'Estocart had also set to music in 1582.[43] Le Jeune's *Dodécacorde* (1598), another Calvinist collection on poetry by Marot and Bèze, uses traditional melodies with accompaniments in the twelve modes.

It was in the second half of the sixteenth century that, under the influence of Italians such as Vicentino and humanistic ideas in general, French composers began to use chromatic progressions, chiefly in secular music, but also in some

[43] Reese, *Renaissance*, p. 377, 384.

religious works, by Guillaume Boni, Costeley, Le Jeune (who
may have been the first to use it in French Catholic church
music, in his motete *Nigra sum sed formosa*, 1565),[44] and
Caietain. Some chromaticism was not humanistic in origin,
and was simply the result of progressive transpositions of a
motif—which could already be found in the latter part of the
fifteenth century (as Lowinsky has shown in several studies), or
the transposition of a whole piece to a level requiring a
different signature. The Renaissance-oriented chromaticism
was of the type which looked back to the Greek genera for
inspiration, or which was used for coloristic or expressive
purposes, such as in late Italian madrigals.

One of the boldest experiments in French chromaticism is
Costeley's chanson *Seigneur Dieu ta pitié*, an isolated example of
its kind. It was written *ca.* 1558, but published in 1570, with
the octave divided into nineteen tones; thirds of tones are
considered not only for voices but for instruments, requiring
split keys. There was an attempt to use the Greek genera
in Baïf's *Académie*, and it has been suggested that Costeley,
who was connected with it, had a part in these experiments.
Claude Le Jeune, in such works as *Qu'est devenu ce bel oeil
vainqueur* and *Helas mon Dieu ton ire*, uses Greek chromatic
tetrachords as melodic material, which lead to daring
modern harmonies.[45]

Anthoine de Bertrand, who was also influenced by
Vicentino, tried to recapture the spirit of the Greek genera in
pieces from his settings of Ronsard's *Amours*, published in 1578
but possibly written earlier—particularly *Ces liens d'or* and *Je
suis tellement amoureux*, set in chromatic and enharmonic
modes. In a later edition he abandoned the quarter-tones,
which he had used in only one chanson, judging them im-
practical. Chromaticism he used throughout. Bertrand's
method did not necessarily involve a revival of the tetrachord
itself—only the selection of intervals from it, in order to
improve modern music. The composer lived in Toulouse,
where he frequented circles such as the *Académie de poésie* and the
humanistic milieu of Cardinal d'Armagnac. These men

---

[44] Lesure, in *New Oxford*, IV: p. 249.
[45] Levy, *Costeley*, p. 213–248.

contributed in their own way to the ideal of perfect union of poetry and music. Bertrand reported the use of an instrument especially built to accompany enharmonic music, and it has been suggested that possibly Toulouse was not the only French city to possess one.[46]

Perhaps one of the most important new trends in French Renaissance music was the increasing attention paid to the literary text and the efforts made to have it heard clearly. Josquin is one of the first composers to articulate the text reasonably clearly and respectfully in a consistent manner. The movement towards homophony and eventually accompanied monody had as its purpose to have the text well understood. This occurs in secular as well as in religious music—quite independently of the Council of Trent, which was to prescribe this aim for Catholic church music. Calvin shows, in his preface to the Genevan Psalter of 1542, that music is closely linked with prayer and can enhance the literary text; but it has to be subordinate to the word of God, which must be fully understood. The music helps to accomplish this. The idea is similar to some of the thoughts expressed by humanists such as Pontus de Tyard, except that these men do not discuss them within a religious context, whereas Calvin naturally does.

Specific word-painting, which one associates so often with the Italian madrigal, is present in a less developed form but still exists to a remarkable degree in French music. Black notes are sometimes used to portray sadness—such as in Josquin's déploration on Ockeghem's death, throughout the composition. We find it at the end of the sixteenth century in chansons by Anthoine de Bertrand. Daring dissonances and chromatic progressions for the purpose of musical depiction, however, are not the rule in France.

Finally it is during the Renaissance that a repertoire of idiomatic instrumental music emerges. We know, of course, that instruments could and did participate in any work that might also be sung. Works such as Dufay's *Gloria ad modum tubae*, with its canon at the unison in the two upper voices and an *ostinato* alternating between the two lower ones, forming the

[46] Carruth, *Bertrand*, p. 4–35, 129–140, 330.

instrumental-sounding interval of the fourth, suggest that perhaps there was an instrumental style that could be imitated. However, with the publication of an important corpus of music for keyboard, lute, and other instruments, with written-out ornamental figures, we have music that can hardly be duplicated by the human voice.

9

Musical genres
and their performance:
sacred, secular, vocal, instrumental

Roman Catholic church music in plainchant and polyphony
was the most usual type of religious music that could be heard
in the Renaissance. One could not speak of French Protestant
church music before some time during the sixteenth century.
It is not that Frenchmen had not protested against the
established church before that time—indeed they had—but
not enough to also found a distinctive musical movement that
was to become, under the Calvinists, an intrinsic part of the
new religion; but it was strong enough to lead eventually to a
counter-reformation in Catholic music. As for Jewish music,
we realize that it was the main source of Christian plainchant,
but during the Renaissance, not too many people seem to
have been aware of it. Specifically Jewish music must not have
been heard in many places in France, with the exception of the
Southern communities. We shall return to non-Catholic music
shortly.

The composition of polyphonic Masses gradually replaced
that of isolated Mass movements, and pairs of movements
although one finds archaic publications of an isolated
movement or two well into the sixteenth century—a *Credo* by
Maillard, or a *Kyrie* by Sermisy. Isolated *Introits, Offertories*
and *Graduals*—all sections of the Proper—are set polyphonically (mostly by Layolle) in Guaynard's *Contrapunctus*
(1528). A particular type of Mass fragment found in the
fifteenth century is the 'Credo de village.' Seven of them, by
Busnois, Josquin, and others, are published in Petrucci's
Fragmenta Missarum (1505[1]); three exist in manuscripts. All ten
are based on *Credo I* of the liturgy. Why they are designated as
'de village' no one is sure. Van den Borren points out that they
are hardly simple music geared to the level of a village choir;
on the contrary, they consist of highly refined polyphony,

which must have been performed on solemn occasions by *maîtrises* of important localities, such as *villages royaux*, or market towns which included a royal residence.[1]

Whereas most Masses came to have the Ordinary set polyphonically, but not the Proper, exceptional ones, plenary Masses, have sections of both parts included in the polyphony. Requiem Masses are of that type. Before the first known polyphonic Requiem Mass was written, however, plenary Masses existed. Reginald Liebert's *Missa De Beata Virgine*[2] is an example as is Dufay's *Missa Sancti Jacobi*. It has been noted that 'most cyclic settings of the Ordinary are not really Ordinaries. From the earliest of the cyclic Masses most chants which underpinned the music were taken from Propers.'[3]

Regardless of who wrote the first cyclical polyphonic Mass, the practice became prevalent on the Continent at the time of Dufay, whose first Mass in that style may have been the one on *Se la face ay pale*,[4] with the *cantus firmus* in long notes in the tenor. Polyphonic Masses were not the only ones or the first ones to use the cyclical principle. Some plainchant manuscripts were organized in cycles (rather than in groups of similar movements, such as a series of *Kyries*, or a series of *Glorias*, which was the usual arrangement) already in the Middle Ages. Hoppin shows that plainchant Masses from the Turin manuscript (*ca.* 1413–20) were also arranged in cycles and that they were 'not mere compilations of pre-existing chants, but were, rather, conceived and created as unified musical entities.' None of them are in the *Liber usualis*. All of them have unity of mode. Their presence in a predominantly

[1] Borren, *Enigme*, pp. 48–54.

[2] Reaney, *Fifteenth*, III: pp. ii–iii; transcription, pp. 64–94. The first polyphonic *Requiem* was probably written by Dufay, but it is not extant. The next one was by Ockeghem and consists of *Introit, Kyrie, Gradual, Tract,* and *Offertory.* The *Dies irae* did not become an established part of the *Requiem* Mass in France until the middle of the sixteenth century (Reese, *Renaissance*, p. 130). Others who wrote Requiem Masses in France include Prioris, Févin, Sermisy, Certon, and Mauduit.

[3] Crawford, *Masses*, p. 89.

[4] Planchart (*Dufay*, pp. 19–20) discusses the chronology and authenticity of some of Dufay's Masses; he believes that the true ancestors of his *cantus firmus* Masses may not be earlier Masses, but motets such as *Nuper rosarum flores*.

polyphonic source implies to Hoppin that they were regarded as a new addition to the plainchant repertory in which the five sections of the Ordinary were unified by musical means. These certainly antedate continental polyphonic cycles, though they were not necessarily their models. It is not impossible, however, that Dufay saw the Cypriot-French manuscript after Anne de Lusignan became duchess of Savoy in 1434. Cypriot origin is not claimed for the cyclical principle. 'More important is the evidence we now have that in the early fifteenth century, composers were writing true cyclic Masses, perhaps the most characteristic, and certainly the most astonishing musical contribution of the Renaissance.'[5] The Turin manuscript also contains a polyphonic cyclical Mass (lacking the *Agnus Dei*), which seems to have been added after the rest of the manuscript had been compiled. Although the date of the addition is not known, Hoppin considers that even if it were 1425, the melodic and harmonic writing would be archaic for the time. The Mass is unified both by repetitions of a tenor (said to be an English innovation), and by the suggestion of head-motives at the beginning of several sections (said to be a continental innovation, *ca.* 1425). It has been noted that, whereas English composers used plainchant melodies as *cantus firmi*, the anonymous Turin Mass has an unidentified tenor which is lively and dance-like, and 'seems suspiciously secular.' Although it is difficult to tell who first unified a Mass by means of a *cantus firmus*, we can only agree with Hoppin that 'a reliable history of continental music cannot be written without taking into account this [French] repertory from the court of Cyprus.'[6]

Van den Borren summarizes the importance of the cyclical mass by comparing it to a fresco which is substituted for a miniature and which makes it possible to put polyphony 'at the service of a work of art of ample dimensions, the realization of which requires the sense of grandeur and the spirit of synthesis.'[7]

The *cantus firmus* may not always have been very audible, since it was usually in the tenor voice—an inner part—and in

[5] Hoppin, *Mass*, pp. 85–91.
[6] Hoppin, *Cypriot* (article), pp. 123–125.
[7] Borren, *Etudes*, p. 120.

long notes, unless it was pounded by a brass instrument; therefore, a secular *cantus firmus* in a fifteenth-century Mass probably was not as objectionable and incongruous as might be expected. It was simply a compositional basis. The same cannot be said of the borrowed chanson material in many French parody Masses of the sixteenth century, by Claudin, Certon, or Janequin. There the original material appears with little distortion or reworking, and is fairly easy to follow. The typical French Mass of the sixteenth century is short and simple, mostly syllabic, with somewhat unorthodox Latin accentuation, and contains homorhythmic and freely imitative passages. The dactylic motif is found in many sections. The predominant number of voices is four, with passages for two and three parts, such as in the *Benedictus*, and for five parts, as in the *Agnus*.[8] Borrowed material is not limited to chansons; it also includes motets, and in the case of non-parody Masses, single lines of music. Some Masses quote from more than one source. Sermisy's *Missa plurium motetorum*, based on motets by Gascongne, Consilium, Févin, and others, has been claimed as the 'only mass of the Renaissance under that title, and [it] may well be the only Mass . . . composed on many motets.'[9] The same composer's *Missa plurium modulorum* includes material drawn from some of his own chansons.

Parody Masses were sometimes published with the motets on which they were based. Attaingnant's *Missarum . . . cum suis motetis* (1540²) is an example of this practice. It has been observed that in some of these Mass-motet pairs the motet may have been written later than the Mass; if this is so, the Mass, of course, is not necessarily of the parody variety. Crawford conjectures that Moulu's *Missa Stephane gloriose*, which seems to paraphrase several chants of the Proper of Saint Stephen, was not based on Layolle's motet *Stephanus autem plenus gratia*, which appears with it in a print by Moderne, and that when Layolle, who was the printer's musical adviser, prepared Moulu's Mass for publication, he may have tried to imitate it in a motet which he placed with it.[10]

Some Masses 'ad placitum' were not based on known pre-

[8] Allaire, *Masses*, pp. 47–51, and Lesure, *Religieuse*, p. 63.
[9] Allaire, *Masses*, pp. 152–60.
[10] Crawford, *Masses*, pp. 83–89.

existent material. Examples are those by Cadeac, Sermisy, and Le Jeune.

The Mass service was not always kept free of other forms, such as motets. From *ca.* 1500 it became customary to sing a motet during the transubstantiation, in honor of the Sacrament. Reese points out that this practice is related to Josquin's substitution of the first part of his motet *Tu solus qui facis mirabilia* for the *Benedictus* of his *Missa D'ung aultre amer,* and Pierre de la Rue's replacement of *Osanna I* in his *Missa de Sancta Anna* by his motet *O salutaris hostia.*[11]

The earlier mentioned *motetti missales (also known as loco* motet cycles, or substitution Masses), of which Compère wrote several during his stay in Milan, probably for Galeazzo Maria Sforza, are a series of motets which were substituted for certain sections of the Ordinary and Proper of the Mass, and designated as 'loco Introitus, loco Gloria,' etc. The texts of the *motetti missales* were usually centered on a general theme, such as the Blessed Virgin, or Christ, but were not related to the Mass texts they replaced, except in the case of Elevation motets. Compère's three cycles—*Missa Galeazzescha, Ave Domine Jesu Christe*, and *Hodie nobis de Virgine*—have all of their movements designated as 'loco,' unlike some of the cycles of other composers, which have only partial substitutions. This replacement of traditional texts was short-lived and does not seem to have influenced the course of the Mass in France.[12]

Motets, however, were used in addition to the normal Mass movements, particularly at the end of the Ordinary. Charles the Bold wrote a motet which was sung after Mass at Cambrai in 1460. Much later, in 1520, during the meeting between Francis I and Henry VIII at the Field of the Cloth of Gold, the Mass was concluded with the performance of several motets. It was also customary to interpolate motets during the Canon, either at the Elevation or immediately after it, or in place of sequences. Snow has shown that Mass-motet cycles were prevalent between 1440 and 1460, and that they may have been composed by Englishmen working on the Continent. They are considered to be experiments in the development

[11] Reese, *Renaissance*, pp. 245, 270.
[12] Noblitt, *Motetti*, pp. 1–15.

and expansion of the cyclic Mass Ordinary—though they did not enjoy widespread usage.[13]

Large-scale polyphonic pieces for the Offices, such as Passions (which are distinct from small motets on Passion texts), Lamentations, and Magnificats were written during the Renaissance. in 1438, Binchois received twenty-four *livres* for a book of 'Passions in the new style,' which have not survived.[14] These may antedate the first known English polyphonic Passions, from Brit. Mus.: *MS. Egerton 3307*, which may have been written towards the middle of the fifteenth century.[15] The sixteenth-century Passions show a change from the motet type, such as Longueval's Passion, to the dialogued dramatic type, such as Sermisy's and the other anonymous Passion from Attaingnant's tenth book of motets (1535[2]).

Dufay was among the first to set *Lamentations* polyphonically; other early settings were included in Montecassino *MS. N 871*, which also contained a lost Passion. Whether any of their composers were French we do not know, since they are not listed. Important settings of the Lamentations were written in the following century by Genet, Claudin, Cadeac, Phinot, and Leleu. Many of these contain significant passages that are homorhythmic.

The first known polyphonic Magnificat (incomplete) appears to be English, and may date from the fourteenth century.[16] On the Continent, Dufay and Binchois wrote several, with *fauxbourdon* passages. Busnois wrote at least one. At the time, the entire text was set polyphonically, although later on, alternate versicles were to be sung in plainchant. Numerous Magnificat settings were written in France in the sixteenth century—including those of Sermisy, Maillard, and Goudimel.

Other polyphonic music for the Offices includes hymns and antiphons—many of which were composed by Dufay, Binchois, and others of their generation. The earliest Vesper hymns of the fifteenth century are found in the Apt manuscript, which dates from *ca.* 1400 and must reflect the

[13] Snow, *Mass,* pp. 301–313.
[14] Marix, *Musiciens,* pp. xv, xvii.
[15] Reese, *Renaissance,* pp. 364.
[16] Kanazawa, *Vespers,* I: p. 12.

musical practice of the papal court of Avignon. These include a setting of *Sanctorum meritis* for three voices in note-against-note style. The same text had appeared with different music and meter, but also in a three-part chordal version, in Brit. Mus. *MS. Egerton 2615* (thirteenth century), and it has been suggested that this earlier version was the first polyphonic hymn for Vespers. The Apt hymns seem to have found no immediate successors, and it took some thirty years before more were to appear in North Italian manuscripts. Although the connection between the Apt repertory and Italy appears to be slight, one piece, *Iste confessor*, is shared by both Apt and Trent *MS. 87*, but with a new contratenor in the latter version. Among the first polyphonic psalm settings is Binchois's *In exitu Israel*.[17] In the sixteenth century, Attaingnant's ninth book of motets (1535[1]) is devoted to Latin psalms, and his twelfth (1535[4]) to Marian antiphons.

Motets are sometimes grouped according to certain church celebrations. Attaingnant's seventh book of motets (1534[9]), for example, has to do with the Nativity. Much earlier, in the Turin manuscript, nine motets, related to Advent antiphons but with no musical relationship to plainchant, which were presumably performed at the court of Cyprus, form what Hoppin calls 'a fifteenth-century Christmas Oratorio.'[18]

Motet publication became significant in the sixteenth century, beginning with Attaingnant's thirteen books of these compositions, and Moderne's nine. French motets are often based on plainchant melodies derived from psalms, antiphons, or sequences in all voices, and are treated in two or more successive sections. Like the French Mass, the motet, though it no longer combines chanson texts with a liturgical tenor, seems to show the influence of the chanson in its frequent use of dactylic meter and other rhythms, in its use of syllabism, and the attention given to proper accentuation of the literary text. Among the subjects treated in non-liturgical motets of the French Renaissance was music itself, as well as those who practiced the art. *Frequentatio*, the rhetorical practice of listing several varieties of a species—such as Molinet's enumerations of musical instruments, or Rabelais's list of

[17] *Ibid.*, pp. 6, 17–24, 91, 377.   [18] Hoppin, *Christmas*, pp. 41–48.

dance tunes, or dishes—is sometimes applied to composers. The best-known compositions in which this occurs are probably Josquin's *Deploration* for Ockeghem and Compère's *Omnium bonorum plena/ De tous biens plaine*, sometimes referred to as the singers' prayer to the Virgin. Other similar motets include Binchois's *Nove cantum melodie/ Tanti gaude germinis*, for the birth of Antoine of Burgundy, in which the composer names Fontaine, Foliot, and other musicians from the ducal chapel, and Moulu's *Mater floreat*, in which twenty-four composers from several generations sing the praises of the king and queen of France.[19] One might perhaps call these pieces catalogue motets, just as one refers to certain enumerative secular pieces as 'catalogue quodlibets.'

Latin religious publications by Frenchmen suffered a decline after 1570, although works by Flemings, such as Lassus, were issued. In 1583, Le Roy et Ballard printed the psalms and canticles sung at the Chapelle de la Congrégation by a confraternity of penitents. Some of the French manifestations of the Counter-Reformation will be mentioned after a few words about Protestant church music which prompted them.

Protestant music stems largely from plainchant, which was the source of several psalm melodies or psalm fragments, and from secular songs, which were used as *timbres* for contrafacta. The *Kyrie cunctipotens*, for example, served as melody for *Psalm 20* of the Huguenot Psalter (*Le Seigneur ta prière entende*) and *A solis ortus cardine* for *Psalm 31* (*J'ay mis en toy mon esperance*). Pidoux has shown that on the whole, the melodies of the Huguenot Psalter do not derive from a systematic adaptation of secular melodies, contrary to earlier theories.[20] A possible antecedent for the tune known in the English-speaking world as the 'Old Hundredth' and its French text, *Or sus, serviteurs du Seigneur*, has been suggested in the tenor of Binchois's *Veneremur Virginem* (a sequence from the Proper of the Mass *De Assumptione BMV*).[21]

The original repertoire of Calvinist Church music stemmed

[19] Marix, *Musiciens*, pp. 212–217, and Lowinsky, *Medici* (edition), III: no. 17.   [20] Pidoux, *Psautier*, I: p. xiii, and Honegger, *Pidoux*, p. 242.
[21] Parris, *Binchois*, pp. 55–56.

from Strasbourg, as we have seen earlier. The translations which Calvin made there were not retained in the definitive Geneva Psalter. As early as 1543, he himself replaced them with Marot's translations. Some of Marot's psalms were used in the Strasbourg Psalter of 1539. How they reached Calvin, no one knows. The translation for the definitive Genevan Psalter was completed by Théodore de Bèze.

Calvin had unkind things to say about music which aimed to please the ear only, such as polyphony in general: it was characteristic of Papists, those people who 'bray in a language unknown to the people, and often to themselves.' All this probably applied to music for the cult. There is reason to believe that Calvin tolerated polyphony outside of the church.[22]

It is undeniable that Loys Bourgeois had an important part in establishing the definitive melodies of the Huguenot Psalter. Although it was once believed that he was solely responsible for the codification of the Genevan melodies prior to 1562, and that his polyphonic edition of the *Cinquante Pseaulmes de David* (Lyon: Beringen, 1547) was the first polyphonic setting of Marot's psalms, it now appears that his contributions to the official Genevan Psalter are probably limited to the edition of 1551 (his preface to the fifty psalms of 1547 states that he kept the Genevan melodies intact and would seem to imply that a Genevan ecclesiastical music book existed prior to 1547, with melodies which he took over).[23] As for the polyphonic setting of Marot's psalms, Bourgeois is no longer considered its first author, since two books of Marot's psalms were published by Attaingnant in 1546, with the authorship attributed to Pierre Certon and Antoine de Mornable respectively.[24] Certon's psalms were transcribed for voice and lute by Guillaume

[22] Rokseth, *Chants*, pp. 11–20, Pidoux, *Psautier*, I: p. xvi, and Honegger, *Dictionnaire*, I: pp. 167–168.

[23] Pidoux, *Mornable*, pp. 190–198, and Teuber, *Psautier*, p. 114.

[24] They are nos. 142 and 143 in Heartz, *Attaingnant*; the author attributes the first to Certon and gives his reasons on p. 347. Pidoux (*Mornable*, pp. 179–198) on the other hand, ascribes both collections to Mornable. In 1546, Mornable was director of the chapel of Guy XVII de Laval, nephew of Anne de Montmorency and brother-in-law of Gaspard de Coligny, leader of the French Protestants. Pidoux (*Mornable*, p. 198) notes that in such a circle the psalms must have been greatly appreciated.

Morlaye (Paris: Fezandat, 1554). Other polyphonic settings of psalms in French include those by Janequin (dedicated to Catherine de' Medici), Arcadelt, Goudimel (in note-against-note style as well as motet style), Philibert Jambe de Fer (mostly on texts by Jean Poitevin), Richard Crassot,[25] Jean Servin, Claude Le Jeune, and Pascal de L'Estocart. Lesure mentions a mysterious collection, *Psalmes a 3 parties de Cottier*, listed in a catalogue from Plantin.[26] Not all of these composers were Protestants. Arcadelt was not. Certon and Janequin were Catholic churchmen all their lives. But then, psalms in French were not limited to the Huguenot cult. They were very much in vogue at the court of Francis I and his son. Clément Marot dedicated a manuscript copy of his thirty psalms to Francis I (possibly *MS. 3632* of the Bibliothèque de l'Arsenal, Paris).[27] Earlier than this, an inventory of the libraries at the court of Burgundy made in 1487 lists 'Sept saulnes en françois, historiées et couvertes d'un baldequin de soye verde doublée de satin noir. . . .'[28] These psalms in French were, of course, for private devotion and were not intended for the church service—as they were later used by the Huguenots. Psalms were translated into French by Baïf late in the sixteenth century; Courville and Mauduit were said to have set them to music. Although the Pléiade poets were Catholics, and Baïf's *Académie* was on the whole for the Counter-Reformation, it included Protestants, such as Claude Le Jeune, who was forced to flee to La Rochelle in 1590 on account of his beliefs. It was then that his friend Mauduit saved his manuscripts, including the *Dodécacorde*.[29]

French psalms were transcribed by Adrian Le Roy for a single voice with lute accompaniment, or for solo cittern. Again this was for private rather than liturgical use. A psalm was sung by a prisoner at the Bastille shortly before his

[25] Unlike Goudimel, Crassot apparently was not murdered on Saint Bartholomew's day 1572, as it was believed formerly, for Lesure (*Minor*, p. 540) locates him at the cathedral of Saint-Martin de Tours in 1581.

[26] Lesure, *Pidoux*, p. 243.

[27] Rokseth (*Chants*, p. 13) notes that Gastoué, in the catalogue of that library's music collection, ascribes the date 1527 to this manuscript without stating his reasons.

[28] Barrois, *Bibliothèque*, p. 289.   [29] Yates, *Academies*, pp. 66–75.

execution in 1559, and he accompanied himself on the lute.[30]

In addition to psalms, canticles, and various material for the cult, Huguenots sang other spiritual songs, some of which are of a rather polemic nature. Among the early Protestant sacred songs in French are the *Premier livre de chansons spirituelles* of Didier Lupi 2d (on texts by Guillaume Guéroult, Lyon: Beringen, 1548), who also set to music thirty psalms of Giles Daurigny, and Antoine de Hauville's *La lyre chrestienne* (Lyon: Gorlier, 1560), now lost. The same composer had also written two-voiced prayers to be sung before and after meals, which were inserted at the end of the volume of Crassot's psalms. Other spiritual compositions include collections by Jean Servin, Pascal de L'Estocart, and Claude Le Jeune.[31]

Many religious texts were not set to polyphony, but were sung to pre-existent *timbres*, presumably in a monophonic version.[32] An outstanding collection of these poems is Eustorg de Beaulieu's *Chrestienne resjouyssance* (1546).[33] Many of these popular texts are anonymous, and they are directed against various aspects of Catholicism. A particularly colorful one, to be sung to the tune of *C'est a grant tort que moy povrette endure* (probably Claudin de Sermisy's musical version) is entitled *Chanson nouvelle de la messe desespérée et enragée voyant approcher sa fin et horrible ruyne*. This attack on the Mass begins with the verse 'C'est à grand tort que moy, messe, tant dure,' which is made to rhyme with 'ordure.'[34] It is only fair to add that these expressions of opinion had their counterpart in the Catholic popular repertoire. In the song 'Quatre grosses bestes/ Font un Huguenot,' for example, Calvin, Luther, Marot, and Bèze

[30] Lesure, *Musicians*, p. 52.

[31] Honegger (*Pidoux*, p. 239) mentions in addition Pierre de Courcelle's *Cantique des Cantiques de Salomon et Lamentation de Jérémie* (Paris, 1564). It has been noted by G. Dottin (*Janequin*, p. 133) that a few of Janequin's abnormally austere spiritual songs, such as *Doulens regretz* and *En la prison*, seem to foreshadow L'Estocart's *Octonnaires*.

[32] The practice of adapting religious words to a secular tune—or pre-existent polyphonic composition—was not limited to Calvinist music, needless to say. The *sainctes chansonnettes* of Busnois and others of his time were Catholic examples of the same idea. (*See* Reese, *Renaissance*, pp. 89, 107, 110.)

[33] *See* Bridgman, *Beaulieu*, for details on this staunch believer.

[34] The text is given in Barbier, *Histoire*, I: pp. 98–100, and in H. Bordier's edition of the Huguenot *chansonnier*.

are irreverently compared to various anatomical portions.[35]

Huguenots were not always allowed to sing their songs in public. Many specific popular pieces were proscribed in the ecclesiastical province of Toulouse in the mid-sixteenth century.[36] Prohibitions were often ineffective, however, as we can see from the following account of Huguenot psalm-singing in the provinces, given by a citizen of Bourges:

> Since the beginning of April 1559 and throughout the following summer, large groups of people sang the Psalms of David every night, on feast days as well as on working days, at the place called Pretz Fichault; and every night innumerable persons, men as well as women, gathered there and sang the psalms most melodiously. Several interdictions were made by public proclamation, to the effect that the psalms were no longer to be sung, under penalty of hanging; and a gallows was raised in the middle of the Pretz Fichault. . . . In spite of everything that was said above, however, the singing at the said place did not cease all summer long.[37]

Catholic manifestations, musical and other, had their counterpart among the Huguenots, and vice versa. Just as Goudimel was killed by the Catholics in Lyon (1572), Anthoine de Bertrand met the same fate at the hands of the Protestants in Toulouse, several years later, as a result of the religious conflicts there.[38] Yet in spite of these struggles, many persons in France were working to promote unity between Catholics and Protestants. Catherine de' Medici herself wanted, at one time, to unite all factions under the crown. Cardinal de Lorraine, though a member of the house of

---

[35] Barbier, *op. cit.*, from Paris: Bibl. de l'Arsenal, *MS. 3118*.

[36] Fréville, *Index*.   [37] Lesure, *Pidoux*, p. 243.

[38] Vaccaro, *Bertrand*, p. 43. The author suggests that Bertrand was killed because he had set to music ecclesiastical hymns in French; these included songs about the Virgin, the saints, and the Eucharist, which were anti-Reformation in spirit. Toulouse was an important center of the Counter-Reformation, under the influence of the Jesuits and Cardinal d'Armagnac. The movement promoted conversions, charitable works, and confraternities of penitents.

Guise, wanted to influence the Council of Trent on the lines of tolerance. The Council proceeded differently, of course; yet its decrees were not officially accepted at the Parlement, or the Sorbonne, or the royal household. Jean de Montluc, bishop of Valence, preached against violence and for unity in 1560, at Fontainebleau. In 1561 a national meeting was held at Poissy for the same purpose. Ronsard, who approved of these ideas, as did his fellow poets from the Pléiade, attended the unsuccessful colloquium.[39]

A suggestion was made to Pope Pius IV in the name of Charles IX and his mother, probably by Jean de Montluc, that psalms in French be sung in Catholic churches. The latter had already been in favor of French psalms at court, to replace 'wild songs.' The French delegation to the Council of Trent proposed the singing of French psalms during Mass and at other times. It may have been during his stay in Trent in 1562 that Baïf was inspired to write measured psalms in French for use outside the church, in order to counteract the Huguenot psalms peacefully.[40]

A musical aspect of the Counter-Reformation in France in the later sixteenth century was the writing of spiritual songs in French by Catholics. The movement was encouraged by Le Roy and Ballard. Among the favorite texts set to music by such composers as Guillaume Boni and Jean Planson were the quatrains of Guy du Faur de Pibrac. Psalm translations and other spiritual texts by Philippe Desportes were used by Denis Caignet and Anthoine de Bertrand. Although opinion was divided about how beneficial French sacred texts were to Catholics—and even among Jesuits, who on the whole promoted the trend—they were liked by most people. Sainte Jeanne de Chantal (1572–1641), founder of the Order of the Visitation, before entering the convent, used to carry with her a volume of Desportes's French psalms 'when she went across the fields on horseback, so as to be able to sing along the road.' They had been recommended to her by Saint François de Sales.[41]

Father Auger, confessor of Henry III, encouraged such

[39] Yates, *Academies*, pp. 199–205.
[40] *Ibid.*, pp. 76, 201–209.
[41] Brenet, *Couvents*, p. 12, and Verchaly, *Desportes*, p. 290.

Counter-Reformation manifestations as the religious processions mentioned earlier. He did not, however, promote
the singing of French psalms in church. He and many of his
fellow Jesuits, who were very devoted to the pope, advocated a
liturgy in keeping with Roman use and free from Gallican
peculiarities.[42] Psalm singing outside the church was another
matter. The question of their suitability led to some polemics,
but in the first decade of the seventeenth century, the Jesuit
Michel Coyssard, author of a *Traicté du profit que toute personne
tire de chanter en la Doctrine Chrestienne et ailleurs les hymnes et
chansons spirituelles en vulgaire et du mal qu'apportent les lascives et
hérétiques, controuvées de Satan*, notes that if one were to condemn
psalms in French, one would have to condemn many
Catholics, including theologians from the Sorbonne, who
allowed their printing.[43]

Rules formulated between 1576 and 1587 for a Parisian
Jesuit college give attention to the role of instruments and
polyphony in religious music. Works with too much musical
development and repetition of words are forbidden. In this
category are included Masses and motets of Lassus. Motets in
general are not permitted, except by permission of the rector.
In their place is prescribed an antiphon to the Virgin with
fauxbourdon. Sacred works are not to be sung to light secular
tunes.[44]

In matters of liturgy, the *Pontificale Romanum* of 1596, with
mensuration applied to plainchant, became the model for
similar French publications, although Roman use was not
immediately accepted in all of France. Michel Huglo has given

[42] Deslandes, *Auger*, pp. 35–36. The author sees Auger as the precursor
of Dom Guéranger, who was to promote a return to Roman liturgy and
Roman pronunciation of Latin.

[43] Verchaly, *Desportes*, p. 288. Father Coyssard's *Hymnes sacrez* included
French paraphrases of the *Credo* (which Virgile Le Blanc set for four voices
in 1592), *Pange lingua,* and other liturgical pieces; and Lesure (*New Oxford,*
IV: p. 251) suggests that they may have been sung to plainchant melodies.

[44] Paris, Bibl. nat., *MS. lat. 10989. See* Lesure, in *New Oxford,* IV: pp.
250–252, and *Religieuse*, pp. 71–72. Other examples of homorhythmic
settings of plainchant include the *Magnificat* in the eight tones, and *In exitu*
in Laurens Dandin's *Instruction pour apprendre à chanter à quatre parties selon le
plain chant les pseaumes et cantiques* (1582), and Le Longis's *Nouveaux cantiques
spirituels* (1587).

a convincing example of this in his study of Du Caurroy's *Missa pro defunctis* (published in 1606 but written about 1590). This work contains several textual and melodic variants from the Roman rite. They agree, however, with Parisian practice of the time. The absence of a polyphonic *Dies irae*, although the sequence was admitted in several French churches at the time, and was well-known in Paris (it was included in the Missal of Sens, printed in Paris in 1529), is explained by the fact that it was not yet part of the official liturgy of the Parisian church.[45] Also meeting with the approval of the Jesuits were sacred dramatic presentations with music, such as the *Céciliade* (1606), with four-part homophonic choruses by Abraham Blondet.[46]

All these manifestations of the Counter-Reformation led to the intense mysticism of the French Catholic church in the early seventeenth century.

One hears little about Jewish music in France during the Renaissance.[47] Few Jews lived there, since their expulsion at the end of the fourteenth century, and again in 1501, in the case of the Provençal Jews, following the annexation of Provence to the crown in the latter part of the fifteenth century.[48] The most important Jewish community was in the papal territories of Avignon and the Comtat Venaissin, where it maintained itself continuously from the Middle Ages to the French Revolution.

Thomas Platter, a student from Basel who visited Avignon in 1599, describes the morning service at the synagogue and notes that the faithful sing prayers 'and often drawl on a single word for a half hour and even a full hour.' Outside of the synagogue, music was part of various festivities, such as wedding banquets. Local authorities drafted statutes which set limits on the frequency of these affairs and the number of

[45] Huglo, *Requiem*, pp. 201–206.

[46] Lesure, *Religieuse*, p. 72.

[47] Adler (*Pratique*, p. 34) states that *MS. 4096b*, E. N. Adler Collection of the Jewish Theological Seminary in New York, which contains religious poetry with neumatic notation (twelfth to fourteenth centuries) may be of French origin.

[48] Maître Petit, in his funeral oration for Anne of Brittany, praised the queen for her services to the church. 'After having worked towards the expulsion of the Jews, she had a large number of them baptized and had given them pensions' (Fouché, *Grandioses*, p. 264).

participating guests. One such ruling from 1490 in the Comtat Venaissin allowed for only eight persons at circumcision dinners. Still, many of these receptions were far from austere. Platter reports that wedding festivities ordinarily lasted for eight days. One of them, which he attended, included singing and dancing of gaillardes and branles—without stringed instruments.

Instrumental music, though often frowned upon, was often performed. Statutes of 1558 at Avignon forbid the presentation of farces and dances 'with instruments or drum' during Holy Week, unless one had obtained permission from the authorities. This has been interpreted as an effort to maintain good relations with the Christian neighbors.[49]

French secular music of the Renaissance shows a gradual division of labor between poet and musician. Persons such as Guillaume de Machault, or the trouvères and troubadours before him, who wrote both words and music are becoming the exception rather than the rule. Busnois undoubtedly wrote his own poems. It has been suggested that Gilles Mureau and Hayne de Ghizeghem may have done the same.[50] Jean Molinet is known to have composed some music (*Tart ara mon cueur*, for example), but was far better known as a poet, chronicler, and historiographer. His friend Compère mentions him in his *Omnium bonorum plena*. It is Jean Rollin's thesis that Clément Marot probably composed music to his own chansons,[51] but it is difficult to find evidence to support this. Jean Servin's acrostic on his own name, in his *Meslange* (Lyon, 1578), which is written in the first person and gives a clue to his character (it states that he likes good men and dislikes bad ones), implies that the composer was the author of the words.

In spite of this distinction between poet and musician in the majority of instances, writers had a high regard for music and composers, and often alluded to them in their works. Humanistic poets such as Ronsard and Baïf actively sought the

[49] Adler, *Pratique*, pp. 159–160.

[50] Reese, *Renaissance*, p. 99, on Ghizeghem. Droz (*Poètes*, pp. 9, 43–48) points out that Mureau's name appears in acrostic in the chanson *Grace attendant ou la mort pour tous mes*, and infers from this that the composer was also the poet of the piece. It is probably true, although it is not impossible that someone else wrote the poem in honor of Mureau.

[51] Rollin, *Marot*.

collaboration of musicians in an effort to achieve unified works of art in the manner of the ancients. Even without such ideals in mind, however, poets invited composers to set their works to music by labeling some of their poems 'chansons.'[52]

That poetry and music were closely allied was recognized long before the age of humanism. Johannes de Garlandia considered poetry a type of music, and Machault's nephew, Eustache Deschamps (*L'Art de dictier*, 1392) found that poetry was best when sung. 'Musique naturelle,' which was reserved for an elite—i.e., persons naturally inclined to learn it—Deschamps defines as 'musique de bouche en proférant paroles métrifiées, aucunefois en laiz, an balades, autrefois en rondeaulx cengles et doubles, et en chançons baladées.' As for Molinet, he defines rhetoric as 'une espèce de musique richmique.'[53] Long lists of instruments which appear in literary works, such as Molinet's *Le Naufrage de la pucelle*, and *Le Trosne d'honneur*, foreshadow the enumeration of composers and musical works in Rabelais. The latter author (or whoever wrote the fifth book of *Pantagruel*), however, places his allusions in a much more cheerful context than the *rhétoriqueurs*. Composers from several generations are portrayed as picnickers singing a song with double meanings which is not listed in music bibliographies. *Plus ne peut musique son secret taire*, from Chantilly *564* uses music as its subject. Tributes to musicians, or to music patrons, by poets were not infrequent. Random examples include Busnois's musico-poetic homages to Jacqueline d'Hacqueville.[54] His motet

[52] Defaux (*Charles*, pp. 232, 241) maintains that there is a structural difference between the pure *rondeaux* of Charles d'Orléans and those which he designates as *chansons* in Paris: Bibl. nat., *MS. fr. 25458*. The literary *rondeau* may have an interior refrain of only one verse, whereas the *rondeau* labeled 'chanson' must have more, so as to allow for the prescribed musical repetition. The author sees the first type as strictly poetic ('the poetry of secret') and the other as musical, decorative, and courtly.

[53] Quoted in MacClintock, *Molinet*, pp. 112–113, 120. See also Shipp, *Lorraine*, p. 70.

[54] Two of the pieces, *A vous sans autre me viens rendre* and *Je ne puis vivre*, form acrostics, and *A que ville et abhominable* is a pun on the lady's name. (*See* Droz, *Chansonniers*.) Fifteenth-century poems often contained acrostics, most of which were respectable. A notable exception is the acrostic of the following *rondeau cinquain* with music by Hugo de de Lantins (Oxford: Bodleian, *MS. Canonici 213*, fol. 46vo; transcribed in Borren, *Pièces*, pp.

to Saint Anthony contains references to his own name. Molinet, in a letter to the composer, uses rhymes in *bus* and *nois* exclusively.[55] The Bayeux manuscript (Paris: Bibl. nat., *MS. fr. 9346*) bears the name of Charles de Bourbon in acrostic.[56] Charles Edinthon, of Scottish origin, lutenist to Henry II, was honored in a sonnet by Ronsard, and mentioned in an elegy on the death of another lutenist, Charles Duverdier, by César de Nostradame (1555–1629), son of the famous astrologer. The elegy also praises Francesco da Milano and Valentin Bakfark, who had performed in France.[57] In 1585, Etienne Pasquier wrote a Latin epigram on the collaboration between Baïf and Claude Le Jeune.[58] A sonnet by Remy Belleau and two by Baïf were composed in honor of Guillaume Costeley.[59] Jean Servin's second book of chansons (Lyon: Pesnot, 1578), which is dedicated to Henri de la Tour, contains an anagram on that gentleman's name ('Adroit en l'heur' in the piece *Heureux celui qui porte humaine face*).

Formalistic literary devices sometimes have their musical

48–49). In reading the three words of the acrostic, one must bear in mind that *V* is the equivalent of *U*, and *J* of *I*:

> Plaindre m'estuet de ma damme jolye
> Vers tous amans qui par sa courtoisie
> Tout m'a failly sa foy qu'avoit promis
> Aultre de moy, tant que seroye vis,
> Jamais changier ne devoit en sa vie.
>
> Ne scay comment elle a fait departie;
> De moy certes ne le cuidesse mye
> En tel deffault trouver, ce m'estoit vis.
>   Plaindre . . .
>
> Mais je scay bien que ja merancolie
> Et moy n'ara pour y ceste folye;
> Renouveler volray malgré son vis
> D'aultre damme dont mon cuer est souspris,
> Et renuncier de tout sa compaignye.
>   Plaindre . . .

[55] Borren, *Etudes*, p. 241, and Pirro, *Histoire*, p. 119.
[56] Chaillon, *Louis XII*, p. 68.
[57] Haraszti, *Bakfark*, pp. 170–171.
[58] Levy, *Le Jeune*, p. 14.
[59] Godt, *Costeley*, I: pp. 33, 36–37.

counterpart; retrograde verse, or palindrome, for example, presents parallels with retrograde canon.[60] Busnois's *J'ay pris amours tout au rebours* illustrates the meaning of the last part of the verse by using the cantus of the well-known chanson *J'ay pris amours a ma devise* in the tenor, in free inversion.[61] The analogy between the poetry and the music is not unlike that found in Machault's *Ma fin est mon commencement*, or Arcadelt's (or Maillard's) *Tout au rebours de mon affaire* (see example, pp. 198ff).

Among the poets whose works were set to music in the fifteenth century were Alain Chartier, Christine de Pisan, Molinet, and Jean Lemaire de Belges. Poets from nobility include Charles d'Orléans, Jean II duke of Bourbon, and Jacques, son of Louis, duke of Savoy and Anne de Lusignan of Cyprus; Jacques is the author of *En tous les lieux*, which was set to music by Busnois. In the following century, some of the fashionable poets were Clément Marot, some twenty-two of whose texts were set by Claudin de Sermisy alone, Mellin de Saint-Gelays, Francis I, and Marguerite of Navarre. Ronsard's ideas on the union between poetry and music were put into practice on his part by using strophic regularity and alternation between masculine and feminine rhymes in non-quantitative verse, and were illustrated by the musical supplement to his *Amours* (1552), with ten pieces for four voices by Muret, Certon, Goudimel, and also by Janequin, of an older generation.[62] Two months earlier, Ronsard's ode, *Ma petite colombelle*, had appeared in Du Chemin's *Dixiesme livre* (1552⁴), with music by Muret. Later on, the poet was to have volumes of music devoted entirely to his works. His composers included not only Frenchmen, such as Boni, Bertrand, and Cleaeau, but Flemings such as Lassus and Philippe de Monte. Other poets of the Pléiade also provided poetry for chansons. Baïf's quantitative verse gave rise to the well-known *musique mesurée* movement. Maurice Scève's somewhat obscure poetry was favored chiefly in the Lyon circle. Seventy-four of Desportes's secular poems were set to music from 1569 to 1650 by La Grotte, Costeley, Caietain, Maletty, Le Blanc, Le Jeune,

[60] Maniates, *Mannerism*, p. 283.

[61] Hewitt, *Odhecaton*, no. 39, and commentary, pp. 99–100.

[62] It has been noted (Lesure, *Musicians*, p. 56) that Ronsard seemed to take the lute of his time for the equivalent of the lyre of the ancients.

TOUT AU REBOURS*

* Attaingnant, 1548³, fol. 6ᵛ–7ʳ (attrib. to Arcadelt); Paris: Bibl. nat., *Rés. Vma. MS. 851*, p. 508 (attrib. to Maillard).

Bertrand, and others. They include a *Complainte pour le roi Henri III (Lieux de moy tant aimez)*.[63]

Musicians usually selected works by contemporary poets for their chansons. Only exceptionally did they turn to the immediate past for inspiration. Lassus, for example, used a text by Villon, and Sermisy chose two fifteenth-century poems, *N'arai-je jamais mieux*, and *J'ay prins amours*; the latter seems to have been so out of date at the time, that the printer, who perhaps did not recognize it, transformed it into *J'ay prins a aymer*. Translations and adaptations of Petrarch became fashionable in the first third of the sixteenth century and were sometimes set to music. Sermisy's *Allez souspirs* is such an example. Some chanson collections include settings of Italian texts, such as Janequin's *Si come il chiaro*, or dialect texts, such as Le Jeune's *Villageoise de Gascogne*.

The structure of fifteenth-century music was on the whole dependent upon poetic *formes-fixes*, with the predominance of the *rondeau (quatrain* or *cinquain)*. Also used were the *ballade* and occasionally the *virelai*. The latter was not as prevalent as the other two types, but lingered on in the late Burgundian *bergerette*, which is essentially a monostrophic *virelai*. The *bergerette*, however, did not last much longer than to about 1500. It is also towards the turn of the century that a modification of the *ballade* occurs, with one strophe instead of three, and the omission of the *envoi*. Josquin occasionally uses this type of *ballade*, which is found again in the works of Marot.[64] Some composers used the *formes-fixes* more than others who lived at the same time. Ockeghem's favorite poets were the *rhétoriqueurs*, who produced *formes-fixes*. Josquin, on the other hand, avoided these genres most of the time.

The sixteenth century saw the decline of the old *formes-fixes* and the vogue of free types of chanson texts, such as *quatrain*, *cinquain*, and *huitain*. Chansons had been set to free texts long before the sixteenth century, but not as frequently as afterwards. Du Bellay, in his *Deffense et illustration de la langue française* (1549) refers to the old *rondeaux, ballades, virelais*, and

---

[63] *See* Verchaly, *Desportes*, pp. 271, 279, 340.

[64] *See* Hewitt, *Odhecaton*, Droz, *Chansonniers*, Reese, *Renaissance*, and Baird, *Changes*, for discussions of literary texts as applied to music.

the like as *épisseries* (groceries) 'which corrupt the taste of our tongue and serve no end but to testify to our ignorance,' whereas Jacques Tahureau, writing about the same time, compares them to rusty old ironwork (*vieille quinquaille rouillée*).[65]

Sonnets came into vogue chiefly in the second half of the century, with Ronsard as their most famous exponent. Musical settings of sonnets, by Boni, Bertrand, and many others, were sometimes schematic, and mostly through-composed. Claude Le Jeune, for example, always set them in the second manner.[66] A special category of sonnets which was prevalent in France as well as Italy during the sixteenth century featured the exclamation 'o' more than normally. The prototype for this genre seems to have been Petrarch's *O passi sparsi* in a translation from the 1530s by Marot, and one of the extreme examples is Claude de Pontoux's *O triste chants, o reveils et aubades/ O folle empris, o pensers reperdez . . .* (Lyon, 1579).[67]

The early fifteenth-century chanson repertoire is often characterized by the domination of the treble voice in a light ornamental melody provided with a text, over an independent tenor and contratenor—both textless. Passing dissonances are frequent, and the meter is mostly ternary. The rhythm is relatively clear, in spite of more than occasional use of *hemiola*. In the second half of the century, the upper voice is still important, but not more so than the tenor. Pieces featuring this trait are said to show the discant-tenor technique. The contratenor becomes less individual than before and often serves as a quasi-harmonic 'filler.' Dissonances are fewer and the lower parts seem somehow more singable than before. The meter becomes predominantly binary, although certain pieces contain ternary sections. Perhaps the most marked change is the progressive use of free non-systematic imitation. As the imitation is used at narrower distances, it can detract from the rhythmic clarity of a piece. The pervading imitation which will become prevalent in the more nordic type of sixteenth-century music is hinted at in some mid fifteenth-century compositions, in all three voices. Canons were used in chansons as early as Dufay's time, and also in Josquin's, as we

[65] Levy, *Le Jeune*, p. 159.
[66] *Ibid.*, p. 197.   [67] *Ibid.*, p. 203.

can see from such collections as Petrucci's prints. Fast-moving syllabic settings are more frequent in later music than in the earlier period. The same is true of word repetition, and it has been noted that passages such as 'mary, mary' and 'pendu, pendu,' from Dufay's *La belle se siet* are rare for their time.[68] In sixteenth-century programmatic chansons, on the other hand, such procedures are the rule. Other traits, such as *ochetus*-like (hocket-like) writing for comic effects are foreshadowed in such a late fifteenth-century work as Compère's *L'autre jour*.[69] The *ochetus* in paired voices on repeated notes, which occurs occurs on the exclamation 'hé,' is similar in many ways to Sermisy's treatment of 'ha' several years later, in *Hari, bouriquet*.

The chansons of the earlier sixteenth century are on the whole shorter and lighter than those of the preceding era—though certain composers, such as Sermisy, are able to write in a lyrical vein. Musical phrases are usually parallel to verses of text, with cadence points occurring at the end of a line of poetry, regardless of whether or not it contains an *enjambement*. Entire lines can be repeated. By this time, most chansons consist of four real parts. Of course there had been four-voiced chansons earlier, but many of them were essentially conceived for three parts, with the fourth to be sung 'si placet.' Reminiscent of this old practice is Hesdin's *Plaindre l'ennuy de la peine estimée* (Attaingnant, 1538[10]) for four voices and a fifth one in canon at the unison with the contratenor. The piece bears the indication 'A quatre chantez, A cinq si voulez.'[70] Occasionally a composer adds a voice to a pre-existent chanson—as Verdelot did to Janequin's *La Guerre*, or Le Jeune to the same composer's *L'alouette* and *Le rossignol*. Le Jeune added more than a voice, however, and included new sections among the old material.[71]

Paraphrase or parody chansons were not uncommon during both centuries of the Renaissance. The borrowed material could apply to literary text or music, or both. *Ma bouche plaint les pleurs de ma pensée* was based on Ockeghem's *Ma*

[68] Borren, *Etudes*, p. 138.
[69] Finscher, *Compère*, p. 242.
[70] Transcribed in Lesure, *Anthologie*, pp. 42–43.
[71] *See* Levy, *Le Jeune*, p. 136.

bouche rit. J'ay pris amours a ma devise led to the less serious version *J'ay pris ung poul a ma chemise.*[72] Sermisy's *Altro non e'l mio amor* is based on a superius by Costanzo Festa. The earlier pieces often, but not invariably, borrowed the tenor of a well-known chanson, whereas later ones used mostly the superius. This implies a shift of emphasis from the tenor to the superius in the course of the sixteenth century, although it was not achieved immediately. Many pieces of the Attaingnant repertoire—notably pieces by Sermisy—contain tenor lines which are at least as important as the upper parts. By the second half of the sixteenth century, the vogue of parody chansons was almost over, although Claude Le Jeune still occasionally reworked earlier pieces, such as Sermisy's *C'est une dure departie*, Cadeac's *Je suis desheritée*, and Lupi's *Susanne un jour*, which text was to be set about forty times during the course of the century by Flemings as well as Frenchmen.[73]

Chansons are sometimes based on dance rhythms and are often transcribed as instrumental dances with little transformation. This is true of such works as Claudin's *Au joly bois* and Passereau's *Je ne seray jamais bergere.*[74]

It was mentioned earlier that sixteenth-century chansons were generally short. This does not apply to certain programmatic chansons, such as Janequin's, or to cyclical settings of the latter half of the sixteenth century, of which Claude Le Jeune wrote about half. Some of these works could have as many as seven or eight sections.

A special type of chanson is the polytextual *fricassée*—the French version of the quodlibet. Like its Spanish counterpart, the *ensalada*, its nomenclature is derived from gastronomy. Often the subject matter has to do with food and drink, at least in part. The term seems to have been applied to music for the first time in 1531 by Attaingnant to designate an anonymous four-part composition consisting of several pre-existent heterogeneous elements sung simultaneously. Some of these pieces may contain from fifty to one hundred fragments of four or five notes, derived from incipits or middles of single

[72] Reese, *Renaissance*, p. 101, and Kottick, *Cordiforme* (dissertation), pp. 41–42.

[73] Levy, *Le Jeune*, p. 89, and *Susanne*, pp. 375–408.

[74] Lesure, *Eléments*, p. 172.

voices of generally cheerful chansons by Sermisy, Janequin, or others, which are distributed among the several voices. Occasionally a whole superius or bassus line is borrowed and used together with the smaller fragments in the other parts. *Fricassées* were published in Paris and Lyon throughout the sixteenth century and as late as 1597. Jean Servin's *La fricassée des cris de Paris* may reproduce some of the street cries of his time. We cannot be sure that they are always exact replicas of what was sung in the streets, however. Certain fragments of other *fricassées* which have been identified, prove to be slightly altered from their original version, in order that they may fit within the polyphonic texture. (See example in Appendix at end of this chapter, pages 230–236.)

Certain pieces are of the *fricassée* type although they are not so designated. Such is Certon's *Vivre ne puis* (1538[14]), which quotes from three chansons of Claudin: *Vivre ne puis, Languir me fais,* and *Contentez-vous.* It could perhaps be called a parody-chanson. Whether or not Burgundian double chansons and mediaeval polyglot motets necessarily belong in the category of quodlibets, of which *fricassées* are part, is open to question, since some scholars want to limit the term to pieces which contain amusing and incongruous elements. At any rate, possible precursors of the sixteenth-century *fricassée* include the thirteenth-century motet on street cries, *On parole/ A Paris/ Frese nouvelle,* in which all parts have to do with food or drink, and a two-part quodlibet from the Seville *chansonnier,* with Binchois's *Pour prison ne pour maladie* as superius, and a section of a plainchant Passion as bassus.[75]

Towards the middle of the sixteenth century, side by side with the polyphonic chanson, which by now is often composed for five rather than four voices, one finds an increasing number of homorhythmic and strophic pieces, with or without refrain, which will be variously designated as *vaudeville, air, air de cour,* or *chansonnette*—the latter being reserved for *vers mesurés* in the form of airs. This is not to say that Attaingnant's repertoire was not occasionally strophic, for one often finds additional stanzas to a given chanson, but in purely literary collections. They are not as a rule printed with the music,

[75] Plamenac, *Quodlibets,* p. 164. See also Gudewill, *Quodlibet*; Lesure, *Eléments,* and *Anthologie*; Maniates, *Mannerist,* and *Quodlibet.*

however, whereas in many of Le Roy et Ballard's prints they appear at the bottom of the page.

Among the first composers to write homophonic airs in the form of *vaudevilles* were Arcadelt (1547) and Certon (1552). Many such works were intabulated for guitar as an accompaniment to a solo voice in Le Roy's second guitar book (1555). The term itself seems to have been used for the first time in a morality play of 1507, *La Condamnacion de Bancquet*, by Nicole de la Chesnaye. The expression is derived from *voix de ville*, which were probably tunes sung in the streets.[76] In 1537, a translation of the Acts of the Apostles refers to *vau de vire* as dance songs. Le Caron, in his *Dialogues* (1556), mentions vulgar and impudent songs, which have spread like 'un vent de ville.' Towards the end of the century Pasquier calls *vaudeville* a type of political chanson which is sung in all the squares.[77] Adrian Le Roy states in his book of *airs de cour* of 1571 that the genre was formerly called *voix de ville*.

Although works in the style of the *air* were written in the mid sixteenth-century by Clereau, Mornable, and others, the first composer known to have used the term was Costeley in his *Musique* (1570). From 1596 on, the term *air de cour* will be applied to airs for several voices as well as to those for one voice and lute. The term *air* is often used in the meaning of strophic poetry. It was in this sense that the poet Jodelle employed it in 1574, and the composer Caietain in his first book of airs (1576). It is often set to odes, *plaintes, complaintes, stances*, etc., in preference to the sonnet, which was so prevalent in the more polyphonic chanson. Bar-lines are sometimes placed at the end of each verse, as in the *Airs* of Planson (1587), and the compositions are called *airs sans mesure*.[78]

The principles of *musique mesurée* have been stated earlier. Works in that style have included Latin texts, but the overwhelming majority of the repertoire was in French. The

[76] Levy, *Vaudeville*, pp. 186–187, and Frissard, *Chardavoine*, pp. 63–64.

[77] Lesure, *Eléments*, p. 173. Songs from Normandy, such as several in the Bayeux manuscript, including *Reyne des flours/ La plus belle du Vau de Vire* (or Val de Vire) allude to Vire because they probably originated in this Norman town. Gérold (*Bayeux*, p. xxvi) states that the term *Vau de Vire* came to be applied to drinking songs.　　　[78] Verchaly, *Métrique*, pp. 69–70.

use of irregular quantitative meters and limited note-values within a homorhythmic texture differentiated the *chansons mesurées* from the *airs non-mesurés*; yet there is much influence of one on the other in matters of clarity of text, rhythm, and texture, with the result that seventeenth-century *airs de cour* by Guedron and Boesset will bear traces of the *Académie*'s experiments. Many composers have written in both genres.[79] D. P. Walker rightly points out that *musique mesurée* did not hasten the change from polyphony to accompanied solo.[80] It is true that in the days of Attaingnant homorhythmic songs already existed, as did vocal solos with lute accompaniment.

Baïf, who had been the leader of the *musique mesurée* movement, and had intended thus to recapture the spirit of the ancients, does not seem to have participated in the *Balet comique de la royne*, which joined spectacle, music, and dance. The ballet itself, with words by La Chesnaye and music mostly by Lambert de Beaulieu, was put together by Beaujoyeux; the music was not purely *mesurée*. Other sections of the *magnificences*, however, contained *pièces mesurées*; and there Le Jeune and Baïf took part.[81]

An important part of French secular music of the Renaissance is descriptive, although programmatic devices can also be found in some religious music.[82] The best-known

[79] See Walker, *Aspects*, and *Influence*, Levy, *Vaudeville*, and *Le Jeune*, and Verchaly, *Métrique*. Walker maintains that *musique mesurée* may be modeled on the natural stresses of the text and treats the literary text much better than does the *air de cour*—a thesis with which Verchaly does not agree.

[80] Walker, *Influence*, p. 144.

[81] See Lesure, *Musicians*, pp. 104–105, and Yates, *Magnificences*, pp. 248–250. In his discussion of Miss Yates's paper (pp. 250–264), Raymond Lebègue pointed out the double character of such spectacles, at least in the mind of Queen Catherine. She reasoned that while the nobility took part in them, they stayed away from political discussion. Furthermore, the astrological connotations of the *magnificences* were to attract benefits to the kingdom. Catherine, who practiced occult sciences, as did her son Henry III, banished tragedies from her court, because she was convinced that they brought bad luck.

[82] Some examples noted include ascending lines on 'et ascendit in coelum' and descending ones on 'descendit de coelis' in *Credos* by Gembloux, Dufay (*Missa Ave Regina*), and Ockeghem (*Missa Ecce ancilla*). (*See* Borren, *Etudes*, pp. 108, 163, and his *Madrigalisme*, pp. 181–186.) Eye-music in the form of black notes is found in Ockeghem's *Missa Mi-mi* on 'mortuorum' in the *Credo*.

descriptive piece in the French Renaissance is undoubtedly Janequin's *La Guerre*. Among the other favorite subjects imitated in music, chiefly by means of onomatopeia, were animal cries, with bird calls heading the list. The Chantilly manuscript includes Jean Vaillant's *Par maintes foys ay oÿ recorder*, which was later made into a German contrafactum by Oswald von Wolkenstein, and Borlet's *He tres doulz roussignol joly*. (Nightingales have been the subject of countless musical settings, in the Renaissance and later.) The most famous bird song in history is probably Janequin's *Le chant des oyseaux*, which also refers to bells. The text was set again by Gombert. Other bird pieces include Janequin's *Chant de l'alouette*, which was reworked by Claude Le Jeune in his *Le Printemps*, and Certon's *Chant du rossignol*. The same composer, in *Ung laboureur au premier chant du coq* (1538[11]) depicts not only the crowing of the rooster, but the neighing of pack animals. The latter is achieved by the use of the *ochetus* (hocket) technique. The clucking of the hens is imitated in Passereau's *Il est bel et bon, bon, bon . . . commère*.[83]

A lesser subject for imitation was bells, and the two *Quarillons de cloches* (1559) by Fourmentin, or Formentin, which Lesure identifies as Philippe Fromentin, master of the children of the Reims cathedral, are examples of this.[84] The *Balet comique de la royne* included the dance piece *Le son de la clochette*.

Chansons abound with examples of individual word-painting by various means. Etienne Du Tertre's *Puysque je n'ay pour dire aultre nouvelle* has a sequential line proceeding by fourths and thirds to suggest the climbing of a ladder, on the words *Qu'ar veoir grimper au ciel par une eschelle*, and Janequin's version of the same text is also descriptive.[85] Along the same lines is Janequin's setting of the passage 'et pas a pas' from *En la prison les ennuys de ce monde*, in which the progressions in most voices are step-wise.[86] The street cry *A ramonner la cheminée haut et bas*, from Jean Servin's *Fricassée*, shows a descending skip of

[83] *See* Brenet, *France*, for a study of descriptive music of the time. She notes that by the time Claude Le Jeune had written his *Printemps*, birds were no longer depicted musically in as literal a manner as before.

[84] Lesure, *Minor*, p. 540.

[85] *See* Cunningham, *Du Tertre*, pp. 140, 161.

[86] Janequin, *Chansons*, v. 6, no. 242.

an octave from 'haut' to 'et bas,' a procedure which Ockeghem had used in the *Credo* of his *Missa Quinti toni* on the words 'vivos et mortuos.' Melismas are sometimes used to emphasize certain words, such as 'plains' in Claudin's *Las je m'y plains*—in this instance on a descending line. Fast repeated notes are often combined with onomatopoeia in descriptive pieces such as those of Janequin and Passereau, and Costeley's *Grosse garce noire et tendre*. Passages in black notes—eye music to depict some sad element—occur in several pieces.[87] The one aspect of word-painting which is very much present in the Italian madrigal, but which is rarely found in the French chanson is extreme chromaticism.

The subject-matter of chansons was, generally speaking, more varied and more cheerful in the sixteenth century than in the fifteenth. Earlier music, to be sure, included its share of drinking songs and crude songs; but the secular repertoire on the whole was courtly and often sad. Many pieces which include the word *regretz* were written in the second half of the fifteenth century—i.e., *Mille regretz, Tous les regretz*, etc. Elegiac pieces are still prevalent during part of the sixteenth century, from Sermisy's *Tous mes amys, venez ma plaincte ouyr*, or his *Allez souspirs*, and Janequin's *Doulens regrets*—'regret' pieces have obviously not gone out of fashion—to Desportes's *Complainte pour le roi Henri III*, with settings by Tessier, Besard, and Bataille. Serious songs from both centuries include several on the goddess Fortuna.[88] Verjeust's *Au hault de la roue de fortune*[89] and Mittantier's *Puisque fortune a sur moy entrepris* are but two examples. Songs on lighter topics come to share honours with the rest. These include pieces about workmen—plowmen or wine-growers—such as Certon's *Ung laboureur*, and Claudin's *Vignon, vignon, vignette*, or animals, such as Clereau's *Mon petit chien aymé entre tous autres*, or Janequin's *Ung jour Catin venant d'estre batue/ Veid ung gros chat qui mangeait la chosette . . .* Sermisy's *Je ne menge point de porc* refers to the unsanitary eating habits of pigs. *A cent diables la verolle*, with settings by Bon Voisin or Heurteur, and by Certon, has to do with a social

[87] Bernstein (*Couronne*, p. 43) lists several examples in the chanson literature by L'Huillier, Symon, Janequin, Passereau, and Willaert.

[88] *See* Lowinsky, *Fortuna*.

[89] Transcribed by G. Thibault in *Revue de Musicologie* (1926), pp. 187–189.

disease, the ship on which it was contracted, and a few accompanying ailments, such as loose teeth, gout, and ulcers.

An important type is the drinking song, although it is by no means as popular as it will become in the seventeenth century, when it forms part of several collections of *airs sérieux et à boire*. The Bayeux manuscript contains several Bacchic songs, and the more lady-oriented *chansonnier* of Françoise de Chateaubriand appropriately enough contains but one—*Seigneurs, que Dieu vous gard d'ennuy et d'encombrier*[90]—which alludes to drinking in refined language. One of Fourmentin's carillons, *Reveillez-vous tous, gentils compaignons*, encourages everyone to have a drink, except the little children, who had better wait until they are grown up. Claudin's *La, la, Maître Pierre* suggests a bottle of wine as a cold remedy, or rather as preventative medicine. Guiard's *Or ouez les introites de taverne* speaks for itself. A delightful poem set to music by Jean Guyon,[91] which might well have been entitled *Counseils aux musiciens*, for the pedagogical and dietary advice it offers to singers, deserves to be quoted in full:

> Musiciens qui chantez a plaisir,
> Si vous voulez faire valoir la notte,
> Prenez un ton doulx et a loisir
> En escoutant ce que le chant denotte;
> Accordez-vous ainsi que la linnotte,
> Qui prend plaisir a son chant gratieux.
> Soyez expers d'oreilles et des yeux,
> Ou autrement il vauldroit mieux se taire;
> Mais je vous pri que vous soyez soigneux
> De ne chanter si vous n'avez a boire.

The first part seems to anticipate Hamlet's advice to the actors. As for the last two lines, it may be frivolous to suggest that they are neo-Platonist in spirit, but they remind one of Plato's admonition that choir-members over eighteen be given wine (*Laws*, II, ch. 9). It presumably improves the quality of

---

[90] Chaillon, *Françoise*, p. 12.
[91] Du Chemin, 1550[9], pp. x–xi, transcribed in Cunningham, *Chanson*, pp. 13–15 of musical examples.

singing.[92] The chanson also shows the predilection of Renaissance musicians for birds.

Richard Renvoysy, in the preface to his setting of *Quelques odes d'Anacreon* in French (Paris: Breton, 1559) disclaims any similarity with Anacreon; on the other hand he does not wish to be taken for a teetotaler, and concludes that the collection is not meant to teach the reader how to live morally, but to make him laugh.[93]

That many gastronomical subjects were treated in chansons was mentioned earlier in relation to *fricassées* and their models. There is at least one instance of a chanson fragment named as one of the dishes in a gastronomical list from the fifth book of *Pantagruel*—'du botte-luy toy-mesmes.'[94]

Pieces which use hexachordal syllables for the purpose of punning have been mentioned in the section on language and music. There are other songs, however, which use similar syllables with little or no apparent play on words intended. One (see next page) example is the refrain of *Il estoyt ung bon homme qui venoyt de Lyon*, from Paris: Bibl. nat., *MS. fr. 1597*.[95] Another is Clereau's *Sol, fa, mi, re, la*, from Le Roy's *Disieme livre* (1570[9]), in which these syllables are used throughout the piece.

The majority of chansons have to do with love, partly of a noble sort and partly not. The brunette is gradually becoming more fashionable than the blonde, at least in poetry and music of a popular type. In a pastoral chanson by De Bussi (1559[13]), *A rose fleurie*, we are told that 'L'aultrier Corbin vit la brunette bergerette mignonnette . . . Seule gardant sa brebiette et chevrette jolie.' Sermisy's and Villiers's settings of Clément Marot's *Pourtant si je suys brunette (Chanson pour la brune)* are in

[92] Musicians were apparently not reluctant to accept this advice, if we are to believe the anonymous poet of the following lines from *Le Resveur avec ses resveries*, Paris, *ca.* 1525 (quoted in Rokseth, *Orgue*, p. 366): 'Chantres sont tousjours prets a bien boire;/ Organistes les suyvent souvent;/ Tousjours ont souef, cela devez croire.'

[93] Thibault, *Breton*, pp. 302–308.

[94] *Boute ly ty mesme* is a chanson from Attaingnant's *1530[5]*, and occurs as a *fricassée* fragment in *1536[5]*.

[95] In this piece the syllables *la, my* may be interpreted also, and perhaps more appropriately, as *l'amy*, particularly since *la* and *my* do not always correspond with the notes to which they are sung. (See ex.)

praise of dark-haired ladies. It is only fair to add that the poet also wrote a *Chanson pour la blanche*, in which the blonde is given equal treatment; however, that is not the one which was selected by the musicians.

Then came the vogue of the *blasons anatomiques*, poems about various parts of the human body—launched by Marot's *Blason du beau et laid tétin*, with settings of the first part by Janequin and the second by Clemens non Papa. These texts are highly descriptive and rather explicit. Others also use symbolism of an earthy sort. The cuckoo traditionally stands for the cuckold husband. The trumpet has been used to represent one portion of a lady's anatomy—such as in Janequin's *Or vien ca, m'amie Perrette*—and the chimney another. And one can be sure that Hesdin's *Ramonnés moy ma cheminée*, or Briault's *Je te preste ma cheminée* are not *chansons de métier* in the usual sense.

The *mal mariée* theme has been current since the Middle Ages in songs about the young wife unhappily married to an old, unpleasant husband, who is jealous to boot, and not without reason. *Un orrible*, from Chantilly 564 (fol. 13vo) and Sermisy's *Il est jour, dit l'alouette* are but two examples, though far apart from each other in terms of time.

Chansons often refer to pairs of lovers. Some of them are anonymous shepherds and shepherdesses, such as in Revez's *Le berger et la bergere*, or Janequin's *Ung gay bergier prioit une bergiere*, and the anonymous *Une pastourelle gentille et ung berger*. Occasionally their profession is not entirely clear, such as in Passereau's *Ung compaignon gallin gallant et une fillette jolye*. Sometimes the lady is simply addressed as *ma dame*, or more unceremoniously as *grosse garce noire*—in tribute, perhaps to her dark locks. In many instances, however, the couples have names. The best-known pair, and probably the oldest, dating from the Middle Ages, consists of Robin and Marion, who appear in *Petite Camusette* and other songs. In the course of the sixteenth century, Marion is sometimes transformed into Margot, as in Janequin's *Ung jour Robin vint Margot empoingner*. Other lovers from the chanson repertoire include Perrin and Perrinette, Martin and Alix, Colin and Colette, Jehanne and Janinet, Gaultier and Janeton. As for Guillot, a familiar character in the chanson literature, one can only surmise that he was fickle, because he appears with different ladies in various pieces—with Helène in Claudin's *En entrant en ung jardin*, with Babeau in a piece by Janequin, and with Cathin in one by Decapella.

Many of these chansons were of the narrative type and contained dialogue by several characters, such as *Martin menoit son pourceau au marché*, with settings by Sermisy and Janequin. Marot called them 'chansons avec propos.' Lesure notes that 'thus the chanson became a miniature theatre, while the farce in turn was filled with chansons. It would be difficult to determine which of these two genres influenced the other.'[96] Anecdotal songs were not limited to the crude variety. They include some of the more spiritual types, such as *Susanne un jour*, by the poet Guillaume Guéroult, about Susannah and the Elders.[97] Some of the subjects of the chansons, particularly in the sixteenth century, are mythological. They include l'Huillier's *O ma Venus a ton Vulcain fidele*, Sermisy's *Ung grand plaisir Cupido me donna*, and Servin's madrigalesque *Les Regrets de Didon*.[98]

It is obvious that certain chansons were particularly well-liked in the Renaissance. Some enjoyed several musical settings, or were borrowed for Masses or contrafacta. Many were listed in literary works. Jean Molinet quotes some eighty incipits in his *Oraison a Nostre Dame, La Collaudation a Madame Marguerite*, and *Le Debat du gendarme et du vieil amoureux*. And there are Rabelais's aforementioned lists. Villon's *Testament* contains allusions to popular songs of his time.[99] *Fricassées* and farces quote chansons. Jenin le Racowatier, who had stolen more than twenty chalices in his lifetime, marched to his execution singing *Hé, Robinet, tu m'as la mort donné* in a loud voice.[1] Ockeghem's *Prenez sur moy*, was also quoted, but without text, in Glarean's *Dodecachordon*. In spite of the popularity of the chansons, or perhaps because of it, the state occasionally tried to prevent the singing of some of them. In 1580, for example, the Parisians were forbidden to provoke peaceful people 'par cris et dictz de chansons.[2]

Iconographic sources and the accounts of chroniclers and

[96] Lesure, *Musicians*, pp. 30–34.
[97] *See* Levy, *Susanne*.
[98] *See* Gagnepain, *Servin*, p. 125.
[99] Droz, *Villon*, pp. 29–32.
[1] Droz, *Poètes*, p. 6.
[2] Breton, *Chanson*, p. 80.

poets make us aware of the important role of instrumental music in the French Renaissance. Although the presence of a literary text under a given piece of music did not preclude its performance by instruments, compositions specifically designated for instruments are rare in the French written repertoire of the fifteenth century. The *Tuba Gallicalis* from *MS. 222 C 22* of the Strasbourg Library, with its fanfare-like tenor on a broken chord, and the Escorial *MS. V III 24 version of* Pierre Fontaine's *J'ayme bien celui qui s'en va*, with its *contra tenor trompette* are well-known exceptional examples of music presumably written for wind instruments.[3] French chansons were transcribed for keyboard outside of France in such collections as the Faenza codex and the Buxheim organ book. The chief sources for fifteenth-century French dance music are the Brussels manuscript (facsimile edition by Closson), and Michel de Toulouze's *L'Art et l'instruction de bien dancer.*[4]

With the advent of music printing on a large scale in the sixteenth century, collections of pure instrumental music in France are plentiful, though by no means as numerous as those of music provided with a text. Some of these instrumental works were found in instruction books, beginning with Attaingnant's *Tres breve et familiere introduction* of 1529, which combined vocal notation and lute tablature. Other collections were not preceded by any method. Attaingnant, and later his widow, published some twenty books for lute (partly solo and partly with voice), keyboard (*orgues, espinettes et manicordions*), flutes and recorders, and unspecified ensemble. The repertoire included transcriptions of chansons and dances. Three keyboard books from 1531 contain sacred instrumental music, based on various chants for the Mass and Vespers, as well as thirteen motets and were presumably intended for the church organist. Although the transcribers and composers of the instrumental collections are rarely stated in Attaingnant's prints, notable exceptions are Claude Gervaise, Etienne Du Tertre, and Consilium for ensemble *danceries*, and a mysterious P. B. for some of the lute basses danses, gaillardes, and pavanes of 1530[7]; he was

---

[3] *See* Borren, *Pittoresque*, pp. 92–98, and Reese, *Renaissance*, p. 35.
[4] *See* Bukofzer, *Studies*, pp. 190–216.

formerly thought to be the Italian lutenist Pietro Paulo Borrono, but Daniel Heartz has since suggested that he was Pierre Blondeau.

From 1536 to 1553, Moderne published five collections for harpsichord (lost), lute, and unspecified ensemble. From 1556 to 1564, Du Chemin issued five books, for lute and for ensemble (Jean d'Estrées's four books of *danseries*). Other publishers of instrumental music include Fezandat, who printed seventeen volumes, between 1550 and 1562, for lute, guitar, or cittern by Albert de Rippe and Guillaume Morlaye, and Simon Gorlier, with eight collections for guitar, lute, cittern, transverse flute, and harpsichord (1551–156–?). The most prolific publisher of tablatures for plucked instruments—lute, guitar, cittern, mandora—in the second half of the century was Adrian Le Roy, himself a lutenist and guitarist. (The other famous guitarist of the time was Brayssing, from Augsburg.) And it was Le Roy's firm that printed the music to the *Balet comique de la royne*. Arbeau's *Orchésographie* (Langres: J. des Preyz, 1589) gives mostly monophonic dance tunes. Manuscripts of instrumental music are rare; they include an organ fantasia by Nicolas de la Grotte, on Rore's madrigal *Anchor che col partire*, and a fragment of another by Costeley, for keyboard. Other composers of instrumental fantasias include Eustache du Caurroy, Claude Le Jeune, and Charles Guillet.

The lute in France seems to have had more noble connotations than some of the other plucked instruments. By the middle of the sixteenth century it had reached the peak of its popularity, largely through the attention given to it by the poets of the Pléiade and the work of virtuosi, some of whose ornate versions of pieces are reflected in mid-century prints. Under the reign of Henry II, the guitar began to share honours with the lute and almost supplant it among all classes of society. The author of an anonymous method for lute and guitar (Poitiers, 1556) attempts a hierarchy of several instruments. The *vielle* is for beggars, the rebec and viol are for *ménétriers*, and the lute and guitar for musicians. 'In my earliest years,' he says, 'we used to play the lute more than the guitar, but for twelve or fifteen years now everyone has been guitaring, the lute is nearly forgotten for Heaven knows what kind of music on the guitar which is much easier than for lute.'[5] The guitar was considered a Spanish instrument—invented by the Catalans, according to Tinctoris. It was supposed to have been played mostly by women; the Catalan men, however, used it as an accompaniment to love-songs.[6] The best-known sixteenth-century makers of guitars in France was the Bavarian Gaspard Duyffoprucgar (Tieffenbrücker), the supposed inventor of the violin, who worked in Lyon, *ca.* 1559. He was so well rated that his trademark was appropriated by a contemporary of his, Benoit Le Jeune, for his own instruments, which led to his arrest and imprisonment.[7]

The cittern's reputation was by no means at the same level as that of the lute and guitar, at least in France, where it seems to have been 'a simple instrument associated especially with simple people.'[8] By the seventeenth century, the lute seems to have overshadowed all the other plucked instruments.

Keyboard instruments, with the exception of the church organ, seem to have been played mostly by non-professional musicians in the home. We do not hear of any harpsichord virtuosi. The extant music published for keyboard in France is not too difficult to play and consists largely of transcriptions of vocal music in which the model can be readily followed. Organs were used both in the home and in church. Dates at which they were admitted in various French churches are highly divergent. Portable organs were also used for various outdoor ceremonies.[9]

Harps were undoubtedly well regarded—Clément Marot, in *Dieu gard de mon cueur la regente*, writes of 'son de voix ou herpe

---

[5] Heartz, *Parisian*, p. 460.   [6] Reese, *Fourscore*, p. 35.

[7] Lesure, *Guitare*, pp. 189–195.

[8] Waldbauer, *Cittern*, p. ii. The author explains (p. 170) that 'in Paris the popularity of the guitar and the cittern started in the 50's with the guitar slightly ahead both in time and importance; in the late 80's the mandora began to claim an increasing share of popular favor; and by the first decade of the 17th century the vogue of the guitar and the cittern all but vanished.' See also Charnassé, *Cistre*.

[9] *See* Rokseth, *Orgue*. Becker (*Maîtrise*, p. 111) notes that although Gerson, who gave symbolic connotations to instruments, accepted all of them, they may or may not have been used at Notre-Dame de Paris; and they were probably not favoured in the churches of the Northern provinces, since their practice was not taught in the *maîtrises*, nor are they mentioned in their archival documents.

doulcette'—but no French music specifically designated for that instrument is extant.

Viols were played in the homes of respectable people, most of whom took a long time to accept the violin on an equal footing with the older instrument.[10] Although viols were played by aristocrats, violins were played exclusively by professional musicians of a relatively low social class. The violin probably originated about the 1530s. It was used mostly for dance music and spectacles, which covered the 'whole social gamut from village fete to court functions.'[11] Philibert Jambe de Fer states, in his treatise of 1556, that most people considered it too strident for chamber use. Even after 1638, Pierre Trichet, in his treatise on instruments, states that violins are mainly used for 'dances, balls, ballets, mascarades, serenades, aubades, feasts and other joyful pastimes, having been judged more proper for these recreational exercises than any other sort of instrument.'[12]

Francis I had French violinists among his court musicians. Six of them played at his funeral. After his death, Catherine de' Medici imported a band of Italian violinists under Baldassare da Belgiojoso, who later under the name of Beaujoyeux organized and choreographed the *Balet comique de la royne*. In this spectacle, incidentally, is found the first extant music for violin. These instruments had taken part, however, in the ballet of the Polish ambassadors in 1573. Catherine's son, Charles IX, is reported to have ordered a number of violins from Andrea Amati. Under his reign the violinists were promoted from the *écurie* to the king's chamber.[13]

Not all instrumentalists were attached to a particular household, royal or aristocratic. Most of them belonged to the confraternity of Saint-Julien-des-ménétriers, and were hired for particular occasions by people from all walks of life. They formed small bands of indeterminate numbers of musicians, and their partnership could last any length of time from a few

[10] Jacques Mauduit, according to Mersenne, added a sixth string to the viol, which formerly had only five. (*See* Brenet, *France*, pp. 232–233.)

[11] Boyden, *Violin*, p. 3.

[12] Lesure, *Trichet*, p. 228.

[13] Boyden, *Violin*, pp. 3–57. Other high-ranking dignitaries, such as Cardinal de Lorraine, employed violinists on a regular basis. (*See* Pirro, *Histoire*, p. 323.)

days to thirty-five years. The occasional membership of a royal musician (such as Jean Fourcade, oboist to the king in 1560) in a private band created a large demand for the services of that particular group, and so the king's musicians were exempt from the ruling which forbade the other members from performing with other bands for the duration of their legal association. Although contracts generally do not mention obligatory rehearsals, perhaps because the repertoire was familiar and not too difficult, rehearsals were sometimes held as frequently as twice a week by the very end of the sixteenth century. Sick-pay was provided unless the musician had contracted a dishonorable disease, 'maladie de vérolle, pullins ou bosse chancreuse,' or unless he feigned illness and was seen in town attending to other business instead of staying in bed. Musicians could be fined for blaspheming, swearing, or insulting their associates.

Bands played in the provinces as well as in Paris, but they were fewer in number than in the capital, and they were generally more stable. In general the groups consisted of four persons until the end of the sixteenth century, when a fifth player was often added. Exceptionally, as in Amiens, 'gens mécaniques et artisans' were allowed to hire only two musicians for their festivities.

These popular musicians probably played the familiar tunes of their time largely from memory, and with added improvised ornamentation, perhaps. An early seventeenth-century tablature from the south of France (Paris: Bibl. nat., *Rés. Vmb. MS. 5*) includes two branles provided with texts, of which one is in dialect from Gascogne or Béarn. This collection shows that the southern repertoire was much the same as that which was performed in Paris and at the court.[14]

How did French music of the fifteenth and sixteenth centuries sound at the time and how was it performed? It is not possible to answer this categorically, because the performance practice for a given piece probably was not the same each time it was played or sung. And there must have been differences from

---

[14] Lesure, *Orchestres*, pp. 39–54. The author notes (p. 52) that the orchestra of the twenty-four violins of the king will be the transposition to the court of the instrumental arrangements of the Saint-Julien confraternity.

region to region, from institution to institution, and from individual to individual in styles of performing.

For one thing, it is not easy to determine what kind of singing pleased most people during the French Renaissance. Perhaps the manuscript copies or reprints of older theoretical works made during this time imply tacit approval of their authors' opinions on the subject. The author of the *Livre des proprietez des choses*, invoking the authority of Isidore of Seville, considers the perfect voice to be high, strong, clear, and suave at the same time. Suavity alone denotes weak spirit, such as may be found among women and children. A thick voice, on the other hand, implies goodness and strength of spirit, as found in perfect men.[15]

Guillaume Guerson, in his *Utilissime musicales regule*, accepts many kinds of voices and gives sensible advice to singers, so that they may achieve natural-sounding results:

> The singer should consider the quality and ability of his voice: whether its range is wide, so that it may easily run through the various degrees of the scale, or whether it is of narrow range. He should also consider the agility and flexibility of his voice, and whether he is able to sing low or high. He should sing or chant without any trouble or violence or corruption, and without any unforeseen disturbance, in order to avoid singing too high or too low—in sum, he should sing according to what his voice can bear.[16]

Cambraisian parishioners may have had sensitive ears, and they do not seem to have liked loud voices. On 26 May 1498, one of the cathedral singers, Verjus, was asked to moderate his voice so as not to frighten people, and another, Craspournient, was admonished not to sing so much louder than the rest, because it was displeasing to the listeners.[17] Many years later, in 1536, one of the music masters of the *maîtrise* was told to teach his students to sing *submissa voce* (which Pirro interprets as *falsetto*).[18]

[15] Barthélemy l'Anglais, *Livre*, fol. 340ro.
[16] Ferand, *Guerson*, p. 263.
[17] Pirro, *Cornuel*, p. 195.
[18] Pirro, *Histoire*, p. 316. Choirboys of the *maîtrises* from the Northern

From time to time, one finds allusions to a new manner of singing, which is not explained. A tenor from Maximilian's chapel, named Cordier, is mentioned in Molinet's chronicles as particularly well recommended because of his knowledge of 'the new mode of singing.'[19] Whatever the style was, it was probably widespread and not limited to Austro-Burgundian chapel. Since Cordier was reported to have sung at the courts of the duke of Milan and the king of Naples before coming to Maximilian, he may have learned the method in Italy. Whether it refers to voice production or to a special kind of improvisation we cannot tell.

As early as 1550, Loys Bourgeois, in his *Le droict chemin de musique* suggested the possibility of singing successions of equally notated semiminims and *fusae* in dotted rhythm. Two years later, in his *Tiers livre de tabulature de luth contenant vingt et un pseaumes*, Le Roy notates the voice part of a psalm in equal notes and its doubling by the lute in dotted notes. This has been interpreted to mean that Le Roy trusted the singer to dot the notes, but felt the need to indicate the rhythm with precision for the benefit of the amateur lutenist.[20] Why the lutenist was considered more ignorant of unwritten practice than his singing colleague is not clear. The possibility that both singer and lutenist performed the notes exactly as written should perhaps not be entertained, on the grounds that the results would be too ugly—at least to some twentieth-century ears. But it would be rash to try to determine with any degree of precision what constituted beauty to most French sixteenth-century listeners. As late as 1623 some of them presumably enjoyed hearing the royal singer Le Bailly produce quarter-tones, and others perform chromatic and enharmonic music.[21]

That good singers were highly regarded in France, during the Renaissance, is undeniable. Lambert de Beaulieu, who

provinces were supposed to have had their mutation of voice generally later than those of the Seine and Loire valleys (Becker, *Maîtrises*, p. 93, after J. Samson, *La Polyphonie sacrée*, Paris: Schola, 1953, p. 66).

[19] Linden, *Molinet*, p. 169. The lines 'C'est luy qui bien sceut choisir et attaindre/ Tous les secrets de la subtilité/ Du nouveau chant . . . ,' from Crétin's *Deploration* on the death of Ockeghem, undoubtedly refers to a compositional process rather than to a style of singing.

[20] G. Thibault, in Roland-Manuel, *Histoire*, I: pp. 1314–1315.

[21] According to Mersenne (*see* Levy, *Costeley*, p. 248).

sang to the lute, was celebrated in 1559 in a poem by Olivier de Magny. Later in the century, the castrato Etienne Le Roy, abbot of Saint-Laurent, became the favorite singer of Charles IX and sang in court spectacles.[22]

In church, plainchant was sometimes performed as a single line, and other times with improvised discant. The foundation of a High Mass at the Sainte-Chapelle of Dijon in 1431 stipulated that it should be performed in descant except when it was a *Requiem*. Then it should be done in unaccompanied plainchant.[23] Fauxbourdon became rare by the end of the sixteenth century. In 1584, a singer from the cathedral of Chartres asked permission to have several psalms sung in fauxbourdon. He was allowed to have 'the psalm *In exitu Israel de Egypto* during some Sundays in the year, and also the psalm *Memento Domino David* on the day of the dead, and a few other days . . . extraordinarily sung in fauxbourdon.' Polyphonic music was called 'musique' in contrast to plainchant and fauxbourdon.[24]

Churchmen seem to have favored doubling of individual parts. The *Livre des proprietez des choses* suggests that all good melodies should have 'several voices well in tune, for a single voice is not so pleasant to hear as the voice of the choir.'[25] Adult sopranos—i.e., castrati—sometimes helped the choirboys sing their part, and were used as vocal models.[26]

It is certain that in the fifteenth century, if not much earlier, there was contrast in performance of church music between small and large groups. Certain sections of works by Ciconia, Binchois, and others, are marked 'chorus' to alternate with 'unus' or other small combinations, such as duets or trios.[27]

Alternation between equal performing groups, or double chorus, for which Willaert and his Venetians followers became famous, was also practiced by Frenchmen. Performances with dialogue undoubtedly took place during previously described occasions—international meetings such as the interview at the Field of the Cloth of Gold, or the local celebration of the

[22] Lesure, *Musicians*, pp. 78–79.   [23] Rokseth, *Orgue*, pp. 33–34.
[24] Goldine, *Chartres*, p. 170.   [25] Barthélemy l'Anglais, *Livre*, fol. 339vo.
[26] Becker, *Maîtrises*, p. 94.
[27] Borren, *Etudes*, pp. 90 ff., 105, and Kanazawa, *Vespers* I: pp. 44–48.

Peace of Vervins at Notre-Dame de Paris in 1598. In order to mark the visit of Henry IV at Rouen, on 25 December 1596, the king's singers performed a 'messe en musique' accompanied by high instruments, together with the singing personnel of the cathedral.[28] There is little doubt that the performance there too was done in alternation.

Josquin's use of paired imitation, within a piece pre-dominantly in unpaired polyphony, may foreshadow the double chorus, on a restricted scale, to be sure. Mouton, Willaert's teacher, has antiphonal sections of four voices in his motet *Verbum bonum*. This is also true of Rousée's eight-part *Regina celi letare* (1535⁴).[29] Dominique Phinot published five motets in polychoral style—including Lamentations (Lyon: Beringen, 1548), two years before the appearance of Willaert's *Salmi spezzati*.[30] For some time Phinot's nationality was uncertain—he was thought to be Italian or southern French—but it now seems that he was considered French in his time, at least by one Italian writer.[31]

Later composers of polychoral music in France include Claude Le Jeune and Eustache du Caurroy. Le Jeune's work in that genre includes a ten-part echo on a Latin text, *Quae celebrat thermas*, an eight-part French echo, *O voix, o de nos voix*, which may date from the 1560s, although it was not published until 1612, and a spiritual dialogue of 1564 entitled *La Religion*. The latter is divided into two unequal choirs. The four lower voices sing the questions and the three upper the answers. The piece may be inspired by similar dialogues from Willaert's *Musica nova* (1559).[32]

---

[28] Mlle. Launay (*Motets*, p. 177) also points out that in church it was normal for the choirboys to sing in alternation with the clergy or the faithful.

[29] Hertzmann, *Mehrchörigkeit*, pp. 140–147.   [30] *See* Hansen, *Phinot*.

[31] Jerome Cardan, in his *De tranquillitate*, refers to 'the French Dominique Phinot, a distinguished musician,' and states that he was beheaded and burned because of his penchant for young boys (Miller, *Cardan*, p. 416).

[32] Levy, *Le Jeune*, pp. 4, 59–63. The dialogue is transcribed in Hamersma, *Pseaumes*, pp. 231–269. Miss Yates (*Magnificences*, p. 246) suggests that Le Jeune's bi-choral *Epithalame*, from his *Airs* of 1608, was performed at the *magnificences* of 1581 with the principal character, Hymen, accompanied by a chorus of boys and one of girls, all dressed in costumes of classical antiquity.

Another aspect of performance practice about which we do not know as much as we would like to is the extent to which instruments accompanied voices or substituted for them when the manuscripts or prints do not so specify. Here again there was probably no fixed rule. The absence of literary text in certain voices of a manuscript or print has sometimes been interpreted to suggest instrumental performance, but that alone does not necessarily preclude singing. Perhaps a scribe or printer wanted to save time and assumed that a singer would know the missing words or could obtain them from a word-book. Conversely, the presence of words under a musical line does not inevitably entail vocal performance. Iconographical documents such as the often-reproduced portrait by the master of the three-quarter figures, of three ladies performing Claudin de Sermisy's *Jouyssance* with one voice and two instruments, show that there is more than one way to perform a given piece of music. Other contemporary pictures show motets being performed by viols alone during the journey of Louise of Lorraine from the Louvre to the Faubourg Saint-Marceau, or choir singers with instrumenta-lists at their side.[33]

Publishers occasionally tell us that a piece of music is 'convenable tant a la voix comme aux instruments.' Attaingnant considers his *Vingt et sept chansons* (1533[1]), all of which are provided with a text, 'convenables a la fleuste d'Allemant . . . et a la fleuste a neuf trous.' Long before the Renaissance publisher, Guillaume de Machault, in *Le Livre du Voir-dit*, tells Péronne d'Armentières: 'J'ay fait un chant à votre commandement . . . et qui la pourroit mettre sur les orgues, sur cornemuses ou autres instrumens, c'est sa droite nature.'[34]

The rubrics of certain pieces suggest performance by a brass instrument. In this category are the textless and anonymous *Tuba gallicallis*, Fontaine's *J'ayme bien celuy qui s'en va*, Dufay's *Gloria ad modum tubae*, and a Mass by Etienne Grossin, which is

---

[33] Alexander, *Moduli*, pp. 125–126, referring to M. Pincherle, *Illustrated History of Music,* 1959, pp. 56–57, and Lesure, *Du Chemin*, p. 308. We realize, of course, that not all iconographical sources are equally reliable as guides to performance practice.

[34] Quoted in Marix, *Musiciens*, p. xxi.

unified by the use of a *trompetta* in all of its movements.[35]

That instruments were played in French Roman Catholic churches during the Renaissance is well-known, but it would be more difficult to assert that they were used uniformly in all of the country. In the fifteenth century, the organ was used only for important feasts, whereas during the course of the following century, it came to be gradually played every Sunday. By 1600 Clement VIII decreed that this practice was obligatory. In certain instances, the organ might double the vocal parts, give the intonation, or substitute for the chorus if necessary. Otherwise it might alternate with the singers, particularly in the Ordinary of the Mass. Its use in the *Introit* was already established by the end of the fifteenth century. The question has been raised exactly how the alternation was applied—between organ and plainchant, or among vocal polyphony, organ, and plainchant.[36] Attaingnant's organ books give us an idea of the organists' repertoire—transcriptions of motets, pieces on liturgical *cantus firmi*, and independent preludes to be played at the church service. The use of the organ spread to convents, where the nuns learned to play the instrument.[37]

One hears not only that organs participated in religious music, but occasionally other instruments as well. About 1480, the cathedral of Saint-Maurice in Vienne (Dauphiné) used *cantores* and a *banda*. The latter term is probably southern French in origin and designates instrumentalists—mostly wind

[35] Reaney (*Fifteenth*, III: p. ii) states that 'presumably this is a genuine trumpet, for there is no mention of imitating the trumpet vocally. Still the old reference to a form called *trumpetum* should not be forgotten, even in this case. Paulus Paulirinus of Prague, writing about 1460, says that "trumpetum is a kind of measured music for four voices. All voices except the fourth proceed normally, but this latter is sung after the manner of the French trumpet (*ad modum tube gallicalis*)."'

[36] See Rokseth, *Orgue*, Lesure, *Religieuse*, pp. 73–74, and Gombosi, *Organ*, pp. 51, 55. Brenet (*Instruments*, p. 280) points out a description of a purely vocal performance of Ockeghem's *Missa Mi-mi* in Crétin's *Deploration* on the composer's death (1495): 'Tous instruments cesserent/ Et sur ce point les chanta commencerent/ . . . Lors se chanta la messe de My, my.'

[37] Brenet, *Couvents*, p. 8. In France the practice was not frowned upon. In Florence, however, Savonarola tried unsuccessfully, in 1495, to make the nuns of the Annunciation stop playing the organ and burn their music books (*loc. cit.*).

players. Their services were required only for important feasts.[38] Most French churches did not use instruments other than the organ. Exceptions to this tradition occurred, however, when a monarch came to a given church for an important celebration, with all of his household musicians—chamber, *écurie*, and chapel. Consecration ceremonies for Henry IV at Chartres (1594) were performed to the accompaniment of 'all sorts of musical instruments, including clarions, oboes, trumpets, and drums.'[39] Mauduit's Requiem, which was sung for Ronsard's funeral service on 24 February 1586 at the chapel of the Collège de Boncour, was 'animated by all sorts of instruments.'[40]

On the whole, Parisian churches were more strict than provincial ones in regard to the acceptance of instruments. Churches from Provence and the Comtat Venaissin—Aix, Avignon, and Arles, for example—employed semi-permanent groups of instruments (cornets, serpents, bassoons, and violins) during the course of the sixteenth century.[41] Other countries may have used instruments in church earlier than France, where they were considered somewhat of a novelty. Marguerite de Valois, in her memoirs, mentions a 'Mass in the Spanish manner, with music, violins, and cornets,' which Don Juan of Austria had her attend in Madrid, in 1577.[42]

Finally, it was in Baïf's *Académie* that one finds some of the earliest performances in what amounts to concert form—with a genuine separation between performers and audience.[43] These were still a far cry from public concerts, open to anyone willing to pay the price of a ticket—as we know, they were strictly limited to members of the *Académie*—but they represent an important step in that democratic direction.

[38] Rokseth, *Instruments*, pp. 206–207. During the Mass celebrated at the Field of the Cloth of Gold (1520), the *Credo*, sung by the French, was accompanied by organ, sackbuts and fifes. Before Mass, the English had sung *Terce*.

[39] Brenet, *Instruments*, pp. 282–283.

[40] Brenet, *France*, p. 234.

[41] Durand, *Avignon*, pp. 73–74.

[42] Brenet, *Instruments*, p. 282.

[43] Lesure, *Musicians*, p. 100.

APPENDIX
Fricassée

Attaingnant, 1531[1] fol. 11ᵛ–12ʳ

Puis - - que vou - les — qu'en
- rez pas, J'ay con - ten - té, La ro - sée du moy de may, Se -
le mar - ché d'Ar-ras, La ou pre - tend, Du vin a une o - reil -
- con-tray ung for - ge - ron, El - le s'en va, Mon cueur est

ce tour - ment il meu - re, qu'en ce tour - ment il meu -
cre - te - ment, N'est - ce pas grant dom - ma - ge, Pas -
le, Por - tes pour moy, Qui ro - bent tout lais - sant les lourds, hel - las,
sou - vent bien mar - ry, Ma - da - me jo - li - et - - te, C'est

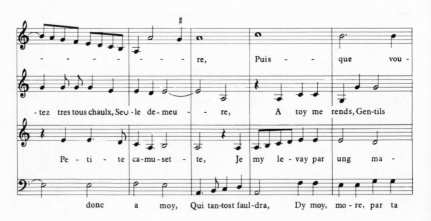

- - - - - re, Puis - - que vou -
- tez tres tous chaulx, Seu - le de-meu - - re, A toy me rends, Gen-tils
Pe - ti - te ca-mu-set - te, Je my le - vay par ung ma -
donc a moy, Qui tan-tost faul-dra, Dy moy, mo - re, par ta

The following fragments have been identified. RISM numbers are used whenever possible. A title in italics indicates that the fragment is not an incipit; the incipit of the piece from which it derives appears underneath in parentheses. An asterisk implies that the fragment has been modified somewhat. S, C, T, B represent the voice-part of the *fricassée* in which the fragment appears.

Fragment	Composer	Source
*A la mort m'avez mys (C) (Petite camusette)	Josquin	Attaingnant, *36ᵉ Livre,* 1549
A l'endurer (T) (C'est a grant tort)	Claudin	1528³
A toy me rends (C)		Attaingnant, *Tres breve introduction,* 1529, under title: *Alsowerdemont*
Amy souffres (C)	[Moulu or Claudin]	1529⁴
Au pres de vous (S) (Complete superius part)	[Claudin or Jacotin]	1528³
C'est a grant tort (B)	Claudin	1528³
C'est donc a moy (B) [i.e., C'est donc par moy]		Cambrai, Bibl. de la ville, *MS. 125–128*
Ce fut amours (T)	Passereau	1529³
*Changeons propos (B)	Claudin	1528³
Croyez de vray (T)		1528⁵
*Damoiselle (B) (Petite damoyselle)	Janequin	Attaingnant, *31ᵉ Livre,* 1549
D'amour je suys (C)		1529⁴
De retourner (T)		1529³
Dessus le marché d'Arras (T)	Willaert	1528⁹
Dont vient cela (C)	Claudin	1528³
Du vin a une oreille (T) (Ung jour Robin)	Claudin	1528³
Elle s'en va (B)	Claudin	1529²
Et bien heureux en ce temps cy (C) (Le content est riche)	Claudin	1528³
Et ne me plains fors seulement (T) (J'ay contenté ma volunté)	Claudin	1528³
*Et vous vivrez (C) (Le content est riche)	Claudin	1528³

Fragment	Composer	Source
Fringuez-moy tant tant (T) (Au joly boys je rencontray m'amye)	[Clemens non Papa]	1529^4
Gentils galans (C)		Paris: Bibl. nat., MS. *9346* (Bayeux)
Hola hay (C)		1530^4
*Il m'est advis (Celle qui m'a tant)	Claudin	1529^3
Ils se sont endormis (T) (Petite camusette)	Willaert	Le Roy, *Livre de* *Meslanges*, 1560
J'ay contenté (C)	Claudin	1528^3
J'ay mis mon cueur (B)	Gascongne	Cambridge: Magdalene College, MS. *Pepys 1760*
*Je my levay par ung matin (T) [i.e., M'y levay par ung matin]	Janequin	1529^2
Je ne scay pas comment (B)		1529^4
La ou pretend (T) (Jouyssance vous donneray)	Claudin	1528^3
La rosée du moys de may (C)	Richafort	1578^{15}
Le cueur est bon (C)		1528^3
Le content est riche en ce monde (B)	Claudin	1528^3
Le doux acueil (T)		1528^4
Ma dame joliette (B) (*Or sus, vous dormez trop,* i.e., *L'alouette*)	Janequin	Attaingnant, *Chansons de* *Janequin,* [1528]
Mais la puissance est bas (B) (Le cueur est bon)		1528^3
Mon cueur est souvent bien marry (B)	Claudin	1528^3
On a mal dit (C)	Févin	Cambridge: Magdalene College, MS. *Pepys 1760*
On ne fait plus (T) (i.e., On n'en fait plus)		1529^4
Oubly, oubly (T)		1528^5
Pastez trestous chaulx (C) (Voulez ouyr les cris de Paris)	Janequin	*ca.* 1528^9
*Petite camusette (T)	Josquin	Attaingnant, 36e *Livre,* 1549

Fragment	Composer	Source
Portes pour moy (T) (i.e., *Pour moy porte*, from *Amy souffres*)	[Moulu or Claudin]	1529⁴
Povre cueur tant il m' ennuye (T)		1528⁴
Puisqu'en amours (C)	Claudin	1529²
Puisqu'en deux cueurs (B)		1528⁷
*Qui la dira la douleur de mon cueur (C)		1542⁸
Secourez moy (T)	Claudin	1528³
Secretement (C) (Aupres de vous)	[Claudin or Jacotin]	1528³
Seule demeure (C)	Deslouges	1529²
Si de nouveau (B)	Consilium	1572²
Si je my plains (C)	Richafort	1572²
Sonnes my donc quant vous yres (B)		1530⁴
Viens tost despiteux desconfort (C, B)	[Claudin or Appenzeller]	1528⁵
Vignon, vignon (C)		1528⁷
Vivre chez soy (T) (Le content est riche)	Claudin	1528³
Vous ne l'aurez pas (C)	Josquin	1545¹⁵
Vray Dieu d'amours (B)		London: Brit. Mus., *MS. Harley 5242*

10

Influences

It seems undeniable that French music of the Renaissance was not entirely autonomous and came under the influence of other countries to some degree. In trying to determine how much of a debt of gratitude France owes to foreign powers, however, it is often difficult to find out whether certain types of music originated in one country and were transplanted into another, or whether we have cases of parallel manifestations of an independent nature; and so we cannot always establish who influenced whom, and the validity of the idea that any influence, one-sided or mutual, necessarily existed in particular instances.

Some authors are convinced that everything good in fifteenth century French music came from England; others believe it came from Italy. Reese takes a sensible attitude when he states that

> while in the early fifteenth century as in the thirteenth and fourteenth, the French were a great nation in the field of music, their international position was no longer so exclusively that of disseminators; they were also recipients. They combined Italian and English elements with French elements, producing a music that may be called international and bring about a shift from the more pronounced nationalism of fourteenth-century music.[1]

Without entering into the controversy over which country exerted the most influence on fifteenth-century French music, it seems safe to say that, taken as a whole over two centuries, French Renaissance music had more in common and benefited most from its relationship with Italian culture. And so it seems fitting to mention Italy before some of the other pertinent regions.

It has been suggested that *trecento* madrigals and *ballate*, with

[1] Reese, *Renaissance*, p. 9.

their supple melodic lines consisting of fast-moving notes of short values, prefigured ornate treble parts on a liturgical *cantus firmus*, such as in paraphrase Masses.[2] Indeed, Italian music on the whole was more rounded than its French counterpart, and it was to become simpler, with a more harmonic texture. The many northern composers who worked in Italy—the two Lantins brothers, Dufay, Josquin, and Compère, to name only a few—incorporated some of these features in their compositions on Italian texts. Although Josquin called himself a disciple of Ockeghem, not everyone believes that he actually studied with him. It was probably the Milanese Santino Taverna, *prior biscantorum* at the cathedral, who contributed most to Josquin's musical education.[3]

Among the Italian centers which favored French-speaking singers were the papal chapel and the Milanese and Ferrarese courts. Galeazzo Maria Sforza of Milan liked singers more than any other prince in the world, according to Molinet's *Chroniques*. His chapel numbered among its members Josquin, Compère, and Jacotin.[4] A very cordial relationship existed between Ferrara and France, until well into the sixteenth century, and the dukes had their singers recruited in France.[5] Sometimes their singers worked for both courts. Josquin worked for the duke of Ferrara and Louis XII simultaneously in 1501, though we do not know precisely in what capacity he served the French court. Ghiselin-Verbonnet, who was a singer in the Ferrarese chapel, continued to send compositions to the duke, even after entering the service of the French king.[6]

It has been said that the homorhythmic and syllabic frottola

[2] Borren, *Etudes*, p. 64.
[3] Bridgman, *Quattrocento*, p. 123.   [4] Fischer, *Compère*, p. 17.
[5] In a letter of 1491, Isabella d'Este wrote from Mantua that she had sent Verbonnet, her father's singer in Ferrara, 'ad partes Galie' to recruit two singers for her chapel. In 1501, Josquin went on a similar mission for Ercole d'Este (Gottwald, *Ghiselin*, p. 108). Many years later, Alexandre Milleville tried to enlist the help of Claudin de Sermisy in finding boy singers for the duke of Ferrara, but Claudin was too ill to oblige.
[6] Gottwald, *Ghiselin*, pp. 109–110. A pavane and gaillarde 'Ferrareze' were published by Phalèse in 1571[14]. Of the pavane, Gombosi (*Masque*, p. 17) says: 'This is a strange cross between the passamezzo antico and the romanesca. But, after all, the French hardly ever knew what to do with an ostinato bass.'

influenced the sixteenth-century French chanson, and perhaps it is true in a limited sense. Still, it is possible to find antecedents for the new chanson style in older French sources, as has been shown earlier, and they would seem likely to have been more direct models than songs from across the border. The similarity of French and Italian pieces may have represented parallel currents. Regardless of their importance as influences on French music, the frottole were known to certain French musicians who wrote some while in Italy (Josquin's *El grillo*, for example), and their patrons. Whether they were imported on a large scale is another matter. When the marquis of Mantua was at the court of France in August 1516, Marchetto Cara sent him four books of frottole, which he must have shared with his French hosts.[7]

Marguerite of Navarre, in her *Heptameron* (no. 19), translates *Che fara la, che dira la*, the music of which appears in Antico's *Canzoni* (1513[1]).[8] French composers from the first part of the sixteenth century manifested interest in Italian texts by setting some to music. Also in favor with musicians were translations or adaptations of Petrarch. Sermisy's *Allez souspirs* (from *Ite caldi sospiri*) and *Bien heureuse est la saison et l'année* (Francis I's version of *Benedetto sia il giorno*), and Boyvin's *Mort sans soleil* (Clément Marot's paraphrase of *Lasciato hai morte*) are examples of these.[9] The French instrumental repertoire also reflects the love for Italian music. Examples are *La gatta en italien*, and *La scarpa my faict mal*, from Attaingnant's *Neuf basses dances*, from 1530. Attaingnant published several Italian pieces in his collections, and so did Moderne—many more, in fact. But it should come as no surprise, since Moderne was of Istrian origin.

From the time of Charles VIII at least, French kings had taken an interest in things Italian, because they had seen and heard them during their Italian campaigns. In order to repair and embellish his castle of Amboise, Charles brought and sent for painters, stone cutters, and other artisans from the kingdom of Naples. All in all, he had twenty-two Italian workmen

[7] Heartz, in Haar, *Chanson*, p. 115.

[8] Pirro, *Pour l'histoire*, p. 52.

[9] The pieces by Janequin and Boyvin appear in Lesure, *Anthologie*, pp. 26 ff. and 44 ff.

in his residence. He was particularly impressed with Italian ceilings, and once wrote from Italy that 'the ceilings of Beauce, Lyon and other places in France do not begin to compare with the beauty and richness of those from here. That is why I shall obtain some and will take them with me to make some at Amboise.'[10] He was also interested in Italian musical contributions, apparently, because, after his first Italian campaign, he brought with him the organ builder Giovanni da Grana.[11]

In 1502, Louis XII brought back six musicians from Milan, whom he engaged at the rate of 120 *livres* per year. They included sackbut players and oboists. He had already had two Italian trumpeters in his service.[12] Francis I also imported Italian musicians, particularly violinists.[13] It has been noted that on the whole, these kings of France seemed to be more interested in Italin instrumentalists than in Italian composers.[14] The composer Albert de Rippe, from Mantua, was a favorite among royalty, to be sure, but it may have been because of his prowess on the lute rather than his creative ability.[15] French kings on journeys to Italy were usually accompanied by their personal chapel, whose singers often doubled as composers. The monarchs seem to have been happy with the work of their own composer-singers, and so did not try to hire Italian rivals. In fact, Louis XII appreciated Févin so much that he occasionally promoted his music abroad. In a letter dated 7 April 1507, he asked that one of Févin's chansons be sent to him, so that he could have the Italian ladies hear it.[16]

[10] Commynes, *Mémoires*, III: p. 110, note 2, and p. 302, note 3.

[11] Heartz, in Haar, *Chanson*, p. 91.

[12] Chaillon, *Louis XII*, p. 65.   [13] Boyden, *Violin*, p. 21.

[14] Brown, in Haar, *Chanson*, p. 36. Benvenuto Cellini, whom Francis I attracted to his court, used to play the flute as an avocation, when he was in Florence, and rather well at that (Bridgman, *Quattrocento*, p. 53). We shall not try to claim, however, that he was called to the court for his musical talent. Not everyone was entranced with the vogue for things Italian. Some took a dim view of Cardinal de Tournon's predilection for Italian arts and letters and of his apparent sympathy for Italy. In a letter dated 2 March 1558, Jean de la Vigne, Henry II's ambassador to Constantinople, refers to 'ceste mauldicte Italie dont nous n'avons jamais rapporté qu'une infinité de vices et mauvaises opinions' (François, *Tournon*, p. 494).

[15] Ronsard dedicated poems to him as well as to Ferrabosco (Lesure, *Musicians*, p. 54).   [16] Chaillon, *Louis XII*, p. 66.

Marsilio Ficino's writings were well-known to the circle of humanists associated with Marguerite of Navarre. As late as 1582, Guy Le Fèvre de la Boderie, translator of Ficino's *De triplici vita*, and an ardent Catholic of the Counter-Reformation, included in his *Hymnes ecclésiastiques* the translation of three Orphic hymns by Ficino, one of which is a hymn to the sun.[17] Miss Yates has shown that the influence of Ficino's Orphic chant was still felt well into the sixteenth century, in such works as Claude Le Jeune's *O Reine d'honneur* (*Airs*, 1608), with its incantation to the heavenly bodies, and the *Balet comique de la royne*, with its astrological connotations.[18]

Italian influence was manifested in French music until the end of the century and even later. Petrarchan adaptations such as Claude Le Jeune's chanson *Un jour estant seulet* are still published in 1586, and the neo-Petrarchan sonnet maintains itself in the work of Desportes, whose models include, in addition to Petrarch, Cariteo, Tebaldeo, and Ariosto.[19] Airs on Italian words appear side by side with French pieces in collections by Le Roy et Ballard. Composers of *canzonette*, *villanelle*, airs, and occasional madrigals include Le Jeune, Caietain, and Tessier.[20] Madrigalism in French music from the second half of the sixteenth century—that of Caietain and Maletty, for example, probably echoes its Italian counterpart.[21] Some word-painting was nevertheless present in chansons by Sermisy and his contemporaries from Attaingnant's era. Jean Servin used the style of the dramatic madrigal in his *Regrets de Didon*. Many *airs de cour* contain pastoral themes, which could be derived from Italian pastoral madrigals. Or perhaps they should be considered offshoots of the mediaeval *pastourelles* and earlier Renaissance chansons such as *Bergerette savoysienne* or cruder ones, such as *Le bergier et la bergiere*. Still, these airs seem closer to the preciosity of the Italian pastoral madrigals than to the earlier, more direct French chansons.

[17] Walker, *Chant*, pp. 24–25.   [18] Yates, *Magnificences*, pp. 249, 254–255.
[19] Verchaly, *Airs*, p. 47.
[20] *Ibid.*, pp. 45–46. See also Levy, *Vaudeville*, pp. 199–201. In the discussion, Miss Yates mentions that Baïf's mother was Venetian, and suggests that *vers mesurés* are of Italian origin.
[21] Many examples are given in Levy, *Le Jeune*, pp. 196–197.

Whether French polychoral music by Le Jeune, Du Caurroy, and seventeenth-century composers owes more to the earlier French experiments in that style or to Willaert and the Venetians is hard to tell. Although there were double choruses in France in the first half of the sixteenth century, as we have seen, it is mainly in Italy that the genre was developed, and it is not impossible that it in turn influenced later French composers. Only one book of Marenzio's madrigals was published in Paris (1598); it was for four voices instead of the more common five.[22] The chromatic madrigal *Passa la nave mia* by Vicentino, who may have come to France, was published by Le Roy et Ballard in 1572, and could be one of the pieces which Adrian Le Roy showed Charles IX in 1571–72.[23] Several prints show the taste for Italian genres already on the title-page—such as Caietain's *Second livre d'airs, chansons, villanelles napolitaines et espagnoles* (Le Roy, 1582), or Guillaume Tessier's *Premier livre d'airs tant François, Italien qu'Espagnol* (Le Roy, 1552). Verchaly sees the possible influence of *passagi*, as exposed in Bovicelli's *Regole* (Venice, 1594), on the French air.[24]

The mascarade, by whatever name—it was sometimes called *momerie*—was Italian in origin. The custom of masquerading was developed at Ferrara and Modena under the patronage of the Este family. Francis I, who saw some of these spectacles in Italy, imported Italian dancers and musicians to Fontainebleau. His successors, and particularly his daughter-in-law Catherine, continued the trend and promoted what came to be called the *ballet de cour*. Balthasare de Beujoyeux, organizer of the *Balet comique de la royne*, was an Italian, though other participants, such as La Chesnaye, probable author of the words, and Lambert de Beaulieu, composer of the songs, were French.[25] An Italian group, the *Comici gelosi*, gave theatrical spectacles under the reign of Henry III.[26]

[22] Verchaly (*Airs*, p. 48) points out that the polyphony is simple and does not contain daring harmonies. Perhaps that is why it was considered suitable for French ears. Alexander (*Moduli*, p. 89) notes that 'despite the possibilities of cross-fertilization during the Renaissance, Palestrina's influence appears not to have been important in France. . . . Neither Du Chemin nor Le Roy et Ballard printed his works.'

[23] Levy, *Costeley*, p. 248.   [24] Verchaly, *Métrique*, p. 73.

[25] Gombosi, *Masque*, p. 5, and Dent-Sternfeld, in *New Oxford*, IV: pp. 804–807.   [26] Verchaly, *Airs*, p. 46.

It was not only Italian practical music which was appreciated in France, but also theory; and Zarlino seems to have been honored above all contemporary theorists. In a hymn to music (1582), the poet Jean-Edouard Du Monin writes: 'Boèce prend tout pour soi l'honneur du présent âge/ En laissant un rameau au Zarlinois visage.'[27] Mersenne, in his *Harmonie universelle* (L. 5, p. 283), gives credit to Zarlino, from whom Du Caurroy 'et tous les autres, médiatement ou immédiatement, ont puisé tout ce qu'ils sçavent de pratique.'[28]

It was mostly during the fifteenth century that the influence of English music was felt in France. The English occupation of a large part of the country after the battle of Agincourt led to the establishment of English musical chapels on French territory. Musicians such as Dunstable, of 'frisque concordance' fame, travelled to the Continent. The chapel of the duke of Bedford, at the time of his regency, included Frenchmen and Englishmen. Henry V and Henry VI brought their chapel with them during their stay in France. Binchois was in the service of the duke of Suffolk, and perhaps also worked for the duke and duchess of Gloucester. It was probably as a result of his contact with the English that he derived stylistic traits similar to those of some of the composers represented in the Old Hall manuscript, and his apparent predilection for the Sarum ritual and chant.[29]

Dufay may have been working in English-dominated Rouen from 1438 to 1441. Robert Morton, who went to the Burgundian court in 1457, and was appreciated by Tinctoris and Hothby, was at Rouen as early as 1429–30.[30] It seems therefore that French music must have been tinged with 'contenance angloise' for some time before 1441, when Martin Le Franc mentioned it in his *Champion des dames*. Among the continental practices for which English origins have been claimed are:

[27] Quoted in Lesure, *Minor*, p. 541.
[28] Quoted in Cohen, *Survivals*, p. 83.
[29] Pirro, *Charles VI*, pp. 34–36, and Parris, *Binchois*, pp. 19, 248.
[30] Parris, *Binchois*, pp. 21–22. Kanazawa (*Vespers*, I: p. 114) notes that Binchois's polyphonic hymn *Ut queant laxis*, unlike hymns in fauxbourdon by Dufay, which generally have their *cantus firmus* in the upper voice, has its third voice 'to be performed a fourth above, not below the cantus, a procedure akin to the so-called "faburden" of English compositions of slightly earlier date.'

polyphonic cyclical Masses, the use of *cantus firmus* in the upper voice, ornamentation of the *cantus firmus*, and the practice of *fauxbourdon*.[31]

Certainly English music was well-liked on the Continent. Walter Frye's music, for example, found its way into several manuscripts otherwise comprising Burgundian repertoire. French composers sometimes used English melodies; the *Missa Caput*, with settings by Dufay and Ockeghem among others, is based on an English model.[32] The musical entertainment at the Field of the Cloth of Gold included exchanges of masked visits between English and French parties, to musical accompaniment.[33] At least one Englishman sang *haute-contre* at the Sainte-Chapelle in the 1580s. He is presumed to be Nicholas Morgan, a former member of the English Chapel Royal, and a penniless fugitive from his country 'because he wanted to die a Catholic and refused to join the Huguenots.' From time to time the authorities of the Sainte-Chapelle allotted him the sum of ten *écus* as a charitable gesture.[34]

Other countries besides Italy and England contributed to French musical life. Flemish music has been so closely linked to French music that musicologists have spoken of a Franco-Flemish style, which is too well known to bear elaboration here. There are differences, however, which we have seen, between Flemish and French traits. Northerners are generally more strict and heavy in their polyphony, and they use more *ostinato* lines than do the French, who specialize in a simpler,

[31] Kenney, *Frye*, pp. 5–6, 93. Mme Clercx (*Faux-bourdon*) states unequivocally that fauxbourdon originated in Italy, where Dufay probably heard it. Mrs Scott (*Fauxbourdon*, pp. 345, 363) summarizes the arguments for and against the English origins of the practice and concludes that 'there was a tradition of improvised polyphony in England that involved three voices and that necessarily required a parallel style. With the c.f. in the middle voice, the technique differed from fauxbourdon but produced similar results. . . . The technique known vaguely as a species of organum, perhaps as "trebill song" travelled to the continent where it was embraced, adapted, and given a name. In turn the English willingly adopted a corrupt version [faburden] of the French label.'

[32] Planchart (*Dufay*, p. 11) suggests that Dufay's version, including the *Kyrie*, which was added later for the use of Cambrai, may have been entirely English.

[33] Gombosi, *Masque*, p. 5.

[34] Brenet, *Sainte-Chapelle*, pp. 136, 139.

more homorhythmic style, with clearer declamation. Often the only thing they seem to have in common is a predilection for French poetic texts. Composers born in regions corresponding to present-day Belgium, however, have worked in France and have been appreciated there. Lassus, whom Ronsard called 'le plus que divin Orlande,' had a reputation among the French such as perhaps only Josquin had enjoyed earlier.[35]

German instrumentalists were in demand in several centers. The court of Savoy engaged some between 1391 and 1410 at least.[36] Several drummers and one flutist who played at the wedding festivities for Anne of Brittany and Charles VIII in Rennes were German. Gregor Brayssing, Protestant lutenist from Augsburg, whose guitar book was published by Le Roy et Ballard in 1553, lived in Paris from 1553 to 1560. There he entertained friendly relations with French musicians and became godfather to a child of Etienne Du Tertre and a daughter of Loys Bourgeois.[37] Gaspard Duiffoprugcar, maker of stringed instruments and some particularly beautiful viols, became a naturalized Frenchman in 1558.

Two famous lutenists who came to France from Central Europe were Jacob le Polonais and the Transylvanian Valentin Bakfark. Both were associated with the French court.

At least one Spanish composer, Guerrero, was considered important enough to have a whole volume devoted to his Masses (Du Chemin, 1566). The Spanish tune *Conde claros* was used by Guillaume Morlaye in works for guitar and for cittern, under the titles *Conte clare* and *Contreclare*.

Music in France was undoubtedly the richer for the contributions of foreign musicians who came to its shores, or whose publications reached French circles.

France was not only on the receiving end, in terms of Renaissance music, but, we believe, also gave its share to the musical life of Europe. It seems that it was in the countries which most influenced France that French music and

---

[35] C. Marot's *D'ung nouveau dard*, in an anonymous setting (1528[4]). advises the singing of 'Allegez moy, doulce playsant brunette'—doubtless a reference to Josquin's *Allegez moy*. This is one more example of Josquin's popularity.

[36] Pirro, *Histoire*, p. 26.   [37] Lesure, *Guitare*, p. 192.

musicians were most welcome; and so we can surmise that the influence must have been mutual.

Already in the early fifteenth century, French musicians found work in various Italian centers and were much in demand there. When the papal court left Avignon and returned to Rome, it brought along many French singers. Later on, and for several years after 1410, chapel members were recruited almost exclusively in the dioceses of Northern France. Many of the papal singers came from Cambrai—Grenon, Dufay, and Jean Cornuel, to name only a few. One of the most musical popes of the Renaissance, Leo X, a Medici, asked Louis XII several times for French singers, and thereby gained Elzéar Genet as director of his chapel. Other French members have included Josquin, Mouton, Longueval, Bidon, and Conseil.[38] The latter was recommended by the pope to Francis I for a prebend, in 1517.[39] Costanzo Festa, who became a papal singer after 1517, was probably at the French court in 1514, when he wrote his funeral motet for Anne of Brittany, and may have brought French music with him to please the pope.[40]

French singers were welcome in Milan. Beltrame Feragut, from Avignon, was 'tenorista' and director of the Milanese cathedral choir from 1425 to 1430. Later in the century, under the leadership of Gafori, the cathedral personnel, which had included several French singers since 1460, became largely Italian, in contradistinction to the ducal chapel, which favored *oltramontani* such as Josquin and Compère. It was probably Galeazzo Maria Sforza who had promoted the hiring of French musicians at the cathedral. When he formed his private chapel in 1471, he took over foreign singers from the *duomo* and recruited others abroad. He enlisted the help of Ockeghem for that purpose in 1472. The duke's predilection for French culture in general—including French music—can be ascribed to his French education. His wife, Bona of Savoy, sister of Charlotte, Louis XI's queen, may have been responsible for Josquin's Milanese sojourn.[41] Understandably, French

[38] *See* Borren, *Etudes*, pp. 18–19, Pirro, *Leo X*, pp. 4–11, and Chapman, *Antico*, p. 303.   [39] Pirro, *Pour l'histoire*, p. 52.

[40] Perkins, *Lowinsky*, pp. 263–264.

[41] *See* Bridgman, *Quattrocento*, pp. 109–110, 119–120, Pirro, *Histoire*, p.

influence, political and cultural, continued to be felt in the Milanese region during the time of Charles VIII's and Louis XII's Italian expeditions and occupation.

There was cooperation between the courts of France and of Ferrara in matters musical. This was particularly true when Renée of France, sister of Queen Claude, was duchess of Ferrara.

Florentine circles accepted French musicians and French musical ideas. Piero de' Medici admired Dufay, as did his son Lorenzo, who sent him one of his poems to set to music. In 1467, Antonio Squarcialupi thanked Dufay for sending good singers from Cambrai to the chapel of the Medici.[42] The Florentine cathedral and baptistry included personnel with French names well into the sixteenth century. Carlo d'Argentina, listed in a roster of 1525, may have been the Frenchman Charles d'Argentil. Philippe Verdelot, choirmaster at the baptistry of San Giovanni from 1523 to 1525, contributed in no small way to the history of the early Italian madrigal.[43] In later years, the circle of Count Bardi, whose discussions and experiments led to the development of opera and oratorio, was similar in many ways to Baïf's *Académie*, particularly in the linking of music and morals.[44]

Venetian printers including Petrucci, Antico, Scotto and the Frenchman Gardane published countless pieces by French composers. Music by Sermisy, Janequin, and other composers of the sixteenth century was printed in Venice before it

103, and Clinksdale, *Josquin*, p. 68. The latter also quotes from C. Sartori (*Annales Musicologiques*, IV: p. 68), and S. Clercx (*Revue belge de musicologie*, XI (1957), p. 155.

[42] Bridgman, *Quattrocento*, pp. 109–111.

[43] D'Accone, *Chapels*, pp. 18–22.

[44] *See* Yates, *Academies*. Dent-Sternfeld (*New Oxford*, IV; pp. 805–806) note that concerning the interest of Baïf and his *Académie* in recreating classical dance based on classical prosody, it is uncertain whether their ideas were derived from Italian choreographers such as Fabrizio Caroso, who mention classical meters in their treatises, or whether it was the Italians who were influenced by the French. The fact that Rinuccini and Caccini spent some time at the French court may have had some bearing on their operatic work. H. Prunières, in his study of Monteverdi, suggests that the composer's *Scherzi musicali* were inspired by *musique mesurée* (*Damigella*, for example, is metrically similar to Le Jeune's *Revecy venir du printemps*)—a thesis with which Schrade strongly disagrees.

appeared in France—but then it was prior to Attaingnant's first print of polyphonic music in 1528. In 1536, the Venetian Francesco d'Asola asked permission to reprint several French books, among them 'uno libretto di canto canzon 29 di Paris'—presumably by Attaingnant (1530³).[45] Some Venetian prints such as *La Courone et fleur des chansons a troys* (A. Dell'Abbate, A. Antico, 1536¹) are devoted entirely to French pieces; others, such as Gardane's *Di Costantio Festa il primo libro di madrigali* (1541¹³) include French and Italian pieces. It is falsely claimed on the title-page of this collection that the thirty songs are by Janequin—so as to attract buyers—whereas in reality they are not, as Lesure has shown.[46] French chansons were sung not only in private homes, but in the street, and one of the most popular of these, according to Andrea Calmo, was Passereau's *Il est bel et bon*, with its onomatopoetic imitation of the clucking of hens.

French musicians were in demand in the Aragonese kingdom of Naples, at the court of Alfonso el Magnanimo and Fernando I; in 1487 the latter sent Tinctoris to recruit singers in France and elsewhere.[47]

Numerous manuscripts from various regions of Italy or of presumably Italian provenance include French works or pieces in the French style. Among the important ones are Modena: Bibl. Estense, *M. 5. 24*, with many French ballades by Italian composers, Florence: Bibl. del Conservatorio, *Basevi 2439* and *2442*, consisting entirely of French music, Oxford: Bodleian Libr., *Canonici misc. 213,* Bologna: Civico Museo Bibliografico Musicale, *Q 19*, Montecassino *N 871*, and the Medici codex. Certain Florentine manuscripts contain a mingling of French and Italian refrains.[48]

Translations and adaptations of French texts have been used in Italian *laude*.[49] Transcriptions of French chansons have been made in Italian collections of instrumental music. The original name of the Italian *canzone*—the *canzone alla francese* is self-explanatory. Various Italians have set French texts to

[45] Thibault, *Vogue*, pp. 61–65.
[46] Lesure, *Janequin*, pp. 193–198.
[47] Pope, *Montecassino*, p. 129.
[48] Ghisi, in Lesure, *Eléments*, p. 181.
[49] Pirro, *Histoire*, p. 168.

music. They include Fabrice Marin Caietain, who emigrated from Italy to France, where he served in the chapel of the dukes of Lorraine. He studied with Thibaut de Courville and Lambert de Beaulieu. His contribution to the development of the French *air de cour* is known. Ingegneri, Monteverdi's teacher, composed two chansons in 1580.[50]

Certain well-known French tunes found their way into Italy. *Roti boulli gioioso* is a translation of the French basses-danse *Roti bouilli joyeux*.[51] The popular *l'Homme armé* melody was used by Palestrina.

Various Italians paid tribute to French musicians. Pietro Bembo, poet, cardinal, and secretary to Leo X, considered one of the pope's French choirboys 'the most skillful, and the one endowed with the most agreeable and flexible voice.'[52] Castiglione depicts people admiring a motet only after they have been told that it is by Josquin. The poet Folengo likes a *Chirie* by Josquin better than what he calls Italian *merdagalli*.[53] Gafori, in his *Practica musica*, mentions Compère, Josquin, and Brumel among celebrated contrapuntalists. A treatise by the seventeenth-century theorist G. B. Doni (Paris: Bibl. nat. *MS. fr. 19065*) mentions the music of Claude Le Jeune as moderately easy to perform—more difficult than that of Lassus and Marenzio, and simpler than that of Gesualdo.[54] The fact that Le Jeune was mentioned at all, among the other famous composers, shows in what esteem he was held abroad. It should be noted that Doni, though Florentine born, received part of his education in Bourges, and returned for a time to France, after his studies. His principal solution to the problems of writing opera—that only certain parts should be set to music and the rest recited—seems to echo French ideas; it was not accepted in his own country.

To a lesser degree, French music must have made its mark among the British. The duke of Suffolk, who wrote poems in French and numbered among his friends Charles d'Orléans, had French music performed at his court.[55] Binchois's *ballade*

---

[50] Lesure, *Musicians*, pp. 82, 102.   [51] *See* Heartz, *Rôti*.

[52] Pirro, *Leo X*, p. 8.   [53] Bridgman, *Quattrocento*, p. 110.

[54] Levy, *Le Jeune*, p. 7.

[55] Marix, *Musiciens*, p. xviii.

Dueil angoisseus served as basis for a Mass by Bedingham. It has
been suggested that Picard, one of the most representative
composers featured in the Old Hall manuscript may have been
French, or of French descent.[56] As Martin Le Franc had paid
tribute to Dunstable and English music towards the middle of
the fifteenth century, John Hothby returned the politeness
almost a half century later by mentioning Dufay, Busnois,
Ockeghem and other Frenchmen in his *Dialogus . . . in arte
musica*.[57] Several English composers including Walter Frye,
Robert Morton, and William Cornysh wrote music to French
texts. Manuscripts such as London: Brit. Mus., *Add. 31922* and
Royal 8. G. vii contain French music.[58] Some of it must have
been performed at the court of Henry VIII. Much as we accept
the idea that the most direct influence on the late sixteenth-
century English madrigal was the Italian madrigal and the
publication in England of *Musica Transalpina* and *Italian
Madrigals Englished*, it does not seem unreasonable to suppose
that the French chanson may have had a small part in the
early stages of the English madrigal.

The French pavane and chansons in pavane rhythm may
have had some bearing on Dowland's works of the same
type.[59] Similarities have been noted between English *ayres* and
French *airs de cour*. Dowland visited France in 1579 and may
have met some exponents of the genre. That there was some
interest in the French air in England is suggested by Guillaume
Tessier's dedication of his first book of airs (Paris, 1582) to
Queen Elizabeth, and the printing in London of Charles
Tessier's first book of chansons and *airs de cour* (1597) by
Dowland's publisher Thomas East.[60] Translations of Le Roy's
instrumental methods appeared in England.

British visitors to France were often exposed to musical
spectacles of the courtly type. In February 1585, for example,
an English delegation came to France to bestow the Order of
the Garter upon Henry III. This was the occasion for many
celebrations with ballets and mascarades in honor of the

[56] Borren, *Etudes*, p. 99.
[57] Brooks, *Busnois*, p. 8.
[58] Harrison, in *New Oxford*, III: pp. 304, 347.
[59] Borren, in *New Oxford*, IV: pp. 3–4.
[60] Dart, *Ayre*, p. 205.

English lords, who 'must have heard the last performances of ballet music by the team which had produced and executed the *Ballet comique de la reine.*'[61] The influence of this work on the English masque was felt well into the seventeenth century. Up to about 1605, the British still used the *Balet comique*'s characteristic 'dispersed scenery' for its masques; and in 1631, in a similar spectacle presented before Charles I and his queen Henrietta Maria, daughter of Henry IV of France, references were made to astrological influences and to Circe, as in the *Balet comique.*[62]

Scottish manuscripts contain some French pieces in the original, such as Dufay's *L'Homme armé* Mass, or as contrafacta. The only known British Mass on *L'Homme armé* is by Robert Carver, canon of Scone, and dates from about 1546.[63]

Persons of Flemish origin or with Flemish names, from Hayne de Ghizeghem to Philippe de Monte, have set French words to music, and Belgian publishers, such as Susato in Antwerp and Phalese in Louvain, have disseminated French works—preferably by Northerners. Some French tunes, such as *Sur le pont d'Avignon* and Sermisy's *Dont vient cela*, were used for the Flemish psalter, the *Souterliedekens*. Belgians such as Lassus, Monte, and Jean de Castro wrote music for Ronsard's poetry. An inventory of the library of the Belgian duke Charles de Croy made in 1614 lists music by Guillaume Morlaye and a collection by Certon.[64]

Flemish musicians occasionally worked or studied in France

[61] Yates, *Processions*, p. 259.

[62] Dart-Sternfeld, in *New Oxford*, IV: p. 814.

[63] *See* Harrison, in *New Oxford*, III: pp. 337–338, and Shire, *Scotland*. There had been Franco-Scottish royal marriages during the fifteenth and sixteenth centuries. Margaret of Scotland was Louis XI's first wife; Madeleine of France, daughter of Francis I, became the wife of James V of Scotland, and his daughter, Mary Stuart, was for a short time queen of France as the wife of Francis II.

[64] Birkner, *Croy*, p. 44. The duke was the author of a lute tablature (Valenciennes: Bibl. municipale, *MS. 429*). Birkner (p. 20) quotes from a letter in which Croy thanks God for having delivered him from his first wife and 'de la captivité, des peines et des travaulx qu'avois enduré avec icelle.' The expression 'peines et travaulx' seems to have been fashionable at the time, and perhaps the duke was familiar with one of the settings of *Pour ung plaisir qui si peu dure/ J'ay enduré peine et travaulx* (by Sermisy or Crecquillon), or one of the several songs beginning with the words *Peine et travail*.

before serving elsewhere. Alexander Agricola spent some years with Charles VIII before entering the service of Philip the Fair in 1500. The scribe Alamire, who visited France in 1516 and 1518, copied, among other things, a choirbook containing many French works, which was sent from the chapel of Charles V to Henry VIII and Catherine of Aragon. It includes a motet originally written for Anne of Brittany and Louis XII, concerning their desire for a son, but with the names changed to Catherine and Henry. Herbert Kellman notes that

> it is not surprising that there is evidence of musical links between the royal chapel of France and the imperial chapel of the Netherlands, despite the necessary role of these chapels in serving political antagonists. . . . The relationship between the two repertoires indicates that the French chapel is the supplier and the Netherlands chapel is the borrower of music that forms an increasingly important component of the imperial repertory.[65]

French musical influence in Germany was probably minimal at the time of the Renaissance, although French music was reprinted by Georg Rhaw in Wittenberg, and by others. French tunes were used in Protestant contrafacta as well as in instrumental transcriptions—sometimes with fanciful titles, such as *Du wentzela* (originally *Dont vient cela*) from Neusidler's lute book of 1540, or *Der Pissepot*. Since Heckel, in his lute book of 1562, designates this as 'ein welscher Tanz,' we had better take his word for it. At least one expression from French manuscripts and prints passed into Germany—'Missa ad imitationem . . .' An anthology published by Schwertel in Wittenberg (1568[1]) labels every one of the Masses thus.[66] Theorists from Adam von Fulda to Seybald Heyden mention Dufay, Busnois, and other French composers with respect.[67]

A French psalter was found in the library of Erik XIV of Sweden, according to an inventory of 1568. The king, who

---

[65] Kellman, *Links,* pp. 23–24. In 1543, Charles V sent his chapel director, Cornelius Canis, to recruit choirboys at Lille (Pirro, *Histoire,* p. 307).

[66] Lockwood, *Parody,* p. 563.   [67] Brooks, *Busnois,* pp. 8, 13.

spoke French, played the lute and composed; he was a personal friend of the Antwerpian publisher Susato. A lute tablature (Uppsala. Univ. Bibl. *MS. 87*) which is probably French in origin and includes psalms by Certon, may have been at one time in the king's possession.[68]

French note-types similar to Attaingnant's were imitated in all of Europe, and as far as Iceland, where a psalter of 1589 was printed from German type, probably cut after French models.[69]

The Bohemian Jacobus Gallus wrote a Mass on Crecquillon's *Ung gay bergier*. Intabulations of French works are found in Poland, which was to have, very briefly, a French king in the person of the future Henry III. (This episode was immortalized in Chabrier's opera *Le roi malgré lui*.) The tablature of John of Lublin contains some French tunes. Roger Pathie, French organist to Mary of Hungary, recruited musicians for her in Lille and Arras in 1542.[70] The French repertoire in fifteenth-century Cyprus was mentioned earlier.

French music was collected on the Iberian peninsula. Two of the best-known bibliophiles were King John IV of Portugal and Ferdinand Columbus, son of the explorer.[71] French chansons were transcribed in Spanish instrumental collections. Fuenllana's *Orphenica lyra* (1554) for vihuela, contains intabulations of French chansons, including Sermisy's *Tant que vivray en age florissant*. Venegas de Henestrosa's *Libro de cifra* (1557) lists *Revellebu*—i.e., Janequin's *Chant des oyseaux* (*Reveillez-vous, cueurs endormis*), and Cabezon's *Obras de musica* (1578) also for keyboard, includes Claudin's ever popular *Dont vient cela*, spelled this time *Duviensela*. Morales composed several Masses based on French motets, two on *L'Homme armé*, and one on Josquin's *Mille regretz*. Guerrero wrote one on Janequin's *La guerre*. In his *Musica pratica* (1482), the avant-garde Spanish theorist Bartolomé Ramos de Pareja mentions Busnois as an authority on music, along with Dufay and Ockeghem.[72] Pierre de Manchicourt, from Béthune, became

---

[68] Hambraeus, *Carminum*, pp. 59–62.

[69] Davidsson, *Isländskt*, p. 108.   [70] Pirro, *Histoire*, p. 307.

[71] *See* Vasconcellos, *Livraria*, and Chapman, *Columbus*. Many works from Attaingnant's time were listed among the holdings of these libraries.

[72] Brooks, *Busnois*, p. 7.

director of Philip II's *capilla flamenca*, which stemmed from the former Burgundian chapel choir. Finally, one brave Frenchman, F. de Caillières, in his *Les mots à la mode* (1692), claimed French origins for the passacaglia, and asserts that 'la passacaille des Espagnols, qui est une composition de musique, était la passerue ou vaudeville des Français.'[73]

Reaction to French music of the fifteenth and sixteenth centuries through the ages has ranged from one of utter neglect to sporadic attempts at revival of the repertoire, and from disapproval of certain aspects of this music to unbounded enthusiasm for it. Albert Cohen finds survivals of Renaissance musical thought in French theory until about 1660–70—particularly in the writings of Mersenne, which reflect a humanistic point of view in the attention given to mathematical and astrological aspects of music. The favorite composers of most theorists were Josquin, Le Jeune, Lassus, and Du Caurroy.[74] Pierre Trichet, in his treatise on instruments (after 1638), refers several times to Adrian Le Roy and his methods for various instruments.[75]

Musicologists such as Alexandre Choron, François-Joseph Fétis, and Joseph Napoléon Ney, prince de la Moskova, were among the first to revive works of the French Renaissance by promoting concerts and musical editions, and by writing about the composers and their works. Choron's *Collection*

[73] Frissard, *Chardavoine*, p. 63. That there was some association between various terms for 'street' is suggested by the sobriquet 'Caillerue,' which was given to one of the Cambraisian ecclesiastics born with the unfortunate name 'Crassequaule' (Pirro, *Cornuel*, p. 202).

[74] A. Cohen (*Survivals*, pp. 82–83) states that 'the abstract, idealized music that formed the theoretical basis for the first part of the century . . . —founded upon Renaissance practice—reflected not only "an age that turned to geometry for an expression of truth and beauty" (Yates, *Academies*, p. 284) but one during which theory and practice were often divorced from each other.' It is true that Mersenne, in his *Questions harmoniques* (1634) decided that 'la spéculation d'un art est inutile . . . si on ne la réduit en pratique,' but, as Cohen notes, 'not without deliberation.' Mersenne, in his *Harmonie universelle*, comments on Glarean's anecdote about Josquin's song for the king of France and seems particularly impressed by Josquin's pedagogical talents. 'Josquin has shown,' he comments, 'that an inflexible and bad voice can sing its part . . . and made the king admit that he could sing in music' (Bibliothèque nationale, *Musique*, p. 38). [75] Lesure, *Trichet*, p. 218.

générale des oeuvres classiques (1806) represented the first practical editions of music by Josquin and Goudimel. His concerts included on the programs Janequin's *La Guerre* and his *Cris de Paris*.[76] Among the works performed by Fétis's groups at the Salle du Conservatoire, in Paris, from 1832 to 1835 were excerpts from the *Balet comique de la royne*, sacred works by Josquin and Mouton, and chansons by Janequin and Goudimel.[77] His writings, and particularly the monumental and much criticized *Biographie universelle des musiciens*, brought to light countless documents about composers, including those from the French Renaissance. The prince de la Moskova, son of one of Napoleon's marshals, and not primarily a musicologist, nevertheless founded a useful *Societé des concerts de musique vocale religieuse et classique*, in 1843, which he directed himself, which specialized in music of the Renaissance and the seventeenth century, and which promoted the edition of music by Josquin, Du Caurroy, and many others. In addition, he helped with the Renaissance concerts of Fétis and Delsarte. It was only in the last decade of the nineteenth century that the Renaissance concerts and editions of Charles Bordes and Henry Expert were organized.[78]

Other musicologists, such as Burney (who, like many others including Fétis, borrowed information from Laborde), were aware of some works of the French Renaissance. Some of them were misinformed, occasionally misattributed compositions, or made errors in judgment. Burney and Maldeghem, for example, have taken Sermisy for Le Jeune or Goudimel, because all of them were named Claude and called Claudin, and their family name was not always given in their musical publications. And there is Eitner's charming and familiar ghost from the *Quellen-Lexikon*, the sixteenth-century 'composer,' Ungay Bergier.[79] In a review of a concert of the *Association chorale professionnelle* under the direction of D. E. Ingelbrecht (*Mercure musical*, 1 March 1914), Josquin's *Mille regretz* was unceremoniously ascribed to Claude Le Jeune.[80]

[76] Haraszti, in Roland-Manuel, *Histoire*, II: pp. 1562–1563.

[77] Wangermée, *Fétis*, pp. 303–308.

[78] Lesure, *Debussy*, p. 242.

[79] Eitner is referring, of course, to Crecquillon's or to Janequin's chanson, *Un gay bergier*.   [80] Lesure, *Debussy*, p. 243.

Fétis did not believe that Ockeghem's thirty-six part canon existed, because 'such a composition was absolutely impossible in Ockeghem's time.'[81] J. R. Sterndale-Bennet believed that Janequin was a Jew, because he had set to music French paraphrases of the proverbs of Solomon.[82] Errors such as these are not the monopoly of musicological pioneers, and equivalent ones could surely be found in more recent works, if one searched diligently enough. (Reviewers do it all the time.) Occasional mistakes, however, are not what earlier musicologists should be remembered by—and these minor flaws are more than compensated for by the positive contributions of these men, who brought Renaissance music to light.

The esthetic reaction to given types of early French music seems to vary from century to century, and sometimes from individual to individual. Programmatic chansons, for example, which, judging from all accounts, were immensely popular in the sixteenth century, have not always pleased listeners from several centuries later. Van den Borren finds them a bit monotonous.[83] Alfred Franklin gives the following criticism of Janequin's *Cris de Paris* in *La vie privée d'autrefois* (1887):

> I have nothing to say about the music—a quartet which would undoubtedly be little appreciated today. It is probable that Janequin was also the author of the words, and if he was proud of it, he was wrong. But Janequin was a musician, not a poet, and it is clear that from one end to the other of the piece, poetry is voluntarily sacrificed to music.[84]

It is understandable that pieces which referred to contemporary events, or quodlibets which used well-known cries or tunes had more meaning for the people for whom they were written than for audiences of a later era.

The subject-matter and language of certain sixteenth-century chansons were of some concern to musicologists and

[81] Quoted from *Biogr. univ.*, 2ᵉ éd., t. 6, p. 365, in Lowinsky, *Ockeghem*, p. 155.

[82] Quoted from *Grove's Dictionary*, 2nd ed., 1906, II: p. 526, in Brenet, *France*, p. 121.   [83] Borren, in *New Oxford*, IV: p. 6.

[84] Quoted in Brenet, *France*, pp. 171–172.

musical editors. Fétis, in his article on Passereau (*Biogr. univ.* 2ᵉ éd., t. 6, pp. 462–463), singles out his chanson *Sur le joly jonc* (1530³) and remarks: 'Ce n'est pas un médiocre sujet d'étonnement que de voir un prêtre mettre en musique des paroles si indécentes.'[85] A solution to which some editors resorted was to bowdlerize literary texts, in full or in part. Maldeghem does it often, in his *Trésor musical*, as Gustave Reese has shown in a remarkable piece of detective work.[86] In his edition to Janequin's *Le chant des oyseaux*, the prince de la Moskova transformed the cuckoo into an owl (because of the cuckoo's association with cuckold husbands) and cut the passage representing the cuckoo's song. In good musico-logical fashion, Brenet reports with disapproval this tampering with the original and resulting historical inaccuracy, and proposes a ladylike alternative to these cuts—that one should 'interpret the meaning otherwise and see in it simply a joyful portrayal of nature in springtime.'[87]

In an item of an exposition catalogue prepared in 1934, we read that Jean Planson's airs 'are charming, but too often written on licentious texts.'[88] Two contemporary opinions on the same work, written within some ten years of each other (1955 and 1964) show that there is probably no such thing as 'the' modern attitude towards the French chanson. In the foreword to his edition of the chansons of Clemens non Papa, Bernet Kempers refers to Clément Marot's 'rather disgusting' *Blaison du beau et laid tétin*, of which Clément Janequin set the first part and Clemens non Papa the second—'a collaboration of three Clemenses.'[89] Lesure, on the other hand, considers Janequin's piece

> one of the chansons which reveals closest understanding of the text. . . . The musician follows the lines of the poem step by step with an extreme finesse and a love for the model

[85] Rousée's *Remues la paille* (1534¹⁴) also contains the verses 'Sur le joly jonc/ Dessus le joly jonc.'

[86] Reese, *Maldeghem*.   [87] Brenet, *France*, pp. 179–180.

[88] Bibliothèque nationale, *Musique*, p. 68. The author of that notice is probably Henry Expert.

[89] Clemens non Papa, *Chansons*, p. vii. Regardless of his opinion of the text, however, Bernet Kempers publishes both versions as they were originally written.

which is still more remarkable than it would be in the case of a painter; and this time the model is entirely devoid of erotic innuendoes. . . . In the diminutive volumes published by Attaingnant and Moderne the most refined lyricism is found alongside the grossest vulgarities, which at that time no one considered shocking. When such subjects were taken up by a true musician, eroticism could become even lyricism.[90]

Nineteenth and twentieth-century composers have manifested interest in poetry and music of the French Renaissance. Works of Villon were set to music by Debussy, Boris Blacher, and Jacques de Menasce; chansons and rondels of Charles d'Orléans by Henri Reber, Charles Koechlin, Debussy, and Werner Egk; poems of Clément Marot by Ravel and Enesco. Delibes's *Avril* is on a text by Remi Belleau, Jean Françaix's *Belaud, mon petit chat gris* on one by Joachim du Bellay, and Massé's *Icare* on one by Philippe Desportes. Of all the Renaissance poets, Ronsard seems to have been the favorite among later composers. Richard Wagner and Victor Massé both wrote music to his beautiful *Mignonne allons voir si la rose*, which had been made famous by Costeley's setting. Other texts by Ronsard were chosen by Gounod, Bizet, Milhaud, Frank Martin, and Lennox Berkeley, to name only a few.[91] Peter Warlock (or Philip Hesseltine)'s *Capriol suite*, based on dance tunes from Arbeau's *Orchésographie*, is an example of the return to the French Renaissance as a source of inspiration.

The numerous publications mentioned at the beginning of this study, all devoted to French Renaissance music, as well as the many successful vocal and instrumental groups (formed of professional musicians or of musicology students from numerous universities with a *collegium musicum* in their curriculum) which specialize in Renaissance works, seem to bear out at least the second part of a statement which I read in a recent concert advertisement: 'Baroque is "out;" Renaissance is "in."' And surely this applies to French music of the fifteenth and sixteenth centuries.

[90] Lesure, *Musicians*, pp. 36–37.
[91] Noske, *Melodie* gives information on nineteenth-century settings of Renaissance verse.

Coda

In the course of the seventeenth century, chansons about the heart were to share honors more than before with pieces on lighter subjects. This came about largely through the work of the house of Ballard, which printed a substantial number of *Livres de chansons pour dancer et pour boire,* and *Recueils d'airs sérieux et à boire,* as well as a *Livre d'airs à boire à deux parties contre les incommoditez du temps; et les fascheuses cérémonies de la table,* and several *Parodies bachiques sur les airs et symphonies des opéras.* But this was another era. Towards the end of the French musical Renaissance, the heart, to be sure was no longer brought out as conspicuously as it had been in the fifteenth and earlier sixteenth centuries. It was far from forgotten, however. A piece from the Duke of Croy's tablature, which was compiled towards the end of the sixteenth century, is entitled *Suffit-il pas que j'ay le cœur noué.*[1] And a chanson in *vers mesurés* by Claude Le Jeune, which was first published in 1594 and again in his posthumous *Second livre des meslanges* (Paris: P. Ballard, 1612) tells us:

> Vous que l'amour n'a touchés de ce trait,
> Trait qui me blesse et me brusle le cœur,
> Chantés ces vers:
> Faites que l'air animé de vos chants
> Puisse à jamais mon amour raconter.
> Ah! que je suis malheureux
> D'adorer celle qui sans fin
> Brusle mon cœur,
> Puisque la fière ne veut.
> Rompre le las,
> Las, qui me tient
> Vivant, mourant, ja transi,
> Sans que je puisse périr
> Ou de nul requerir le secours.

[1] Birkner, *Croy,* p. 34.

Vous que le sort favorable n'a fait
Serfs de ce Dieu qui me rend furieux,
Plaignez mon mal:
Hommes et Dieux, etonnés de mes cris,
Qu'ore ma plainte amolisse vos cœurs.[2]

These verses show us that the symbol of the heart was still very much alive and ever present in the thoughts of French poets and musicians.

[2] Transcription by D. P. Walker in Lesure, *Anthologie*, pp. 144–146.

Sources used

Whenever possible references to sixteenth-century musical publications in the text have been designated by the number assigned to them in RISM (*Répertoire international des sources musicales: Recueils imprimés, XVIᵉ–XVIIᵉ siècles*; F. Lesure, ed.), with superior figures following the year of publication—e.g. 1531^1 and 1535^3, on page 66, which refer to Attaingnant's *Vingt et huit chansons nouvelles,* and *Liber undecimus XXVI. musicales habet modulos* respectively.

Adler, *Musique* Adler, Israel.
  'Musique juive,' in *Encyclopédie de la musique*,
  Paris: Fasquelle, 1959, II: pp. 640–654.

Adler, *Pratique* Adler, Israel.
  *La pratique musicale savante dans quelques
  communautés juives en Europe aux XVIIᵉ et XVIIIᵉ
  siècles,* I, Paris: Mouton, 1966, 334 pp.

Adler, *Traité* Adler, Israel.
  'Le traitè anonyme du manuscrit hébreu
  1037 de la Bibliothèque nationale de Paris,' in
  Yuval, 1968, pp. 1–47.

Aldrich, *Analysis* Aldrich, Putnam.
  'An Approach to the Analysis of Renaissance
  Music,' in *Music Review* XXX (1969), pp. 1–21.

Alexander, *Moduli* Alexander, James H.
  *Nicolas Du Chemin's 'Moduli undecim festorum' of
  1554.* Dissertation, Union Theological
  Seminary, New York, 1967, 367 l.

Allaire, *Masses* Allaire, Gaston Georges.
  The Masses of Claudin de Sermisy. Dissertation,
  Boston University, 1960, 941 l.

Apel, *Fourteenth* Apel, Willi.
  *French Secular Music of the Late Fourteenth
  Century* . . . Cambridge, Mass.: Mediaeval
  Academy of America, 1950, 133pp.

Apollinaire, *Œuvres* Apollinaire, Guillaume.
  Œuvres poétiques. Texte établi et annoté par
  Marcel Adéma et Michel Décaudin. Prèface
  d'André Billy, Paris: Gallimard, 1956, 1,254
  pp.

Baird, *Changes* Baird, Margery Anthea.
  'Changes in the Literary Texts of the Late
  15th and early 16th Centuries, as Shown in the
  Works of the Chanson Composers of the Pays-

	Bas Méridionaux,' in *Musica Disciplina* XV (1961), pp. 145–153.
Barbier, *Histoire*	Barbier, Pierre, and France Vernillat. *Histoire de France par les chansons*, I, Paris: Gallimard, 1956, 164 pp.
Barrois, *Bibliothèque*	[Barrois, J.]
	Bibliothèque prototypographique, ou, Librairies des fils du roi Jean, Charles V, Jean de Berri, Philippe de Bourgogne et les siens. Paris: Treuttel et Würtz, 1830, 346 pp.
Barthélemy l'Anglais, *Livre*	Barthélemy l'Anglais.
	Livre des proprietéz des choses, translaté . . . par Frère Jehan Corbechon. Paris: Bibl. nat., *MS. fr. 22532*, 342 l.
Becker, *Maîtrise*	Becker, Otto Frederick.
	The 'Maîtrise' in Northern France and Burgundy in the Fifteenth Century. Dissertation, George Peabody College for Teachers, Nashville, Tenn., 1967, 301 l.
Bernstein, *Chansons*	Bernstein, Lawrence F.
	'The Cantus-Firmus Chansons of Tylman Susato,' in *Journal of the American Musicological Society* XXII (1969), pp. 197–240.
Bernstein, *Courone*	Bernstein, Lawrence F.
	'*La Courone et fleur des chansons a troys*: a Mirror of the French Chanson in Italy in the Years between Ottaviano Petrucci and Antonio Gardano,' in *Journal of the American Musicological Society* XXVI (1973), pp. 1–68.
Bethel, *Burgundian*	Bethel, Walter Leroy.
	The Burgundian Chanson (1400–1477): a Study in Musical Style. Dissertation, University of Pennsylvania, 1950, 196 l.
Bibliothèque de l'Arsenal, *Musique*	Bibliothèque de l'Arsenal, Paris.
	Catalogue des livres de musique (manuscrits et imprimés) de la Bibliothèque de l'Arsenal à Paris, par L. de La Laurencie . . . et A. Gastoué. Paris: E. Droz, 1936, 184 pp.
Bibliothèque nationale, *Livre*	Bibliothèque nationale, Paris.
	Le Livre. Paris, 1972, 225 pp.
Bibliothèque nationale, *Musique*	Bibliothèque nationale, Paris.
	La Musique française du moyen âge à la révolution: catalogue rédigé par A. Gastoué [et al.] . . . et publié par Emile Dacier. [Paris]: Editions des bibliothèques nationales de France, 1934, 196 pp.
Bibliothèque nationale, *Topographie*	Bibliothèque nationale, Paris, Dept. des Estampes.

Topographie de la France: Paris, 4ᵉ arrondissement (Va. 249d) Plates, in-fol.

Birkner, *Croy* Birkner, Günter.
'La Tablature de luth de Charles, duc de Croy et d'Arschot (1560–1612),' in *Revue de Musicologie* XVIX (1963), pp. 18–46.

Blume, *Musik (MGG)* Blume, Friedrich, ed.
Die Musik in Geschichte und Gegenwart. Kassel, Basel: Bärenreiter, 1949–1968, 14 vols.

Bonnin, *Puy* Bonnin, T., and A. Chassant.
Puy de musique érigé à Evreux, en l'honneur de madame sainte Cécile; publié d'après un manuscrit du XVIᵉ siècle. Evreux: J. J. Ancelle, 1837, 88 pp.

Borren, *Closson* Borren, Charles van den.
'Ernest Closson, l'homme, le savant, le professeur . . . , in *Mélanges Ernest Closson*, Bruxelles: Société belge de musicologie, 1948, pp. 7–17.

Borren, *Enigme* Borren, Charles van den.
'L' énigme des "Credo de village",' in *Hans Albrecht in memoriam*, hrsg. von W. Brennecke und H. Haase. Kassel: Bärenreiter, 1962, pp. 48–54.

Borren, *Etudes* Borren, Charles van den.
Etudes sur le quinzième siècle musical. Anvers: N. V. de Nederlandsche Boekhandel, 1941, 281 pp.

Borren, *Madrigalisme* Borren, Charles van den.
'Le madrigalisme avant le madrigal,' in *Festschrift für Guido Adler* . . . Wien: Universal, 1930, pp. 78–83.

Borren, *Musicologie* Borren, Charles van den.
'Musicologie et géographie,' in *La Renaissance dans les provinces du Nord,* [éd.] par F. Lesure, Paris: Centre national de la recherche scientifique, 1956, pp. 19–25.

Borren, *Pièces* Borren, Charles van den, ed.
Pièces polyphoniques profanes de provenance liégeoise (XVᵉ siècle). Bruxelles: Editions de la librairie encyclopédique, 1950, 75 pp.

Borren, *Pittoresque* Borren, Charles van den.
'La Musique pittoresque dans le manuscrit 222 C 22 de la Bibliothèque de Strasbourg (XVᵉ siècle),' in *Bericht über den musikwissenschaftlichen Kongress in Basel* . . . *26 bis 29 September 1924.* Leipzig: Breitkopf u. Härtel, 1925, pp. 88–105.

Borren, *Tombeaux* Borren, Charles van den.
'Esquisse d'une histoire des "tombeaux"

	musicaux,' in *Festschrift für Erich Schenk*, Graz: Böhlaus, 1962, pp. 56–67.
Bourilly, *Journal*	Bourilly, V.-L., ed.
	Le Journal d'un bourgeois de Paris sous le règne de François Ier (1515–1536), Paris: Picard, 1910, 471 pp.
Boursier de la Roche, *Chasse*	Boursier de la Roche, M.
	Les plus belles fanfares de chasse; transcrites et revues par M. Boursier de la Roche; précédées d'une étude sur les cornures par Jean des Airelles et d'une introduction historique et bibliographique par le Cdt. G. de Marolles. Paris: Librairie Cynégétique, 1930, 186 pp.
Bowles, *Haut*	Bowles, Edmund A.
	'Haut and Bas: the Grouping of Musical Instruments in the Middle Ages,' in *Musica Disciplina* VIII (1954), pp. 115–140.
Bowles, *Processions*	Bowles, Edmund A.
	'Musical Instruments in Civic Processions,' in *Acta Musicologica* XXXIII (1961), pp. 147–161.
Boyden, *Violin*	Boyden, David.
	The History of Violin Playing from Its Origins to 1761 and Its Relationship to the Violin and Violin Music. London, New York: Oxford University Press, 1965, 569 pp.
Brantôme, *Œuvres*	Brantôme, Pierre de Bourdeilles, Seigneur de.
	Œuvres complètes, [éd. par] Prosper Mérimée et Louis Lacour. Paris: Jannet, 1858–78, 7 vols.
Brenet, *Couvents*	Brenet, Michel.
	La musique dans les couvents de femmes depuis le moyen âge jusqu'à nos jours; conférence prononcée le 22 janvier 1898. Paris: Schola Cantorum [1898?], 18 pp. (Extrait de la *Tribune de Saint-Gervais.*)
Brenet, *France*	Brenet, Michel.
	Musique et musiciens de l'ancienne France. Paris: Alcan [1911?], 249 pp.
Brenet, *Instruments*	Brenet, Michel.
	'Notes sur l'introduction des instruments dans les églises de France,' in *Riemann-Festschrift*. Leipzig: M. Hesse, 1909, pp. 277–293.
Brenet, *Méthode*	Brenet, Michel.
	La plus ancienne méthode française de musique; réimpression de l'Art, science et pratique de plaine musique; avec introduction et appendice. Paris: Schola Cantorum, 1907, 32 pp.
Brenet, *Militaire*	Brenet, Michel.

La musique militaire. Paris: H. Laurens [1917], 126 pp.

Brenet, *Molinet*   Brenet, Michel.
'Quelques passages concernant la musique dans les poésies de Jean Molinet,' in *Bulletin de la Société française de musicologie* I (1917), pp. 21–27.

Brenet, *Processions*   Brenet, Michel.
La musique dans les processions; conférence faite à Niort le 26 mai 1896 . . . Paris: Tribune de Saint Gervais, 1896, 12 pp. (Extrait de la *Tribune de Saint-Gervais.*)

Brenet, *Sainte-Chapelle*   Brenet, Michel.
Les Musiciens de la Sainte-Chapelle du Palais. Paris: Picard, 1910, 379 pp.

Breton, *Chanson*   Breton, Guy.
La chanson satirique de Charlemagne à Charles de Gaulle; mille ans de chronique scandaleuse, I. Paris: Perrin, 1967, 441, 28 pp.

Bridgman, *Beaulieu*   Bridgman, Nanie.
'Eustorg de Beaulieu, Musician,' in *Musical Quarterly* XXXVII (1951), pp. 61–70.

Bridgman, *Bourdenay*   Bridgman, Nanie, and François Lesure.
'Une Anthologie historique de la fin du XVIᵉ siècle: le manuscrit Bourdenay,' in *Miscelánea en homenaje a Monseñor Higinio Anglés*, I, Barcelona: Consejo superior de investigaciones científicas, 1958–1961, pp. 161–172.

Bridgman, *Charles Quint*   Bridgman, Nanie.
'La participation musicale à l'entrée de Charles Quint à Cambrai le 20 janvier 1540,' in *Les Fêtes de la Renaissance, II: Fêtes et cérémonies au temps de Charles Quint*, [éd.] Jean Jacquot. Paris: Centre national de la recherche scientifique, 1960, pp. 236–254.

Bridgman, *Echanges*   Bridgman, Nanie.
'Les Echanges musicaux entre l'Espagne et les Pays-Bas au temps de Philippe le Beau et de Charles Quint,' in *La Renaissance dans les provinces du Nord* [éd.] par François Lesure. Paris: Centre national de la recherche scientifique, 1956, pp. 51–61.

Bridgman, *Egenolff*   Bridgman, Nanie.
'Christian Egenolff, imprimeur de musique (à propos du recueil Rés. Vm⁷ de la Bibliothèque nationale de Paris),' in *Annales Musicologiques* III (1955), pp. 77–177.

Bridgman, *Mécénat*

Bridgman, Nanie.
'Mécénat et musique', in *Report of the Eighth Congress [of the] International Musicological Society, New York, 1961*, II, Kassel: Bärenreiter, 1962, pp. 19–30.

Bridgman, *Quattrocento*

Bridgman, Nanie.
La vie musicale au quattrocento et jusqu'à la naissance du madrigal (1400–1530). Paris: Gallimard, 1964, 294 pp.

Brooks, *Busnois*

Brooks, Catherine.
Antoine Busnois as a Composer of Chansons. Dissertation, New York University, 1951, 2 vols.

Brown, *Chansons*

Brown, Howard Mayer. -
'Chansons for the Pleasure of a Florentine Patrician: Florence, Biblioteca del Conservatorio di Musica, MS. Basevi 2442,' in *Aspects of Medieval and Renaissance Music: a Birthday Offering to Gustave Reese*, ed. by Jan La Rue. New York: Norton, 1966, pp. 376–391.

Brown, *Instrumental*

Brown, Howard Mayer.
Instrumental Music Printed Before 1600; a Bibliography. Cambridge, Mass.: Harvard University Press, 1965, 559 pp.

Brown, *Theater*

Brown, Howard Mayer.
Music in the French Secular Theater, 1400–1550. Cambridge, Mass.: Harvard University Press, 1963, 338 pp.

Bukofzer, *Fauxbourdon*

Bukofzer, Manfred, F.
'Fauxbourdon Revisited,' in *Musical Quarterly*, XXXVIII (1952), pp. 22–47.

Bukofzer, *Studies*

Bukofzer, Manfred F.
Studies in Medieval and Renaissance Music. New York: Norton, 1950, 324 pp.

Carpenter, *Rabelais*

Carpenter, Nan Cooke.
Rabelais and Music. Chapel Hill: University of North Carolina Press, 1954, 149 pp.

Carpenter, *Universities*

Carpenter, Nan Cooke.
Music in the Medieval and Renaissance Universities. Norman: University of Oklahoma Press, 1958, 394 pp.

Carruth, *Bertrand*

Carruth, Carroll D.
Anthoine de Bertrand: French Chromatic Chanson Composer of the Sixteenth Century. Dissertation, George Peabody College for Teachers, Nashville, Tenn., 1961, 380 l.

Cauchie, *Guilliaud*

Cauchie, Maurice.
'Maximilien Guilliaud,' in *Festschrift Adolph*

Koczirz zum 60. Geburtstag, hrsg. von R. Haas
und J. Zuth. Wien: Strache [1930], pp. 6–8.

Cauchie, *Psaumes* Cauchie, Maurice.
'Les psaumes de Janequin,' in *Mélanges de musicologie offerts à M. Lionel de La Laurencie.* Paris: Droz, 1933, pp. 47–56.

Cazeaux, *Sermisy* Cazeaux, Isabelle.
The Secular Music of Claudin de Sermisy. Dissertation, Columbia University, New York, 1961, 2 vols.

Chaillon, *Françoise* Chaillon, Paule.
'*Le Chansonnier de Françoise*,' in *Revue de Musicologie*, 1953, pp. 1–19.

Chaillon, *Louis XII* Chaillon, Paule.
'Les Musiciens du Nord à la cour de Louis XII,' in *La Renaissance dans les provinces du Nord*, [éd.] par François Lesure. Paris: Centre national de la recherche scientifique, 1956, pp. 63–69.

Chapman, *Antico* Chapman, Catherine Weeks.
Andrea Antico. Dissertation, Harvard University, 1964, 2 vols.

Chapman, *Columbus* Chapman, Catherine Weeks.
'Printed Collections of Polyphonic Music Owned by Ferdinand Columbus,' in *Journal of the American Musicological Society* XXI (1968), pp. 34–84.

Charnassé, *Cistre* Charnassé, Hélène.
'Sur la transcription des recueils de cistre édités par Adrian Le Roy et Robert Ballard (1564–1565),' in *Revue de Musicologie*, 1963, pp. 184–202.

Church, *Pattern* Church, Margaret.
The pattern poem. Dissertation, Radcliffe College, 1944, 440 l.

Cimber, *Archives* Cimber, L., and F. Danjou.
Archives curieuses de l'histoire de France. Paris: Beauvais, 1834–1841, 30 vols.

Clarke, *Renaissance* Clarke, Henry Leland.
'Musicians of the Northern Renaissance,' in *Aspects of Medieval and Renaissance Music; a Birthday Offering to Gustave Reese*, ed. by Jan La Rue. New York: Norton, 1966, pp. 67–81.

Clemens non Papa, Clemens non Papa, Jacobus.
Chansons *Opera omnia*, XI *(Chansons)*, ed. K. Ph. Bernet Kempers. American Institute of Musicology, 1964, 122 pp. *(Corpus Mensurabilis Musicae, 4.)*

Clercx, *Ardoise*   Clercx, Suzanne.
'D'une Ardoise aux partitions du XVIe siècle,' in *Mélanges d'histoire et d'esthétique musicales offerts à Paul-Marie Masson* . . . , I. Paris: Richard-Masse, 1955, pp. 157–170.

Clercx, *Faux-bourdon*   Clercx, Suzanne.
'Aux Origines du faux-bourdon,' in *Revue de Musicologie*, 1957, pp. 151–165.

Clinksdale, *Josquin*   Clinksdale, Edward.
'Josquin and Louis XI,' in *Acta Musicologica* XXXVIII (1966), pp. 67–69.

Cohen, A., *Fantasie*   Cohen, Albert.
'The *Fantaisie* for Instrumental Ensemble in 17th-Century France—Its Origin and Significance,' in *Musical Quarterly* XLVIII (1962), pp. 234–243.

Cohen, A., *Survivals*   Cohen, Albert.
'Survivals of Renaissance Thought in French Theory, 1610–1670: a Bibliographical Study,' in *Aspects of Medieval and Renaissance Music; a Birthday Offering to Gustave Reese,* ed. by Jan La Rue. New York: Norton, 1966, pp. 82–85.

Cohen, J., *L'Homme armé*   Cohen, Judith.
The Six Anonymous L'Homme Armé Masses in Naples, Biblioteca Nazionale, MS VI. E 40. American Institute of Musicology, 1968, 80 pp. (*Musicological Studies and Documents*, 21.)

Commynes, *Mémoires*   Commynes, Philippe de.
Mémoires; ed. par Joseph Calmette. Paris: Société d'Edition Les Belles Lettres, 1965, 3 vols.

Compère, *Opera omnia*   Compère, Loyset.
Opera omnia, ed. Ludwig Finscher. American Institute of Musicology, 1958, – vols. (*Corpus Mensurabilis Musicae*, 15.)

Coussemaker, *Histoire*   Coussemaker, Edmond de.
Histoire de l'harmonie au moyen âge. Paris: V. Didron, 1852, 349 pp.

Crawford, *Masses*   Crawford, David.
'Reflections on Some Masses from the Press of Moderne,' in *Musical Quarterly* LVIII (1972), pp. 82–91.

Crawford, *Noblitt*   Crawford, David E.
Review of Noblitt: *The Motetti Missales of the Late 15th Century*, in *Current Musicology* X (1970), pp. 102–108.

Cunningham, *Chanson*   Cunningham, Caroline M.
Estienne Du Tertre, Sçavant Musicien, Jean d'Estrée, Joueur de Hautbois du Roy, and the Mid-Sixteenth-Century Franco-Flemish Chanson and Ensemble Dance. Dissertation, Bryn Mawr College, 1969, 2 vols.

Cunningham, *Du Tertre*   Cunningham, Caroline M.
'Estienne Du Tertre and the Mid-Sixteenth-Century Parisian Chanson,' in *Musica Disciplina* XXV (1971), pp. 127–170.

Curtis, *Tricotée*   Curtis, Alan S,
'Josquin and "La belle tricotée,"' in *Essays in Honor of Dragan Plamenac on his 70th Birthday*, ed. by G. Reese and R. J. Snow. Pittsburgh: University of Pittsburgh, 1969, pp. 1–8.

D'Accone, *Chapels*   D'Accone, Frank A.
'The Musical Chapels at the Florentine Cathedral and Baptistry during the First Half of the 16th Century,' in *Journal of the American Musicological Society* XXIV (1971), pp. 1–50.

Dalbanne, *Granjon*   Dalbanne, Claude.
'Robert Granjon, imprimeur de musique,' in *Gutenberg Jahrbuch* XIV (1939), pp. 226–232.

Dart, *Ayre*   Dart, Thurston.
'Role de la danse dans "l'ayre" anglais,' in *Musique et poésie au XVIe siècle*, [éd.] Jean Jacquot. Paris: Centre national de la recherche scientifique, 1954, pp. 203–209.

Davidsson, *Drucke*   Davidsson, Åke.
Bibliographie der musiktheoretischen Drucke des 16. Jahrhunderts. Baden-Baden: Heitz, 1962, 99 pp.

Davidsson, *Isländskt*   Davidsson, Åke.
'Isländskt musiktryck i äldre tide,' in *Studier tillagnade Carl-Allan Moberg, 5 juni 1961*, [Under redaktion av Ingmar Bengtsson et al.]. Stockholm: I. Marcus, 1961, pp. 99–108. *(Svensk tidskrift for musikforskning, 43.)*

Defaux, *Charles*   Defaux, Gérard.
'Charles d'Orléans, ou, La poétique du secret: à propos du rondeau XXXIII de l'édition Champion,' in *Romania* XCIII (1972), pp. 194–243.

Deslandres, *Auger*   Deslandres, Paul.
'Le Père Edmond Auger, confesseur de Henri III (1530–1591),' in *Revue des études historiques* CIV (1937), pp. 28–38.

Dottin, *Janequin* Dottin, Georges.
Review of Janequin, *Chansons polyphoniques*, VI (ed. Merritt and Lesure), in *Revue de Musicologie*, 1972, pp. 133–134.

Droz, *Chansonniers* Droz, E., Y. Rokseth, and G. Thibault, eds.
Trois Chansonniers français du XVe siècle. Paris: Droz, 1927, 124 pp.

Droz, *Poètes* Droz, E., and G. Thibault.
Poètes et musiciens du XVe siècle. Paris, 1924, 86 pp.

Droz, *Villon* Droz, E.
'Les Chansons de François Villon,' in *Mélanges de musicologie offerts à M. Lionel de la Laurencie*. Paris: E. Droz, 1933, pp. 29–32.

Du Fouilloux, *Venerie* Du Fouilloux, Jacques.
La Venerie . . . Poitiers: De Marnefs et Bouchetz, 1566?, [Privilège, 1560], 295 pp.

Dunning, *Staatsmotette* Dunning, Albert.
Die Staatsmotette (1480–1555). Utrecht: A. Oosthoek, 1970, 361 pp.

Durand, *Avignon* Durand, Henri-André.
'Les Instruments dans la musique sacrée au chapitre collégial Saint-Agricol d'Avignon (1600–1660),' in *Revue de Musicologie*, 1966, pp. 73–87.

Eitner, *Chansons* Eitner, Robert, ed.
60 Chansons zu vier Stimmen . . . Leipzig: Breitkopf u. Härtel, 1899, 120 pp. (*Publikation aelterer, praktischer und theoretischer Musikwerke*, XXIII.)

Erlanger, *Diane* Erlanger, Philippe.
Diane de Poitiers. Paris: Gallimard, 1955, 372 pp.

Félibien, *Histoire* Félibien, Michel.
Histoire de la ville de Paris . . . Paris: Desprez et Desessartz, 1725, 5 vols.

Ferand, *Guerson* Ferand, Ernest T.
'Guillaume Guerson's Rules of Improvised Counterpoint (c. 1500),' in *Miscelánea en homenage a Monseñor Higinio Anglés*, I, Barcelona: Consejo superior de investigaciones cientificas, 1958–61, pp. 253–263.

Ferand, *Sodaine* Ferand, Ernest T.
'Sodaine and Unexpected Music in the Renaissance,' in *Musical Quarterly* XXXVII (1951), pp. 10–27.

Finscher, *Compère* Finscher, Ludwig.

Loyset Compère (c. 1450–1518); Life and Works. American Institute of Musicology, 1964, 262 pp. (*Musicological Studies and Documents*, 12.)

Fouché, *Grandioses*   Fouché, Madeleine.
'Les grandioses funérailles de la reine Anne, Duchesse de Bretagne,' in *Revue des études historiques* CIV (1937), pp. 249–268.

Fournel, *Cris*   Fournel, Victor.
Les Cris de Paris; types et physionomies d'autrefois. Paris: Firmin-Didot, 1887, 221 pp.

Fox, *Requiem*   Fox, Charles Warren.
'The Polyphonic Requiem Before About 1615,' in *Bulletin of the American Musicological Society* VII (1943), pp. 6–7.

François, *Tournon*   François, Michel.
Le Cardinal François de Tournon . . . Paris: Boccard, 1951, 557 pp.

Franklin, *Annonce*   Franklin, Alfred.
L'annonce et la réclame; les cris de Paris. Paris: Plon, 1887, 240 pp. (*La vie privée d'autrefois.*)

Fréville, *Index*   Fréville, Ernest de.
'Un Index du XVIᵉ siècle; livres et chansons prohibées par un inquisiteur de la province ecclésiastique de Toulouse (1548–1549),' in *Bulletin de l'histoire du protestantisme français*, I (1853), pp. 355–363, 437–448; II (1854), pp. 15–24.

Frissard, *Chardavoine*   Frissard, Claude.
'A propos d'un recueil de "chansons" de Jehan Chardavoine,' in *Revue de Musicologie* (1948), pp. 58–75.

Fuller, *Bologna*   Fuller, Sarah.
'Additional Notes on the 15th-Century Chansonnier *Bologna Q 16*,' in *Musica Disciplina* XXIII (1969), pp. 81–89.

Gagnepain, *Musique*   Gagnepain, Bernard.
La Musique française du moyen âge et de la Renaissance, 2ᵉ éd. Paris: Presses Universitaires de France, 1968, 128 pp.

Gagnepain, *Servin*   Gagnepain, Bernard.
'Une contribution à la connaissance du XVIᵉ siècle musical en France: Jean Servin' (résumé of a paper read at the Société française de musicologie, 14 February 1957) in *Revue de Musicologie*, 1957, pp. 125–126.

Garside, *Calvin*   Garside, Charles, Jr.
'Calvin's Preface to the Psalter: a Re-

appraisal,' in *Musical Quarterly* XXXVII (1951), pp. 566–577.

Geoffroy-Dechaume, *Secrets*
Geoffroy-Dechaume, Antoine.
Les 'secrets' de la musique ancienne; recherches sur l'interprétation, XVIᵉ–XVIIᵉ–XVIIIᵉ siècles. Paris: Fasquelle, 1964, 156 pp.

Gérold, *Bayeux*
Gérold, Theodore, ed.
Le Manuscrit de Bayeux; texte et musique d'un recueil de chansons du XVᵉ siècle. Strasbourg: Commission des publications de la Faculté des lettres, 1921, LIV, 127 pp.

Gérold, *Religieuse*
Gérold, Theodore.
'La Musique religieuse française au XVᵉ siècle,' in *Revue Musicale CCXXII (1953–54)*, pp. 44–60.

Giuliana, *Magnificat*
Giuliana, Paul.
History and Development of Magnificat Settings in the Fifteenth and Sixteenth Centuries. Dissertation, Union Theological Seminary, New York, 1949, 2 vols.

Glarean, *Dodecachordon*
Glarean, Heinrich.
Dodecachordon; translation, transcription and commentary by Clement A. Miller. American Institute of Musicology, 1965, 2 vols. (*Musicological Studies and Documents, 6.*)

Godt, *Costeley*
Godt, Irving.
Guillaume Costeley: Life and Works. Dissertation, New York University, 1969, 2 vols.

Goldine, *Chartres*
Goldine, Nicole.
'Les Heuriers-matiniers de la cathédrale de Chartres jusqu'au XVIᵉ siècle; organisation liturgique et musicale,' in *Revue de Musicologie*, 1968, pp. 161–175.

Goldthwaite, *Rhythmic*
Goldthwaite, Scott.
Rhythmic Patterns and Formal Symmetry in the Fifteenth-Century Chanson. Dissertation, Harvard University, 1955, 2 vols.

Gombosi, *Masque*
Gombosi, Otto.
'Some Musical Aspects of the English Court Masque,' in *Journal of the American Musicological Society* I (1948), pp. 3–9.

Gombosi, *Organ*
Gombosi, Otto.
'About Organ Playing in the Divine Service, circa 1500,' in *Essays on Music in Honor of Archibald Thompson Davison by his Associates.* Cambridge, Mass.: Harvard University, Dept. of Music, 1957, pp. 51–68.

Gottwald, *Ghiselin*

Gottwald, Clytus.
'Johannes Ghiselin—Janne Verbonnet;
Some Traces of His Life,' in *Musica Disciplina*
XV (1961), pp. 105–111.

Gudewill, *Quodlibet*

Gudewill, Kurt.
'Ursprünge und nationale Aspekte des
Quodlibets,' in *Report of the Eighth Congress [of
the] International Musicological Society, 1961*.
Kassel, New York: Bärenreiter, 1962, I: pp.
30–43; discussion, II: pp. 53–57.

Gülke, *Volkslied*

Gülke, Peter.
'Das Volkslied in der burgundischen
Polyphonie des 15. Jahrhunderts,' in *Festschrift
Heinrich Besseler zum sechzigsten Geburtstag*, hrsg.
von Institut für Musikwissenschaft der Karl-
Marx-Universität. Leipzig: Deutscher Verlag
für Musik, 1961, pp. 179–202.

Haar, *Chanson*

Haar, James, ed.
Chanson and Madrigal, 1480–1530.
Cambridge, Mass.: Harvard University Press,
1964, 266 pp.

Hambraeus, *Carminum*

Hambraeus, Bengt.
*Codex carminum gallicorum; une étude sur le
volume 'Musique vocale du manuscrit 87' de la
Bibliothèque de l'Université d'Upsala;* [traduit du
suédois par Dominique Birmann de Relles]
Uppsala: Almqvist & Wiksells, 1961, 158 pp.
(*Studia Musicologica Upsaliensia*, VI.)

Hamersma, *Pseaumes*

Hamersma, John Edward.
*Les Dix Pseaumes of Claude Le Jeune: a Study in
Sixteenth-Century French Psalmody*. Dissertation,
Union Theological Seminary, New York, 1961,
2 vols.

Hansen, *Phinet*

Hansen, Peter Sijer.
*The Life and Works of Domenico Phinot (ca.
1510–ca. 1555)*. Dissertation, University of
North Carolina, 1939, 115 l. and musical
suppl.

Haraszti, *Bakfark*

Haraszti, Emile.
'Un grand luthiste du XVI⁰ siècle: Valentin
Bakfark,' in *Revue de Musicologie*, 1929, pp.
159–176.

Haraszti, *Paon*

Haraszti, Emile.
'Une Fête de paon a Saint-Julien de Tours en
1457,' in *Mélanges d'Histoire et d'esthétique
musicales offerts à Paul-Marie Masson . . .* , I. Paris:
Richard-Masse, 1955, pp. 127–145.

Heartz, *Attaingnant*	Heartz, Daniel. *Pierre Attaingnant, Royal Printer of Music; a Historical Study and Bibliographical Catalogue.* Berkeley: University of California Press, 1969, 496 pp.
Heartz, *Parisian*	Heartz, Daniel. 'Parisian Publishing Under Henry II: a Propos of Four Recently Discovered Guitar Books,' in *Musical Quarterly* XLVI (1960), pp. 448–467.
Heartz, *Preludes*	Heartz, Daniel, ed. *Preludes, Chansons and Dances for Lute Published by Pierre Attaingnant, Paris (1529–1530).* Neuilly-sur-Seine: Société de Musique d'Autrefois, 1964, LXXXVII, 128 pp.
Heartz, *Rôti*	Heartz, Daniel. 'A 15th-Century Ballo: Rôti Bouilli Joyeux,' in *Aspects of Medieval and Renaissance Music; a Birthday Offering to Gustave Reese*, ed. by Jan La Rue. New York: Norton, 1966, pp. 359–375.
Heartz, *Sources*	Heartz, Daniel Leonard. *Sources and Forms of the French Instrumental Dance in the Sixteenth Century.* Dissertation, Harvard University, 1957, 424 l.
Hertzmann, *Mehrchörigkeit*	Hertzmann, Erich. 'Zur Frage der Mehrchörigkeit in der ersten Hälfte des 16. Jahrhunderts,' in *Zeitschrift für Musikwissenschaft* XII (1929–30), pp. 138–147.
Hervé, *Chasse*	Hervé, A. 'La Chasse et la musique: le cor,' in *Revue Musicale*, VI (1906), pp. 461–466.
Hewitt, *Canti B*	Hewitt, Helen, ed. *Ottaviano Petrucci: Canti B numero cinquanta, Venice, 1502.* Chicago, London: University of Chicago Press, 1967, 242 pp. (*Monuments of Renaissance Music, 2.*)
Hewitt, *Chanson*	Hewitt, Helen. 'A Chanson Rustique of the Early Renaissance,' in *Aspects of Medieval and Renaissance Music; a Birthday Offering to Gustave Reese*, ed. by Jan La Rue. New York: Norton, 1966, pp. 376–391.
Hewitt, *Fors*	Hewitt, Helen Margaret. '*Fors seulement* and the Cantus Firmus Technique of the Fifteenth Century,' in *Essays in Honor of Dragan Plamenac on His 70th Birthday,*

ed. by G. Reese and R. J. Snow. Pittsburgh: University of Pittsburgh, 1969, pp. 91–126.

Hewitt, *Odhecaton* Hewitt, Helen Margaret, and Isabel Pope, eds. *Harmonice Musices Odhecaton A.* Cambridge, Mass.: Mediaeval Academy of America, 1942, 421 pp.

Honegger, *Dictionnaire* Honegger, Marc, ed. *Dictionnaire de la musique.* Paris: Bordas, 1970–.

Honegger, *Pidoux* Honegger, Marc. Review of Pidoux: *Le Psautier Huguenot,* in *Revue de Musicologie,* 1963, pp. 237–243.

Hoppin, *Christmas* Hoppin, Richard H. 'A Fifteenth-Century "Christmas Oratorio",' in *Essays on Music in Honor of Archibald Thompson Davison by His Associates.* Cambridge, Mass.: Harvard University, Dept. of Music, 1957, pp. 41–49.

Hoppin, *Conflicting* Hoppin, Richard H. 'Conflicting Signatures Reviewed,' in *Journal of the American Musicological Society,* IX (1956), pp. 97–117.

Hoppin, *Cypriot* (article) Hoppin, Richard H. 'The Cypriot-French Repertory of the Manuscript Torino, Biblioteca Nazionale, J. II. 9,' in *Musica Disciplina* XI (1957), pp. 79–125.

Hoppin, *Cypriot* (edition) Hoppin, Richard H., ed. *The Cypriot-French Repertory of the Manuscript Torino, Biblioteca Nazionale, J. II. 9.* Rome: American Institute of Musicology, 1960–63, 4 vols. (*Corpus Mensurabilis Musicae,* 21.)

Hoppin, *Mass* Hoppin, Richard H. 'Reflections on the Origin of the Cyclic Mass,' in *Liber amicorum Charles van den Borren.* Anvers: Lloyd Anversois, 1964, pp. 85–91.

Huglo, *Requiem* Huglo, Michel. 'A propos du "Requiem" de Du Caurroy,' in *Revue de Musicologie,* 1965, pp. 201–206.

Huguet, *Dictionnaire* Huguet, Edmond. *Dictionnaire de la langue française du seizième siècle.* Paris: Champion, Didier, 1929–1967, 7 vols.

Janequin, *Chansons* Janequin, Clement. *Chansons polyphoniques,* éd. . . . par A. Tillman Merritt et François Lesure. Monaco: Editions de l'Oiseau-lyre, 1965– .

Jeffery, *Comedy* Jeffery, Brian.

French Renaissance Comedy, *1552–1630*. Oxford: At the Clarendon Press, 1969, 209 pp.

Kanazawa, *Vespers*   Kanazawa, Masakata.
Polyphonic Music for Vespers in the Fifteenth Century. Dissertation, Harvard University, 1966, 2 vols.

Kast, *Camp*   Kast, Paul.
'Remarques sur la musique et les musiciens de la chapelle de François Ier au Camp du drap d'or,' in *Les Fêtes de la Renaissance, II: Fêtes et cérémonies au temps de Charles-Quint*. Paris: Centre national de la recherche scientifique, 1960, pp. 135–146.

Kastner, *Danses*   Kastner, Georges.
Les Danses des morts. . . . Paris: Brandus, 1852, 310 pp., 20 pl., 44 pp.

Kastner, *Militaire*   Kastner, Georges.
Manuel général de musique militaire. . . . Paris: F. Didot, 1848, 409 pp.

Kastner, *Parémiologie*   Kastner, Georges.
Parémiologie musicale de la langue française. Paris: G. Brandus, [1886?], 682 pp.

Kastner, *Voix*   Kastner, Georges.
Les Voix de Paris. Paris: Brandus, 1857, 136, 171 pp.

Kellman, *Choirbooks*   Kellman, Herbert.
Fifty Imperial Choirbooks; lecture given at the University of Pennsylvania, 12 October 1970.

Kellman, *Links*   Kellman, Herbert.
Musical Links between France and the Empire, 1550–1530; paper read at the 36th annual meeting of the American Musicological Society, Toronto, November 1970. Its *Abstracts*, pp. 23–24.

Kenney, *Frye*   Kenney, Sylvia W.
Walter Frye and the Contenance Angloise. New Haven: Yale University Press, 1964, 227 pp.

King, *Printing*   King, A. Hyatt.
Four Hundred Years of Music Printing. London: British Museum, 1964, 48 pp.

Kling, *Cor*   Kling, H.
'Le Cor de chasse,' in *Rivista Musicale italiana* XVIII (1911), pp. 95–136.

Kottick, *Cordiforme* (article)   Kottick, Edward L.
'The Chansonnier Cordiforme,' in *Journal of the American Musicological Society* XX (1967), pp. 10–27.

Kottick, *Cordiforme* (diss)   Kottick, Edward Leon.

| | *The Music of the Chansonnier Cordiforme: Paris, Bibliothèque Nationale, Rothschild 2973.* Dissertation, University of North Carolina, Chapel Hill, 1962, 2 vols. |

Kottick, *Unica*
Kottick, Edward L., ed.
The Unica in the Chansonnier Cordiforme (Paris, Bibliothèque Nationale, Rothschild 2973). American Institute of Musicology, 1967, XIV, 18 pp. (*Corpus Mensuralibis Musicae*, 42.)

La Laurencie, *Bretagne*
La Laurencie, Lionel de.
'La Musique à la cour des ducs de Bretagne aux XIV et XVᵉ siècles,' in *Revue de Musicologie*, 1933, pp. 1–15.

La Laurencie, *Chambre*
La Laurencie, Lionel de.
'Les Débuts de la musique de chambre en France,' in *Revue de Musicologie*, 1934, pp. 25–34.

Lang, *Civilization*
Lang, Paul Henry.
Music in Western Civilization. New York: Norton, 1941, 1,107 pp.

Launay, *Motets*
Launay, Denise.
'Les Motets à double choeur en France dans la première moitié du XVIIᵉ siècle,' in *Revue de Musicologie*, 1957, pp. 173–195.

Leroux, *Anne*
Leroux de Lincy, A.
Vie de la reine Anne de Bretagne . . . , IV. Paris: Curmer, 1861, 238 pp.

Leroux, *Recueil*
Leroux de Lincy, A.
Recueil de chants historiques français depuis le XIIᵉ jusqu'au XVIIIᵉ siècle. . . . Paris: Gosselin, 1841–42, 2 vols.

Lesure, *Anonymes*
Lesure, François.
'Les Anonymes des recueils imprimés français du XVIᵉ siècle,' in *Fontes artis musicae*, 1954/2, pp. 78–84.

Lesure, *Anthologie*
Lesure, François, et al., ed.
Anthologie de la chanson parisienne au XVIᵉ siècle. Monaco: Editions de l'Oiseau-lyre, 1953, 146 pp.

Lesure, *Badonvilliers*
Lesure, François.
'Un Amateur de musique au début du XVIᵉ siècle: Jean de Badonvilliers,' in *Revue de Musicologie*, 1953, pp. 79–81.

Lesure, *Brown*
Lesure, François.
Review of H. M. Brown: *Music in the French Secular Theater*, in *Revue de Musicologie*, 1963, pp. 234–236.

Lesure, *Chanson*
Lesure, François.

'Chanson, (in der 1. Hälfte des 16. Jahrhunderts; in der 2. Hälfte des 16. Jahrhunderts),' in Blume, *MGG*, II, cols. 1055–1081.

Lesure, *Debussy* Lesure, François.
'Debussy et le XVIe siècle,' in *Hans Albrecht in Memoriam*, hrsg. von W. Brennecke und H. Haase. Kassel: Bärenreiter, 1962, pp. 242–245.

Lesure, *Du Chemin* Lesure, François, and G. Thibault.
'Bibliographie des éditions musicales publiées par Nicolas Du Chemin (1549–1576),' in *Annales Musicologiques* I (1953), pp. 269–373; [Ier supplément], IV (1956): pp. 251–253; [2d supplément], VI (1958–63): pp. 403–406.

Lesure, *Eléments* Lesure, François.
'Eléments populaires dans la chanson française au début du XVIe siècle,' in *Musique et poésie au XVIe siècle*, éd. Jean Jacquot. Paris: Centre national de la recherche scientifique, 1954, pp. 169–184.

Lesure, *Epitome* Lesure, François.
'*L'Epitome musical* de Philibert Jambe de Fer (1556),' in *Annales Musicologiques* VI (1958–1963), pp. 341–[386].

Lesure, *Guitare* Lesure, François.
'La guitare en France au XVIe siècle,' in *Musica Disciplina* IV (1950), pp. 187–195.

Lesure, *Janequin* Lesure, François.
'Les chansons à trois voix de Clément Janequin' in *Revue de Musicologie*, 1959, pp. 193–198.

Lesure, *Le Roy* Lesure, François, and G. Thibault.
Bibliographie des éditions d'Adrian Le Roy et Robert Ballard (1551–1598). Paris: Société française de musicologie, 1955, 304 pp. 'Supplément,' in *Revue de Musicologie*, 1957, pp. 166–172.

Lesure, *Marot* Lesure, François.
'Autour de Clément Marot et de ses musiciens,' in *Revue de Musicologie*, 1951, pp. 109–119.

Lesure, *Minor* Lesure, François.
'Some Minor French Composers of the 16th Century,' in *Aspects of Medieval and Renaissance Music; a Birthday Offering to Gustave Reese*, ed. by Jan La Rue. New York: Norton, 1966, pp. 538–544.

Lesure, *Musicians* Lesure, François.

Musicians and Poets of the French Renaissance; translated from the French by Elio Gianturco and Hans Rosenwald. New York: Merlin Press, 1955, 123 pp.

Lesure, *Ockeghem* Lesure, François.
'Ockeghem à Notre-Dame de Paris (1463–1470),' in *Essays in Honor of Dragan Plamenac on His 70th Birthday*, ed., by G. Reese and R. J. Snow. Pittsburgh: University of Pittsburgh, 1969, pp. 147–154.

Lesure, *Orchestres* Lesure, François.
'Les Orchestres populaires à Paris vers la fin du XVIe siècle,' in *Revue de Musicologie*, 1954, pp. 39–54.

Lesure, *Petit* Lesure, François.
'Petit Jehan de Lattre (†1569) et Claude Petit Jehan (†1589),' in *Renaissance-Muziek 1400–1600 (Donum natalicum René Bernard Lenaerts)*. Leuven: Katholieke Universiteit, 1969, pp. 155–156.

Lesure, *Pidoux* Lesure, François.
Review of Pidoux: *Le Psautier huguenot*, in *Revue de Musicologie*, 1963, pp. 243–244.

Lesure, *Religieuse* Lesure, François.
'La Musique religieuse française au XVIe siècle,' in *Revue Musicale* CCXXII (1954), pp. 61–76.

Lesure, *RISM* Lesure, François, ed.
Recueils imprimés, XVIe–XVIIe siècles, I: *Liste chronologique*. München-Duisberg: G. Henle, 1960, 637 pp. *(Répertoire international des sources musicales.)*

Lesure, *Sociologie* Lesure, François.
'Pour une sociologie des faits musicaux,' in *Report of the Eighth Congress [of the] International Musicological Society, 1961*. Kassel, New York: Bärenreiter, 1962, pp. 333–346.

Lesure, *Trichet* Lesure, François.
'Le Traité des instruments de musique de Pierre Trichet,' in *Annales Musicologiques* III (1955), pp. 283–387; IV (1956), pp. 175–248.

Levy, *Costeley* Levy, Kenneth Jay.
'Costeley's Chromatic Chanson,' in *Annales Musicologiques* III (1955), pp. 213–263.

Levy, *Le Jeune* Levy, Kenneth Jay.
The Chansons of Claude Le Jeune. Dissertation, Princeton University, 1955, 343 l.

Levy, *Susanne* Levy, Kenneth Jay.

'Susanne un jour; the History of a 16th-Century Chanson,' in *Annales Musicologiques* I (1953), pp. 375–408.

Levy, *Vaudeville* — Levy, Kenneth Jay.

'Vaudeville, vers mesurés et airs de cour,' in *Musique et poésie au XVIᵉ siècle*, ed. Jean Jacquot. Paris: Centre national de la recherche scientifique, 1954, pp. 185–201.

Linden, *Molinet* — Linden, Albert van der.

'La Musique dans les chroniques de Jean Molinet,' in *Mélanges Ernest Closson*. Bruxelles: Société belge de musicologie, 1948, pp. 166–180.

Linden, *Nord* — Linden, Albert van der.

'Comment désigner la nationalité des artistes des provinces du Nord á l'époque de la Renasissance,' in *La Renaissance dans les provinces du Nord*, [éd.] par F. Lesure. Paris: Centre national de la recherche scientifique, 1956, pp. 11–17.

Lockwood, *Parody* — Lockwood, Lewis.

'On "Parody" as Term and Concept in 16th-Century Music,' in *Aspects of Medieval and Renaissance Music; a Birthday Offering to Gustave Reese*, ed. by Jan La Rue. New York: Norton, 1966, pp. 560–575.

Lowinsky, *Conflicting* — Lowinsky, Edward E.

'Conflicting Views on Conflicting Signatures,' in *Journal of the American Musicological Society* VII (1954), pp. 181–204.

Lowinsky, *Fortuna* — Lowinsky, Edward E.

'The Goddess Fortuna in Music,' in *Musical Quarterly* XXIX (1943), pp. 45–47.

Lowinsky, *Medici* (article) — Lowinsky, Edward E.

'The Medici Codex: a Document of Music, Art, and Politics in the Renaissance,' in *Annales Musicologiques* V (1957), pp. 61–178.

Lowinsky, *Medici* (edition) — Lowinsky, Edward E., ed.

The Medici Codex of 1518; a Choirbook of Motets Dedicated to Lorenzo de' Medici, duke of Urbino. Chicago, London: University of Chicago Press, 1968, 3 vols. (*Monuments of Renaissance Music*, 3–5.)

Lowinsky, *Ockeghem* — Lowinsky, Edward E.

'Ockeghem's Canon for Thirty-Six Voices: an Essay in Musical Iconography,' in *Essays in Honor of Dragan Plamenac on His 70th Birthday,* ed. by G. Reese and R. J. Snow. Pittsburgh: University of Pittsburgh, 1969, pp. 155–180.

Lowinsky, *Scores*   Lowinsky, Edward E.
'On the Use of Scores by Sixteenth-Century Musicians,' in *Journal of the American Musicological Society* I (1948), pp. 17–23.

Luce, *Requiem*   Luce, Harold T.
The Requiem Mass from Its Plainsong Beginnings to 1600. Dissertation, Florida State University, 1958, 2 vols.

MacClintock, *Molinet*   MacClintock, Carol.
'Molinet, Music, and Medieval Rhetoric,' in *Musica Disciplina* XIII (1959), pp. 109–21.

Machabey, *Machault*   Machabey, Armand.
Guillaume de Machault, 130?–1377; la vie et l'œuvre musical. Paris: Richard-Masse, 1955, 2 vols.

Maniates, *Combinative*   Maniates, Maria Rika.
Combinative Techniques in Franco-Flemish Polyphony. Dissertation, Columbia University, 1965, 2 vols.

Maniates, *Dijon*   Maniates, Maria Rika.
'Combinative Chansons in the Dijon Chansonnier,' in *Journal of the American Musicological Society* XXIII (1970), pp. 228–281.

Maniates, *Mannerism*   Maniates, Maria Rika.
'Musical Mannerism: Effeteness or Virility?' in *Musical Quarterly* LVII (1971), pp. 270–293.

Maniates, *Mannerist*   Maniates, Maria Rika.
'Mannerist Composition in Franco-Flemish Polyphony,' in *Musical Quarterly* LII (1966), pp. 17–36.

Maniates, *Quodlibet*   Maniates, Maria Rika.
'Quodlibet Revisum,' in *Acta Musicologica* XXXVIII (1966), pp. 169–208.

Marix, *Histoire*   Marix, Jeanne.
Histoire de la musique et des musiciens de la cour de Bourgogne sous le règne de Philippe le Bon (1420–1467). Strasbourg: Heitz, 1939, 299 pp.

Marix, *Musiciens*   Marix, Jeanne, ed.
Les Musiciens de la cour de Bourgogne au XVᵉ siècle (1420–1467) . . . messes, motets, chansons. Paris: Editions de l'Oiseau-lyre [1937], XXVII, 240 pp.

Marot, *Œuvres*   Marot, Clément.
Œuvres complètes, [éd.] B. Saint-Marc. Paris: Garnier [s.d.] 2 vols.

Marot, J. *Œuvres* Marot, Jean.
Œuvres. Paris: Coustelier, 1723, 263 pp.

Masson, *Humaniste* Masson, Paul-Marie.
'Le Mouvement humaniste,' in *Encyclopédie de la musique et dictionnaire du Conservatoire*, [éd.] A. Lavignac, III. Paris: Delagrave, 1931, pp. 1298–1342.

Meissner, *Susato* Meissner, Ute.
Der antwerpener Notendrucker Tylman Susato: eine bibliographische Studie zur niederländischen Chanson Publikation in der ersten Hälfte des 16. Jahrhunderts. Berlin: Merseburger, 1967, 2 vols.

Merritt, *Chanson* Merritt, A. Tillman.
'A Chanson Sequence by Févin,' in *Essays in Honor of Archibald Thompson Davison by His Associates*. Cambridge, Mass.: Harvard University, Dept. of Music, 1957, pp. 91–99.

Merritt, *Janequin* Merritt, A. Tillman.
'Janequin: Reworking of Some Early Chansons,' in *Aspects of Medieval and Renaissance Music*, ed. by Jan La Rue. New York: Norton, 1966, pp. 603–613.

Meyer-Baer, *Incunabula* Meyer-Baer, Kathi.
Liturgical Music Incunabula. London: Bibliographical Society, 1962, XLIII, 63 pp.

Meyer-Baer, *Spheres* Meyer-Baer, Kathi.
Music of the Spheres and the Dance of Death: Studies in Musical Iconology. Princeton: Princeton University Press, 1970, 376 pp.

Meylan, *Réparation* Meylan, Raymond.
'Réparation de la roue de Cordier,' in *Musica Disciplina* XXVI (1972), pp. 68–71.

Miller, *Cardan* Miller, Clement A.
'Jerome Cardan on Gombert, Phinot, and Carpentras,' in *Musical Quarterly* LVIII (1972), pp. 412–419.

Miller, *Dodecachordon* Miller, Clement A.
'The *Dodecachordon*: Its Origins and Influence on Renaissance Musical Thought,' in *Musica Disciplina* XV (1961), pp. 155–167.

New Oxford III Hughes, Dom Anselm, and Gerald Abraham, eds.
Ars Nova and the Renaissance, 1300–1540. London: Oxford University Press, 1960, 565 pp. (*New Oxford History of Music*, 3.)

New Oxford IV Abraham, Gerald, ed.
The Age of Humanism, 1540–1630. London:

Oxford University Press, 1968, 978 pp. (*New Oxford History of Music*, 4.)

Noblitt, *Ambrosian*
Noblitt, Thomas L.
'The Ambrosian *Motetti Missales* Repertory,' in *Musica Disciplina* XXII (1968), pp. 77–103.

Noblitt, *Motetti*
Noblitt, Thomas Lee.
The Motetti Missales of the Late Fifteenth Century. Dissertation, University of Texas, Austin, 1963, 352 pp.

Noske, *Melodie*
Noske, Frits.
La Mélodie française de Berlioz à Duparc. Paris: Presses Universitaires de France, 1954, 356 pp.

Packer, *Rabelais*
Packer, Dorothy S.
'François Rabelais, Vaudevilliste,' in *Musical Quarterly* LVII (1971), pp. 107–128.

Paris, *Chansons*
Paris, Gaston, and Auguste Gevaert, eds.
Chansons du XVe siècle. Paris: Firmin-Didot, 1875, 175, 78 pp.

Parris, *Binchois*
Parris, Arthur.
The Sacred Works of Gilles Binchois. Dissertation, Bryn Mawr College, 1964, 3 vols.

Pease, *Bologna*
Pease, Edward.
'The Codex Q 16 of the Civico Museo Bibliografico Musicale, Bologna,' in *Musica Disciplina* XX (1966), pp. 57–94.

Perkins, *Lowinsky*
Perkins, Leeman L.
'The Medici Codex of 1518' [review article on Lowinsky's edition], in *Musical Quarterly* LV (1969), pp. 255–269.

Picker, *Agricola*
Picker, Martin.
'A letter of Charles VIII of France concerning Alexander Agricola,' in *Aspects of Medieval and Renaissance Music*, ed. Jan La Rue. New York: Norton, 1966, p. 665–672.

Picker, *Marguerite*
Picker, Martin, ed.
The Chanson Albums of Marguerite of Austria: MSS. 228 and 11239 of the Bibliothèque Royale de Belgique, Brussels. Berkeley: University of California Press, 1965, 505 pp.

Pidoux, *Mornable*
Pidoux, Pierre.
'Les Psaumes d'Antoine de Mornable, Guillaume Morlaye et Pierre Certon (1546, 1554, 1555); étude comparative,' in *Annales Musicologiques* V (1957), pp. 179–198.

Pidoux, *Psautier*
Pidoux, Pierre.
Le Psautier huguenot du XVIe siècle. Bâle: Bärenreiter, 1962, 2 vols.

Pierre, *Chapelle*   Pierre, Constant.
    Notes inédites sur la musique de la chapelle royale *(1532–1790)* . . . Paris: Schola Cantorum, 1899, 15 pp.

Pilinski, *Cris*   Pilinski, Adam.
    Cris de Paris au seizième siècle; dix-huit planches gravées et coloriées du temps; reproduites en fac-similé d'après l'exemplaire unique de la Bibliothèque de l'Arsenal; avec une notice historique sommaire par M. Jules Cousin. Paris: Labitte, 1885, 2 l., 18 pl.

Pincherle, *Violonistes*   Pincherle, Marc.
    Les Violonistes compositeurs et virtuoses. Paris: Laurens, 1922, 126 pp.

Pirro, *Allemands*   Pirro, André.
    'Musiciens allemands et auditeurs français au temps des rois Charles V et Charles VI,' in *Studien zur Musikgeschichte: Festschrift für Guido Adler zum 75. Geburtstag.* Wien: Universal-Edition, 1930, pp. 71–77.

Pirro, *Charles VI*   Pirro, André.
    La Musique à Paris sous le règne de Charles VI *(1380–1422).* Strasbourg: Heitz, 1930, 36 pp.

Pirro, *Cornuel*   Pirro, André.
    'Jean Cornuel, vicaire à Cambrai,' in *Revue de Musicologie,* 1926, pp. 190–203.

Pirro, *Enseignement*   Pirro, André.
    'L'Enseignement de la musique aux universités françaises,' in *Mitteilungen der Internationalen Gesellschaft für Musikwissenschaft* II (1930), pp. 26–32.

Pirro, *Histoire*   Pirro, André.
    Histoire de la musique de la fin du XIVe siècle à la fin du XVIe. Paris: Renouard, 1940, 370 pp.

Pirro, *Leo X*   Pirro, André.
    'Leo X and Music,' in *Musical Quarterly* XXI (1935), pp. 1–16.

Pirro, *Pour l'Histoire*   Pirro, André.
    'Pour l'Histoire de la musique,' in *Acta Musicologica* III (1931), pp. 49–52.

Plamenac, *Autour*   Plamenac, Dragan.
    'Autour d'Ockeghem,' in *Revue Musicale* IX (1928), pp. 26–47.

Plamenac, *Colombina*   Plamenac, Dragan.
    'A Reconstruction of the French Chansonnier in the Biblioteca Colombina, Seville,' in *Musical Quarterly* XXXVII (1951), pp. 510–542; XXXVIII (1952), pp. 85–177; 245–277.

Plamenac, *L'Homme armé*   Plamenac, Dragan.
'Zur "L'Homme armé"-Frage,' in *Zeitschrift für Musikwissenschaft* XI (1929), pp. 376–383.

Plamenac, *Quodlibets*   Plamenac, Dragan.
'The two-part Quodlibets in the Seville Chansonnier,' in *The Commonwealth of Music*, ed. by G. Reese and R. Brandel (in honor of Curt Sachs), pp. 163–181.

Plamenac, *Riccardiana*   Plamenac, Dragan.
'The "Second" Chansonnier of the Biblioteca Riccardiana (Codex 2356),' in *Annales Musicologiques* II (1954), pp. 105–187.

Planchart, *Dufay*   Planchart, Alejandro Enrique.
'Guillaume Dufay's Masses: Notes and Revisions,' in *Musical Quarterly* LVIII (1972), pp. 1–23.

Pogue, *Moderne*   Pogue, Samuel.
Jacques Moderne: Lyons Music Printer of the Sixteenth Century. Genève: Droz, 1969, 412 pp.

Pope, *Montecassino*   Pope, Isabel.
'The Musical Manuscript Montecassino N 871,' in *Annuario Musical* XIX (1966), pp. 123–153.

Prunières, *Chambre*   Prunières, Henry.
'La Musique de la chambre et de l'écurie sous le règne de François Ier, 1516–1547,' in *L'Année Musicale* I (1911), pp. 215–251.

Randel, *Tonality*   Randel, Don M.
'Emerging Triadic Tonality in the Fifteenth Century,' in *Musical Quarterly* LVII (1971), pp. 73–86.

Raugel, *Saint-Quentin*   Raugel, Félix.
'Notes pour servir à l'histoire musicale de la Collégiale de Saint-Quentin depuis les origines jusqu'en 1679,' in *Festschrift Heinrich Besseler zum sechzigsten Geburtstag*, hrsg. vom Institut für Musikwissenschaft der Karl-Marx-Universität. Leipzig: Deutscher Verlag für Musik, 1961, pp. 51–58.

Reaney, *Bodleian*   Reaney, Gilbert.
'The Manuscript Oxford, Bodleian Library, Canonici misc. 213,' in *Musica Disciplina* IX (1955), pp. 73–104.

Reaney, *Chantilly*   Reaney, Gilbert.
'The Manuscript Chantilly, Musée Condé 1047,' in *Musica Disciplina* VIII (1954), pp. 59–113.

Reaney, *Fifteenth*   Reaney, Gilbert, ed.
Early Fifteenth-Century Music. American Institute of Musicology, 1955–1966, 3 vols. (*Corpus Mensurabilis Musicae* 11.)

Reaney, *Postscript*   Reaney, Gilbert.
'A Postscript to "The Manuscript Chantilly, Musée Condé 1047",' in *Musica Disciplina* X (1956), pp. 55–59.

Reaney, *Underlay*   Reaney, Gilbert.
'Text Underlay in Early Fifteenth-Century Musical Manuscripts,' in *Essays in Musicology in Honor of Dragan Plamenac*, ed. by G. Reese and R. J. Snow. Pittsburgh: University of Pittsburgh, 1969, pp. 91–126.

Reese, *Fourscore*   Reese, Gustave.
Fourscore Classics of Music Literature: a Guide to Selected Original Sources on Theory and Other Writings on Music Not Available in English, with Descriptive Sketches and Bibliographical References. Indianapolis, New York: Bobbs-Merrill, 1957, 91 pp.

Reese, *Maldeghem*   Reese, Gustave.
'Maldeghem and His Buried Treasure; a Bibliographical Study,' in *Music Library Association Notes* VI (1948), pp. 75–117.

Reese, *Renaissance*   Reese, Gustave.
Music in the Renaissance, rev. ed. New York: Norton, 1959, 1,022 pp.

Riemann, *History*   Riemann, Hugo.
History of Music Theory, Books I and II: Polyphonic Theory to the Sixteenth Century; translated with a preface, commentary and notes by R. H. Haggh. Lincoln: University of Nebraska Press, 1962, 431 pp.

Ringer, *Chasse*   Ringer, Alexander L.
The Chasse; Historical and Analytical Bibliography of a Musical Genre. Dissertation, Columbia University, 1955, 431 l.

Rokseth, *Chants*   Rokseth, Yvonne.
'Les premier chants de l'église calviniste,' in *Revue de Musicologie*, 1954, pp. 7–20.

Rokseth, *Instruments*   Rokseth, Yvonne.
'Instruments à l'église au XVe siècle," in *Revue de Musicologie*, 1933, pp. 206–208.

Rokseth, *Josquin*   Rokseth, Yvonne.
'Notes sur Josquin des Près comme pédagogue musical,' in *Revue de Musicologie*, 1927, pp. 202–204.

Rokseth, *Orgue*   Rokseth, Yvonne.
    La Musique d'orgue au XVe siècle et au début du XVIe. Paris: E. Droz, 1930, 418 pp.

Roland-Manuel, *Histoire*   Roland-Manuel, ed.
    Histoire de la musique. Paris: Gallimard, 1960, 2 vols.

Rollin, *Marot*   Rollin, Jean.
    Les Chansons de Clément Marot; étude historique et bibliographique. Paris: Fischbacher, 1951, 379 pp.

Rollin, *Religieuse*   Rollin, Jean.
    'La Musique religieuse protestante française,' in *Revue Musicale* CCXXII (1954), pp. 138–156.

Roth, *Business*   Roth, Ernst.
    The Business of Music; Reflections of a Music Publisher. New York: Oxford University Press, 1969, 269 pp.

Rubsamen, *Masses*   Rubsamen, Walter H.
    'Some First Elaborations of Masses from Motets,' in *Bulletin of the American Musicological Society* IV (1940), pp. 6–9.

Saulnier, *Charles Quint*   Saulnier, V.-L.
    'Charles Quint traversant la France: ce qu'en dirent les poètes français,' in *Les Fêtes de la Renaissance, II: Fêtes et cérémonies au temps de Charles Quint,* [éd.] Jean Jacquot. Paris: Centre national de la recherche scientifique, 1960, pp. 207–233.

Saulnier, *Littérature*   Saulnier, V.-L.
    La Littérature de la Renaissance. Paris. Presses Universitaires de France, 1942, 127 pp.

Schavran, *Kottick*   Schavran, Henrietta.
    Review of Kottick. *The Music of the Chansonnier Cordiforme,* in *Current Musicology* X (1970), pp. 92–101.

Scott, *Fauxbourdon*   Scott, Ann B.
    'The Beginnings of Fauxbourdon: a New Interpretation,' in *Journal of the American Musicological Society* XXIV (1971), pp. 345–363.

Seay, *Chansons*   Seay, Albert.
    'Two Datable Chansons from an Attaingnant Print,' in *Journal of the American Musicological Society* XXVI (1973), pp. 326–328.

Seay, *Yssandon*   Seay, Albert.
    'French Renaissance Theory and Jean Yssandon,' in *Journal of Music Theory* XV (1971), pp. 254–273.

Sebastiani, *Bellum*   Sebastiani, Claudio.

Bellum musicale, inter plani et mensuralis cantus reges, de principatu in Musicae Provincia obtinendo contendentes . . . [Argentorati: in officina Pauli Machaeropoei, 1563], 1 vol., sign. A–X³.

Shipp, *Lorraine*   Shipp, Clifford Marion.
A Chansonnier of the Dukes of Lorraine: The Paris Manuscript Fonds Français 1597. Dissertation, North Texas State College, 1960, 580 l.

Shire, *Scotland*   Shire, Helena Mennie.
Song, Dance and Poetry at the Court of Scotland Under James VI; Musical Illustrations of Court-Song ed. by Kenneth Elliott. Cambridge: At the University Press, 1969, 285 pp.

Snow, *Mass*   Snow, Robert J.
'The Mass-Motet Cycle: a Mid-Fifteenth-Century Experiment,' in *Essays in Honor of Dragan Plamenac*, ed. by G. Reese and R. J. Snow. Pittsburgh: University of Pittsburgh, 1969, pp. 301–320.

Spratt, *Févin*   Spratt, John F.
The Masses of Antoine de Févin. Dissertation, Florida State University, 1960, 2 vols.

Strunk, *Source*   Strunk, Oliver.
Source Readings in Music History: The Renaissance. New York: Norton, 1965, 175 pp.

Taut, *Jagdmusik*   Taut, Kurt.
Beiträge zur Geschichte der Jagdmusik . . . Leipzig: Radelli u. Hille, 1927, 190 pp.

Telin, *Louenge*   Telin, Guillaume.
Bref sommaire des sept vertus, sept ars liberault, sept ars de Poesie, sept ars mechaniques, des Philosophies, des quinze ars magicques. La louenge de musique. Plusieurs bonnes raisons a confondre les Juifs qui nyent l'advenement de nostre seigneur Jesuchrist. Les dicts et bonnes sentences des Philosophes avec les noms des premiers inventeurs de toutes choses admirables & dignes de sçavoir, faict par Guillaume Telin de la ville de Cusset en Auvergne. Paris: Galliot du Pré [1533], 135 l.

Terry, *Baïf*   Terry, Barbara A.
'Baïf's Academy and the Critics,' in *Renaissance Papers*, 1967, pp. 1–10.

Teuber, *Psautier*   Teuber, Ulrich.
'Notes sur la rédaction musicale du psautier genevois (1542–1562),' in *Annales Musicologiques* V (1956), pp. 113–128.

Themerson, *Ideograms*   Themerson, Stefan.

	Apollinaire's Lyrical Ideograms. [London: Gaberbocchus, 1968], 40 pp.
Thibault, *Breton*	Thibault, G.
	'Un Recueil de musique imprimé en caractères de civilité par Richard Breton (1559),' in *Humanisme et Renaissance* II (1935), pp. 302–308.
Thibault, *Chanson*	Thibault, G.
	'Chanson (mehrstimmige, von den anfangen bis etwa 1420),' in Blume, *MGG*, cols. 1034–1054.
Thibault, *Maletty*	Thibault, G.
	'Les Amours de P. de Ronsard mises en musique par Jehan de Maletty (1578),' in *Mélanges de musicologie offerts à M. Lionel de la Laurencie.* Paris: E. Droz, 1933, pp. 61–72.
Thibault, *Vogue*	Thibault, G.
	'De la Vogue de quelques livres français à Venise,' in *Humanisme et Renaissance* II (1935), pp. 61–65.
Thoinan, *Origines*	Thoinan, Ernest.
	Les Origines de la chapelle-musique des souverains de France. Paris: A. Claudin, 1864, 97 pp.
Très Riches	*Les très Riches Heures du duc de Berry*; avant propos de Charles Samaran; introduction, légendes de Jean Lougnon et Raymond Cazelles, Musée Condé, Chantilly. Paris: Draeger, 1970, 1 vol.
	Paris: Draeger, 1970, 1 vol.
Tuetey, *Bourgeois*	Tuetey, Alexandre, ed.
	Journal d'un bourgeois de Paris, 1405–1449. Paris: H. Champion, 1881, 393 pp.
Vaccaro, *Bertrand*	Vaccaro, J.-M.
	'Le Livre d'airs spirituels d'Anthoine de Bertrand,' in *Revue de Musicologie*, 1970, pp. 35–53.
Van, *Pédagogie*	Van, Guillaume de.
	'La Pédagogie musicale à la fin du moyen-âge,' in *Musica Disciplina* II (1948), pp. 75–97.
Vasconcellos, *Livraria*	Vasconcellos, J. de, ed.
	Primeira parte do index da livraria de musica do . . . Rey Dom João IV . . . Porto, 1874–76, 525 pp.
Verchaly, *Airs*	Verchaly, André.
	'Les Airs italiens mis en tablature de luth dans les recueils français du début du XVIIᵉ siècle,' in *Revue de Musicologie*, 1953, pp. 45–77.
Verchaly, *Chardavoine*	Verchaly, André.

'Le Recueil authentique des chansons de Jehan Chardavoine (1576),' in *Revue de Musicologie*, 1963, pp. 203–219.

Verchaly, *Desportes*   Verchaly, André.
'Desportes et la musique,' in *Annales Musicologiques* II (1954), pp. 271–345.

Verchaly, *Métrique*   Verchaly, André.
'La Métrique et le rythme musical au temps de l'humanisme,' in *Report of the Eighth Congress [of the] International Musicological Society*, New York, 1961, I. Kassel, New York: Bärenreiter, 1962, pp. 66–74.

Waldbauer, *Cittern*   Waldbauer, Ivan Francis.
The Cittern in the Sixteenth Century and Its Music in France and the Low Countries. Dissertation, Harvard University, 1964, 435 pp.

Walker, *Aspects*   Walker, D. P.
'Some Aspects and Problems of *Musique mesurée à l'Antique*,' in *Musica Disciplina* IV (1950), pp. 163–186.

Walker, *Chant*   Walker, D. P.
'Le Chant orphique de Marsile Ficin,' in *Musique et poésie au XVIe siècle*, [éd.] Jean Jacquot. Paris, Centre national de la recherche scientifique, 1954, p. 17–33.

Walker, *Humanism*   Walker, D. P.
'Musical Humanism in the 16th and early 17th centuries,' in *Music Review*, 1941, pp. 1–13; 111–121.

Walker, *Influence*   Walker, D. P.
'The Influence of *Musique Mesurée à l'Antique*, Particularly on the *Air de Cour* of the Early Seventeenth Century,' in *Musica Disciplina* II (1948), pp. 141–163.

Wangermée, *Fétis*   Wangermée, Robert.
François-Joseph Fétis, musicologue et compositeur . . . Bruxelles: Palais des Académies, 1951, 355 pp.

Wright, *Tapissier*   Wright, *Tapissier*
'Tapissier and Cordier: New Documents and Conjectures,' in *Musical Quarterly* LIX (1973), pp. 177–189.

Yates, *Academies*   Yates, Frances A.
The French Academies of the Sixteenth Century. London: Warburg Institute, Univertsity of London, 1947, 376 pp.

Yates, *Magnificences*   Yates, Frances A.
'Poésie et musique dans les "Magnificences" au mariage du duc de Joyeuse, Paris, 1581,' in *Musique et poésie au XVIᵉ siècle*, [éd.] Jean Jacquot, Paris: Centre national de la recherche scientifique, pp. 241–264.

Yates, *Processions*   Yates, Frances A.
'Dramatic Religious Processions in Paris in the Late Sixteenth Century,' in *Annales Musicologiques* II (1954), pp. 215–270, 20 pl.

Indexes

The index appears in two sections. *Index I* deals with names and titles: persons, places, publications, etc. Titles or incipits of musical works which are discussed in any detail are listed under the composers' names, except for anonymous works which are listed alphabetically by title. Musical examples are indicated by an asterisk following the page number(s). In alphabetizing names and titles, articles and prepositions have been consistently ignored (and hence Claude le Jeune will be found under *J*, and Antoine de Févin under *F*). In alphabetizing the names of rulers, titles such as 'King of' and 'Duke of' have been ignored; Christian names, domains, and cognomens have been taken into account in that order. Names with the form 'Anne of Brittany' are listed by Christian name, while those with the form 'Anne de Pisseleu' are listed by the second name; where this has been thought likely to cause confusion, cross-references have been made, but it would be advisable to check for the names of middle-ranking nobility under both Christian name and regional name. Churches have been listed under the names of the towns in which they are located.

Index II deals with subjects and categories, and includes a list of manuscripts which are arranged alphabetically by the towns in which they are located. Sub-headings in brackets (unless in a main entry or before a colon) relate only to the page number immediately following.

INDEX I